Private Readings in Public

Studies in the
Postmodern Theory of Education

Joe L. Kincheloe and Shirley R. Steinberg
General Editors

Vol. 26

PETER LANG
New York • Washington, D.C./Baltimore
Bern • Frankfurt am Main • Berlin • Vienna • Paris

Dennis J. Sumara

Private Readings in Public

Schooling the Literary Imagination

PETER LANG
New York • Washington, D.C./Baltimore
Bern • Frankfurt am Main • Berlin • Vienna • Paris

Library of Congress Cataloging-in-Publication Data

Sumara, Dennis J.
Private readings in public: schooling
the literary imagination/ Dennis J. Sumara.
p. cm. — (Counterpoints; vol. 26)
Includes bibliographical references and index.
1. Reading. 2. Reader-response criticism. 3. Literature—Study and teaching.
4. Phenomenology and literature. I. Title. II. Series: Counterpoints (New
York, N.Y.); vol. 26.
LB1050.2.S85   428.4'071—dc20   95-40651
ISBN 0-8204-3028-5
ISSN 1058-1634

Die Deutsche Bibliothek-CIP-Einheitsaufnahme

Sumara, Dennis J.:
Private readings in public: schooling the literary imagination/ Dennis J.
Sumara. - New York; Washington, D.C./Baltimore; Bern; Frankfurt am Main;
Berlin; Vienna; Paris: Lang.
(Counterpoints; Vol. 26)
ISBN 0-8204-3028-5
NE: GT

Cover design by James F. Brisson.
Cover art by Rose Montgomery-Whicher.
Cover concept provided by Brent A. Davis.

The paper in this book meets the guidelines for permanence and durability
of the Committee on Production Guidelines for Book Longevity
of the Council of Library Resources.

© 1996 Peter Lang Publishing, Inc., New York

Printed in the United States of America.

For my mother, Celia Oberberger-Pilecki
and my grandmother, Frances Meier-Oberberger

Contents

Foreword

This text invites the reader to think. How hopeful and respectful. And sadly, how unlike so much of what goes under the name of education. That pathetic story (what goes on in the name of education) is part of this text too, but not in ways that are predictable and not in ways that provide the reader an alibi for disengagement, for pointing to the lack of others, for closing the book unaffected. Instead, we are asked to imagine implications: between reading and becoming, between imagination and the everyday, between presence and absence, between the public and the private, between vulnerability and defense, between conceptualization and desire. We are asked to think, in the opening words of our author Dennis Sumara: "what is the experience of living a life that includes the practice of reading?"

The question invites others. Have you ever become lost in a book? What's it like to fall in love with a fictional character? What does it mean to say that a book has saved your life? Have you ever felt unwelcomed in a text? Can you tolerate being in a place not meant for you? Does your reading haunt you? What happens when your friends dismiss the book you love? What is it like for you when you decide not to read a particular book? How has reading a text allowed you to read the world? What does it mean to experience fiction? What does the practice of private reading do to the practices of the social self? What can you now think because you have thought with a book?

That first question raised by Sumara is important for any teacher but as posed, it takes a particular turn when asked to teachers of literature. For there, the fragile problem of meaning is the grounds of pedagogical possibility and impossibility. Is the thing between the student and the teacher in the text? Is the thing between the reader and the text desire? This, too, is what Sumara wonders and in doing so he engages a range of theoretical traditions, a curious mix of literary theory, philosophy, ecology, and curriculum theory. It is a mix that questions the body and what reading has to do with embodiment. The problems he poses, however, are not those that facilitate application, explication, or what we in education call "development." These imperatives of mastery are beside the point even as they miss the point. The problems Sumara offers are the interminable problems of responsibility.

Sumara, then, is interested in the detours of meaning and how meaning takes a detour through lives, histories, affects, through misrecognition and disavowal, through accidental meetings and coincidence. And so, like a crystal, qualities of meaning are made from its flaws, which in turn require meaning to be vulnerable to the very thing that makes it possible. The flaws are not failure, the failure is in refusing the flaws. A class reads a common text but grapples with the thing in common. A teacher desires the text to provoke but cannot say what is provoked and what is left unsaid. A researcher looks into the lives of others and startles his own.

Throughout this text, the reader will encounter that strange mixture of educational theory, practice, and the lives of those who live in classrooms. We are asked to consider the effects that categories brought to literature and to its readers have on the imagination: categories such as the real and the imaginary, the body and the mind, the thought and the affect, the self and the other, the actual and the possible. We are asked to consider what these categories do to teachers and to teachers as readers. The cast of characters assembled (and Sumara becomes one) grapple with the novel experiment of reading a novel together for no other reason than to engage in the work of a common reading, to wander in the margins of a text, to risk the hesitation that reading might require. Their readings are uncommon acts made from ambivalence and uncertainty. They learn something about the desire for mastery and how this desire shuts down identity, renders pedagogy insufficient.

Be forewarned. Sumara offers a cautionary tale in the ways he reminds the reader that such categories of the literary, of education, and—yes—even identity, are imaginary approximations on the lived. The categories bear their own blind spots and passions for ignorance and, sometimes, perhaps, are made vulnerable to the unexpected question. And while the heuristic lenses through which one reads matter in ways that a life might be lived, Sumara's focus is also on the ways the pre-conceived becomes surprised, distressed, discarded, made insufficient. Perceptions cannot guarantee understanding, or insight into what it must shut out to think as it does. But suppose understanding is the work of making a relation. Then identity, mastery, and knowledge are always at stake. Suppose the very fear of putting knowledge, identity and mastery at stake is the unconscious of education.

If understanding is an exchange, then we are asked to consider what happens when understanding is delayed or passionately resisted. This, too, conditions students and teachers of literature: when the text does not sensitize, when insight into one's own dynamic of reading cannot be made from the stuff of the text, the teacher, or the responses of the class. When meaning is reduced to the hunt for symbols, stereotypes, instances of literary terms, when meaning cannot go beyond the thing that delays it, this, too, conditions students and teachers of literature. Such hesitations—where meaning breaks down, is beside itself—are also the subject at stake. Sumara offers neither comfort nor solace in the relations he is able to make. But he offers something far more interesting: stunning metaphors of practice and questions that allow insight into how pedagogy makes and delays the teacher's identity, the student's identity, the text's identity. This text, then, might be read in the tradition of making education inconsolable, in the tradition of ethics of the question. The reader will have to decide.

To encounter what might be called the historicity of fiction is to encounter how its relations are structured and how these relations are subject to change. Suppose an identity is that (other) fiction. In education, we must ask about that strange meeting, when the fiction of identity meets the identity of fiction. This, after all, is the uncanny and seems to reside within the queer definition Michel de Certeau (1986: 27), in his book *Heterologies: Discourse on the Other,* has in mind when he aptly names as fiction "a knowledge jeopardized and wounded by its otherness (the affect, etc.)." We may as well say the same of education.

If education can bear the idea that fiction jeopardizes knowledge, that fiction is curious about its own divisions, differences, wounds—indeed its own otherness—then, I think we might begin to imagine what education can become when what is becoming is the relation, and when the relation refuses to distinguish between education and imagination. Sumara asks us to ponder such problems, to allow for a thought that can exceed its own limits, to tolerate what it does not know.

Deborah P. Britzman
York University
Toronto

Acknowledgments

Both reading and writing are communal acts. Just as the "private" reading is illusory, so too is the single-authored text. This book is no exception. Over the years many persons have influenced the ideas and interpretations included in these pages.

During my decade of teaching in southern Alberta I learned about teaching and reading from the many students who passed through my classrooms. Their faces remain familiar to me even though they have long-since vanished from my life. As all teachers know, the pedagogical relation never really dissipates. It wanders in and out of the remembered experiences of students and teachers.

While completing doctoral studies in the Department of Secondary Education at the University of Alberta, I was privileged to work with Terry Carson. Terry embodies hermeneutic understanding and, like his teacher, Ted Aoki, Terry showed me the importance of living with the ambiguity of not knowing what the next step in my inquiries would be. Through him, I learned that the teacher's most challenging task is the learned ability to bear witness to the student's discomfort with the new and the unfamiliar. For this learning and for our friendship I am deeply grateful.

Other teachers and friends have been equally influential and supportive of this work. I am especially indebted to Margaret Hunsberger at the University of Calgary who, over the course of two years, spent countless hours meticulously responding to my forays into the world of literary theory and hermeneutic inquiry. Her careful and thoughtful attention to my work and my ideas provoked me to unmuddle the often convoluted interpretations that I produced.

The work and friendship of Madeleine Grumet has been important to me, both academically and personally. It was during a course taught by her one summer at the University of Alberta that I learned the importance of reading slowly, of reading carefully, and of making interpretation a wholly embodied activity. As well, I learned from Madeleine's scholarly work that curriculum theory can be written beautifully, and, as well, that curriculum theory can and must find a home in schools.

For one year, in between my Master's and Doctoral degrees, I had the good sense and good fortune to live with my very dear friend Pat Chuchryk. Not only was Pat able to provide a needed sanctuary for me during a difficult time of personal and professional transition, her strong and well-articulated feminist interpretations, developed from a long history of involvement with and study of feminist movements in Latin America, helped me to develop a critical consciousness and analysis. I have fond memories of long prairie evenings spent with Pat on the front porch of her magnificent turn-of-the-century clapboard house, sipping vodka and tonic, learning about the relations between the personal and the professional, the private and the public, the said and the not-said.

Rebecca Luce-Kapler taught me the importance of learning to live the life of a writer. During our shared teaching of pre-service teachers at the University of Alberta I learned from Rebecca the close connection between writing and teaching. It was in the middle of our many conversations that some of the ideas in this book took form. As well, her editing handicraft has provided a finer shape to this text. She has saved me (and the reader) from the contorted sentences I typically create. From her I have learned that complex thoughts can be expressed simply. This is a lesson only a poet can teach.

And, of course, there is my friend, my colleague, my partner in life, Brent Davis who, in every way, is completely woven into this text. From our first "dates" that consisted of many-hour discussions of the work of Merleau-Ponty, Suzanne Langer, and Madeleine Grumet, to our cross-continent forays in the now-gone Ford Tempo that seemed to die at the most inopportune moments, our relationship has always been an interesting bricolage of the theoretical, the personal, the everyday. The ideas presented in this book are as much his as mine, for as this book explains, cognition is always collective and, most certainly, is always embodied. In addition to all this conceptual assistance, Brent—ever the meticulous mathematician— ensured that my many referencing and stylistic errors were corrected and, on the day when my September cold was at its peak, spent an entire day typing in the corrections that Rebecca had made to an earlier draft. Now this is love.

I have been and am privileged to have been influenced by many other teachers and friends: Laurie Walker supervised my Master's work and unrelentingly insisted that I should continue my studies. Max van Manen helped me to learn the craft of phenomenological writing. Margaret Iveson continually reminded me that this work needed to be about teaching. Margaret Mackey was enormously helpful in guiding me to the right books about reading and, through her own influential research, helped me to learn about the experience of reading. Deborah Britzman's scholarship has helped shape this work and continues to influence my writing and teaching. Cynthia Chambers' hermeneutic inquiries and her friendship have helped me to more clearly understand the relation between teaching and self-understanding. David Smith's brilliance as a writer and his life of scholarly meditation has inspired me academically and personally. Tom Kieren not only introduced me to interesting books, but showed me what it means to be excited by ideas. Bill Pinar's immense scholarship has created a location for the very possibility of this book, and his keen sense of what should come next I have come to rely upon. Michael Wright, one of the finest teachers I know, has (without critical comment) borne witness to my ever-shifting selves over the course of our twenty-year friendship. Finally, I am grateful to Shirley Steinberg and Joe Kincheloe for their encouragement and friendship.

I

A Life That Includes Reading

The reaching out for a book needs to become an organic action.... Pleasant words won't do. Respectable words won't do. They must be words organically tied up, organically born from the dynamic life itself.

Sylvia Ashton-Warner[1]

In her book *Teacher*, Sylvia Ashton-Warner[2] suggests the act of reading changes who we are. Reading is not a virtual experience; it is caught up in life itself. Learning about the experience of reading, then, cannot be accomplished in the absence of inquiry into lived experience. As with Ashton-Warner, the interesting question for me is not "What is reading?" but, rather, "What is the experience of living a life that includes the practice of reading?" Because all experiences are unique, answering this question means inquiring into the specificity of particular reading experiences. Reading a text announced as a literary fiction, for example, is not the same as reading a text that is announced as "factual." Because all texts are particular forms that are historically, culturally, and politically effected and situated, the experience of engaging with *this* form rather than *that* form means participating in one complex set of relations rather than another. Furthermore, the place of reading matters. All texts are read in relation to the contexts of reading. And so, understanding the act of reading cannot be accomplished without an inquiry into the relations among forms, readers, and overlapping contexts of reading.

Over the past decade, my teaching and research interests have collected and developed around inquiries into the influence of the literary imagination in school settings. Following those who have inquired phenomenologically into what it means to read literary fictions with others,[3] I have wondered what these experiences contribute to the ongoing project of understanding oneself and one's relations to others within the complex set of relations called the school curriculum. Rather than fixing reading experience with a generalized theory of engagement between a generic reader and generic text, I have been and continue to be interested in the specificity of the act of reading when accomplished by teachers and students in school. This book will present some of my explorations and interpretations of these schooled reading relations.

My interest in the schooling of shared reading can be traced to my ten years as a junior high school language arts teacher. One of my favorite activities during those years was reading novels aloud to my students. Like many teachers, I developed a repertoire of personal favorites which I read to my classes year after year. One of these was Katherine Paterson's novel *Bridge to Teribithia,*[4] the story of a deep and enduring friendship between two ten-year-old children. Because this novel had the power to completely envelop me and leave me at the mercy of any emotion that the experience of reading generated, I was always careful to assign as "silent reading" those sections to which I knew I was particularly vulnerable. However, as Margaret Hunsberger suggests, the experience of re-reading is always a new experience and, because of this, the emotions that are generated by this experience can never be predicted. And so it was that one day in the midst of reading what I thought was a "safe" passage to my grade seven class, I found myself unexpectedly immersed in emotion. The episode in question takes place between ten-year-old Jesse and his teacher who has called him into the hallway. Now, Jesse has never really liked Mrs. Myers and, like many of his classmates, refers to her as "monster mouth Myers." And so, he was surprised when he realized that her purpose for calling him into the hallway was to convey her condolences over the death of his best friend and classmate, Leslie Burke, and, at the same time, to share her own experience of grieving with him:

> She came over so close to him that he could smell her dime-store powder.
> "Jesse." Her voice was softer than he had ever heard it, but he didn't answer. Let her yell. He was used to that.
> "Jesse," she repeated. "I just want to give you my sincere sympathy." The words were like a Hallmark card, but the tone was new to him.
> He looked up into her face, despite himself. Behind her turned-up glasses, Mrs. Myers' narrow eyes were full of tears. For a minute he thought he might cry himself. He and Mrs. Myers standing in the basement hallway, crying over Leslie Burke. It was so weird he almost laughed instead.
> "When my husband died"—Jesse could hardly imagine Mrs. Myers ever

having had a husband—"people kept telling me not to cry, kept trying to make me forget." Mrs. Myers loving, mourning. How could you picture it? "But I didn't want to forget." She took her handkerchief from her sleeve and blew her nose again. "It—it—we—I never had such a student. In all my years of teaching. I shall always be grateful—"

He wanted to comfort her. He wanted to unsay all the things he had said about her—even unsay the things Leslie had said. Lord, don't let her ever find out.[5]

Of course Jesse couldn't unsay those things; he couldn't change what had already passed. But during this moment with Mrs. Myers in the hallway, while grieving over the tragic death of Leslie, a relational bond was established that changed not only the present moment and all future moments, but also all memories of what had gone before. Although their encounter could not change past events, it could not help but affect memories of those events, for memory is a collective phenomenon: past events can only be understood within the space between the remembered event, the present moment, and projections of what might be.

As I read this passage to my class—one that I had read at least a dozen times to other classes—I realized that I was suddenly there with Mrs. Myers and Jesse. I was with them in their grief. It had become part of the life I was sharing with those students during that moment. And, in the middle of this life, I cried with Jesse and Mrs. Myers—a private, intimate moment made public. At that instant I realized that I was no longer simply "the teacher" acting in a location called "the classroom" but, instead, was involved in a situation in which the "fictional" and "real" texts of my lives were united. I was, as Cynthia Chambers has suggested, "bearing witness" to something announced by a text that had gathered my out-of-school life and presented it to me in this event of curriculum.[6] As I finished reading that chapter, I realized that reading *this* book with *these* students had been a moment removed from the dailyness of classroom life. For a few seconds it had been quieter than usual; there had been less shuffling, less movement. Time had slowed down. We had entered the world of what Margaret Hunsberger has called "not-time"—a world where the boundaries between fiction and non-fiction become blurred.[7]

It was during this brief interlude when I realized that my unplanned, public display of emotional response to a fictionalized story had altered the fabric of relationships in that classroom. Just as Jesse would never be able to remember past encounters with Mrs. Myers without thinking of their shared grief, I would never be able to think of the reading of this novel to this class without recalling what had contributed to my unanticipated response. Why would tears arrive on this day and not during other readings? Was I reminded that it had been almost exactly one year since our much-loved school principal had died suddenly from a brain aneurysm? Was I reminded that other people I loved would also die without warning? Or perhaps I was reminded that someday I would die too. Whatever the reason, like numerous other occasions of shared readings of literary fictions in my classroom, this one had created a location—a "commonplace" for interpretation—that moved classroom relations below the usual skin of the school curriculum to another place—a place that Natalie Goldberg suggests is announced by the "root thought":

> Usually we use thoughts to try to get control of a situation, even the situation of our own mind. These are called second and third thoughts, thoughts on thoughts. We have a raw real root thought that comes from the bottom of our mind—"I am going to die someday"—and instead of staying with that and feeling our fear or curiosity or whatever arises naturally, we grab that thought and try to choke it.[8]

I am sorry to report that is exactly what I did on that day. I grabbed that thought and choked it. Like many teachers working in public schools I believed that thoughts like these did not belong in the English classroom. They certainly should not be expressed by the teacher, for that is not what teachers are supposed to do when they are in the classroom. The teacher is not supposed to cry over a story. The teacher is supposed to be neutral. There is not room in the school classroom for life that is infused with the kind of passion that goes along with having a body that expresses emotions. And so, when they surface without permission to do so, those emotions that arrive in tandem with root thoughts are often squelched, squeezed out, choked. It's no wonder that my moment of disclosed grief created such a silent stir. It is unusual to see signs of unteacherly emotion from the teacher. It is unusual to see signs of life.

But, of course, there is life in the classroom. There are living bodies that collect for blocks of time several times a day in locations we call math, social studies, science, and English. In each of these locations we perform various acts, various performances, various rituals. In the math classroom we learn that four multiplied by four is sixteen, not eighteen; in the social studies classroom we learn that Ottawa is the capital of Canada, not Toronto; in the science classroom we learn that water is made of hydrogen and oxygen, not helium and oxygen. There is comfort in the right answer. And so, it is not surprising that in the English classroom we often do not get down to the root thought. It is not surprising that we scurry around gathering up and repeating second and third thoughts, for it is easier to ask whether the character is a protagonist or an antagonist than it is to wonder about dying.

Becoming involved with a work of literary fiction, however, sometimes takes us to unexpected places, places where second and third thoughts dissipate. Although readers can usually integrate these experiences when reading is done in private, they have more difficulty when these experiences present themselves in the public space of the school classroom. For although curriculum is often described as the interaction of various things—teachers, students, texts, activities—I would like to suggest that there is only one thing: the complexity of the lived curriculum that is the result of each student's and teacher's efforts to maintain a viable relationship between themselves and everything that is not themselves. I call this relationship the unity of *us/not-us*.[9] Neither are there a collection of things that constitute the act of reading—reader, text, meaning—but only one: the experience of reading as it becomes part of our remembered, lived, and projected lives. So, although we act as though there are disparate parts to reading and curriculum that can be separated out, examined, and then put back in place, this is an illusion created in order to help us to believe that we can actually subtract ourselves from our own lives. My experience of reading *Bridge to Teribithia* with my grade seven students shows that reading, curriculum, and the lives of those who experience them are inextricable from one another. Just as I cannot pinpoint the complex way in which my life is connected to the intertwined complexity of culture, experience, and language, neither can I trace the beginnings and endings of the effects that reading literary fictions has had on my life. It is a seamless existence that continues to evolve as I move through the experience of living.

Like everything in the world, then, the classroom is relational. Understood in this way, the classroom cannot merely be seen as a place where subject matter is mastered, where curriculum is covered, or where learning is tested. The classroom is the site of complex, interwoven relationships: between teacher and students, students and each other, teachers and texts, students and texts. Moreover, these relationships overlap and intertwine; we are entangled in them. Their beginnings and endings are indiscernible because, as Merleau-Ponty reminds us, "we are ourselves this network of relationships."[10] And, because we cannot subtract ourselves from knowing about ourselves, we must accept the partiality of our understanding and, at the same time, the way in which we are inextricable from the contexts and events we want to interpret. Once we understand this, it becomes clear that the texts that are used in schools are not merely things that are transposed onto already existing relationships. Like any component of curriculum, these texts influence, affect, and change the fabric of all the relations in the classroom. Choosing *this* book over *that* is to choose one complete fabric of relations over another, for in pulling one thread of the curricular fabric we alter the whole thing.

Heidegger has suggested that the distinction between human beings and other life forms on this earth lies in the ability for humans to reflect upon their own existence, to ponder their purpose[11] It is through such reflection that we often have a sense of the complex and intertwined fabric of our lived experiences. We know, for example, that all of our actions in the world count and that each one is somehow linked to the other. Furthermore, we have a deep understanding that it is the specificity of our actions that creates the path of our lived experiences. In his novel *Einstein's Dreams*, Alan Lightman describes the experience of doing *this* rather than *that:*

> Peter Klausen is making his way to the apothecary on Spitalgasse this afternoon of 16 April 1905. Klausen is something of a dandy and hates to have his clothes sullied. If dust messes his clothes, he will stop and painstakingly brush them off, regardless of waiting appointments. If Klausen is sufficiently delayed, he may not buy the ointment for his wife, who has been complaining of leg aches for weeks. In that case, Klausen's wife, in a bad humor, may decide not to make the trip to Lake Geneva. And if she does not go to Lake Geneva on 23 June 1905, she will not meet a Catherine d'Epinay walking on the jetty of the east shore and will not introduce Mlle d'Epinay to her son Richard. In turn, Richard and Catherine will not marry on 17 December 1908, will not give birth to Friedrich on 8 July 1912. Friedrich Klausen will not be father to Hans Klausen on 22 August 1938, and without Hans Klausen the European Union of 1979 will never occur.[12]

Our lived experience in the world is a complex weaving of chance and planned encounters, of deliberate and accidental actions. No matter what the action, what the motive, what the intention, they share their connection to the ecology of collective lived experiences. Does it matter that I chose to read one passage of *Bridge to Teribithia* to my class and not another? Is everything in my life changed because I made connections between a literary fiction and my life? What about my students? Are their lives altered because of our shared reading experiences?

In his book *Hamlet's Castle*, Gordon Mills relates an exchange between Werner Heisenberg and Niels Bohr as they toured Kronberg Castle in Bohr's homeland of Denmark. Heisenberg wonders:

> Isn't it strange how this castle changes as soon as one imagines that Hamlet lived here? As scientists we believe that a castle consists only of stones, and admire the way the architect put them together. The stone, the green roof with its patina, the wood carvings in the church, constitute the whole castle. None of this should be changed by the fact that Hamlet lived here, and yet it is changed completely. Suddenly the walls and the ramparts speak a different language. The courtyard becomes an entire world, a dark corner reminds us of the darkness of the human soul, we hear Hamlet's "To be or not to be." Yet all we really know about Hamlet is that his name appears in a thirteenth-century chronicle. No one can prove that he really lived here. But everyone knows the questions Shakespeare had him ask, the human depths he was made to reveal, and so he too had to be found a place on earth, here in Kronberg.[13]

It is not difficult for us, through reflection, to distinguish between different experiences. The experience of reading *Hamlet* and of visiting Kronberg Castle comprise different events for Heisenberg. Yet, as he suggests, the effects of these experiences are difficult to distinguish from one another. Does having read and heard about *Hamlet* change what he *sees*, or does it only change the *significance* of what is seen? Did I understand the exchange between Mrs. Myers and Jesse differently because of my recent experiences, or did I see my recent experiences differently because of my experience of reading? Did my relationship with my students and their relationship with me change because of this moment of shared response or was it because of the already-established pedagogical relationship that I was able to even continue my reading in the midst of this response? What does it mean to share a personal response to a literary fiction in the school classroom? Of what significance is knowledge about the teacher's life—both in and out of the school classroom—to these questions about reading and teaching?

These are the questions that I have brought to this inquiry into the experience of shared reading of literary fictions in public schools. Although I believe that what we call the curriculum is an infinite array of interwoven and ever-evolving relations, I am not overwhelmed by this complexity but am reassured by it. For although the beginnings and endings of curricular relations can never be located, isolated, or finally fixed—because they are always and already part of each other—they *can* be studied. But they can never be studied in their entirety. As Wendell Berry has reminded us, trying to understand everything is a futile kind of grasping:

> Understand that no amount of education can overcome the innate limits of human intelligence and responsibility. We are not smart enough or conscious enough or alert enough to work responsibly on a gigantic scale. In making things always bigger and more centralized, we make them both more vulnerable in themselves and more dangerous to everything else. Learn, therefore, to prefer small-scale elegance and generosity to large-scale greed, crudity and glamour.[14]

Following Berry, I have resisted large-scale research and have opted, instead, for rather small-scale inquiries into reading and teaching. What follows is a journey of thinking that I suppose began during my years as a junior high school language arts teacher who knew that shared relations with literary texts were sometimes transformative. Over the years, as I continued to wonder about this phenomenon, I began to wander—through books, university courses, conversations. I began to wander through a life that was not *led* by my wondering, but which developed with it. I began to live a life that contained what I have come to call a "focal practice."

The phrase "focal practice" is derived from Albert Borgmann's phrase "focal reality" and Ursula Franklin's description of a "holistic practice." In his book *Crossing the Postmodern Divide,*[15] Borgmann suggests that in order to more clearly understand our situation in the world, human subjects must learn to notice, value, and develop experiences of "focal reality," a term which he defines as "a placeholder for the encounters each of us has with things that of themselves have engaged mind and body and centered our lives."[16] Activities such as the painting of pictures, the writing of poetry, the tending of animals or a garden, Borgmann suggests, are ones that help us to better perceive and interpret the way in which we and the world are involved in a complex, ever-evolving relation. Participation in "focal realism," means engaging in activities that situate us in the middle of what Ursula Franklin, in her book *The Real World of Technology,*[17] calls "holistic practices." As opposed to "prescriptive practices" associated with activities such as the factory production of goods, holistic practices are those activities where skill and knowledge emerge with the process of production. Holistic practices acknowledge that form and content co-specify one another. The phrase "focal practice," when applied to the activities like reading or research, suggests that these are not activities that one simply adds to one's life—one becomes involved in a life that includes these practices. As Madeleine Grumet suggests about reading:

> If reading is a passage between the public and the private world, the journey is fraught with danger. To give oneself up to the text is to relinquish the world in order to have the world; it is a birth and a death. And so it should not surprise us to find a child wary of reading, reluctant to follow that line across the page without knowing where it leads.[18]

Following the line means taking up a life that includes reading. Including the practice of reading in one's life—particularly the practice of reading literary fictions—means being prepared to have the order of one's life rearranged. As I explain in later chapters, the reading of the literary fiction, because it requires the invocation of the reader's imagination, allows the reader to eventually perceive and interpret her or his world differently. As Grumet suggests, the reader must "relinquish the world in order to have the world." This is what it means to include reading as a "focal practice" in one's life. Focal practices are often risky ventures.

This is also what it means to include research into one's life. Like the reading of literary fictions, inquiry into lived experiences means deciding that the research will not simply be reduced to a series of "data gathering" tasks. Rather, it means that the researcher will dedicate her or his life to "learning to see" differently. As I will explain in chapter four, this act of lived cognition means that the researcher must live a life that allows for this shift in perception, a life that includes a particular "focal practice." And, as I will discuss in chapter five, because this work asks that the researcher continue to interpret his or her relation to the subject under inquiry, this kind of work is deeply hermeneutic. And so, like the poet, the painter, the musician, the "bodyreader," the researcher of lived experience must live a life that allows the possibility for interpreting the usually invisible and unarticulated relations among things. This has been my focal practice for the last few years. It is now my task to translate some of these interpretations within the pages of this text which, of course, is another sort of focal practice.

I mention this here because it is important to state at the outset that although there are a great many references to particular research events in this book, I would not say that the interpretations of shared reading in public schools presented in this book are solely derived from those events. Rather, the depictions of teachers reading fictions, of students reading them, of teachers and students reading together are representative of a long journey of inquiry that I have taken. This journey has no clear beginning and it certainly has not ended. What is presented in this book are a series of interpretations that have helped me to more deeply understand the specificity of the event of shared reading in public schools. As already mentioned, I became interested in the interpretive locations announced by shared reading when I worked as a secondary school teacher. But, if I think back further, I suppose I was interested in this even as a student in public schools. Although I have very few specific memories of my time spent in school, I do have very clear memories of reading literary fictions with other students and with teachers. I remember my grade ten math class because the teacher, Mr. Shields, read us what he told us was his favorite book—a well-worn copy of *Jonathan Livingston Seagull.*[19] I remember my grade eleven French class because of our shared reading and discussion of *Le petit prince.*[20] I also remember many English classes where the shared reading was not transformative: tedious excursions through Shakespearean plays, painful excavations of poetry that I could not understand, countless essays explaining THE MEANING of short stories and novels. And, I must confess, as a teacher I participated in the reproduction of many of these practices with my students. Like the parent who is one day shocked to hear him or herself uttering words his or her parent uttered, I found myself dismayed to discover that, in some ways, I had become the English teacher that presented texts as sites for the excavation of meaning. This was one of the reasons that I left public school teaching to pursue graduate studies.

It was during my years in graduate school that I began to more deeply investigate the phenomenon of shared reading in schools. After I had completed my master's degree, my friend and colleague Cynthia Chambers suggested that as a doctoral student I should inquire into a subject that "quickened my pulse, made my face and ears turn red when I spoke about it, and kept me awake at night." Now, it was not immediately apparent to me what this research interest would be. Many things seemed to make my face turn red and, certainly, there were many things that kept me awake at night. However, soon after commencing doctoral studies, I read an article by Madeleine Grumet where she asks the simple but provocative question: "Why do we read books with other people?"[21] Why do we, I wondered? And, like Grumet, I wondered why we read them in school. A focal practice had been announced.

Once I had made the decision that the experience of reading was a subject that needed investigation, I had the problem of deciding how this inquiry could be accomplished. Because I strongly believed that the reading of literary fictions, in itself, created locations for interpretation of the reader's lived situation, I decided that there could be no better way to study the experience of reading and teaching literature than by reading with teachers. Although at that point I was not really sure how my inquiry into the schooling of shared reading would proceed, I knew that I needed to begin with a reading group comprised of teachers who taught English. And so, I made contact with a teacher whom I already knew (Anna[22]) and with her help organized a reading group. As a form of action research,[23] I knew that although I had decided upon an entry point into this inquiry, the actual path of the research would evolve and new questions requiring investigation would present themselves. Looking back, there is now a clear path of research that can be described. Particular things have been done. Some things that might have been done were not. However, like life itself, it is only in the "looking back" that things appear so orderly and clear. During the course of my investigations into the schooling of shared reading there were many times when I felt a bit lost, unsure, confused and wished for the "good old" pre-determined research plan. In retrospect, I am pleased that I chose to put up with the ambiguity of it all, for although many deliberate decisions were made that changed the course of the research path, as many unanticipated things occurred that dramatically altered the course of my own understanding.[24] It indeed has been a path laid down while walking. And that has been a difference that has made a difference.

Generally speaking, the research and interpretations presented in this book are informed by my reading of hermeneutics, literary theory, curriculum theory and postmodernism. It is important for me to say that it is not my desire to attempt to represent the "truthfulness" of others' experiences as readers, teachers, students, or researchers but, rather, to attempt to interpret particular experiences of reading that I have participated in with others. By attempting to find words to describe the phenomenological experience of reading with others in schools, I have attempted to distinguish these from other reading experiences and, at the same time, to explicate the way in which reading and curricular relations co-specify one another. I describe my inquiries as "postmodern" because I am not claiming (or aiming) to present a unified, fixed and or complete theory of reading or of shared reading in schools. I acknowledge that my inquiries evolved from a particular set of historical, cultural, and political situations that shaped not only my research method but my interpretations of the data that was gathered and the life that I lived around these inquiries and interpretations. Nevertheless, even though it is only in retrospect that my research inquiries seem clear (and, I suppose, sufficient) it is important that I detail what they were for the reader.

After that first initiating conversation with Anna, I sent an open written invitation to teachers in a large inner-city high school inviting them to join a reading group. There was a good response, and after several meetings our group became settled with five members—myself and four secondary English teachers. All four were women. We ranged in age from thirty-five to forty-five and had taught from between ten and twenty-five years. Anna, Ingrid, and Mena were teachers at an inner-city high school. Ruth had taught all grades over a twenty-year period and was on leave pursuing a graduate degree during the year of the research. Although I had known Anna and Ruth prior to the initiation of the reading group, I had not known Ingrid or Mena.

For a period of eight months the five of us met once every two to three weeks to share our responses to various literary fictions. Although we began with short stories and poetry, we quickly moved to novels. Later in the year, I interviewed the teachers about their readings of some of the novels and, with Ingrid and Anna, focused specifically on discussions of novels that were eventually used by them as classroom texts. Because I was interested in learning more about the sharing readings of literary fictions with students in schools, I spent some time in Ingrid and Anna's classrooms. In addition, I interviewed about half of the students in each of their classes about their experience of reading literary fiction for school purposes.

Because I wish to resist presenting a unified and seamless report of shared reading events, I have chosen to write a text that is more performative than most on this topic. The chapters that follow are meant to not only depict the path of inquiry, but the evolution of thinking that occurred with and through my inquiries. As a result, each chapter is meant to "show" the evolution of my own thinking as supported by various reading and research experiences. This first chapter, for example, has attempted to not only describe the subject matter of this book but, as well, to announce my own complicity as a former secondary school teacher and a university researcher in shared reading events that constituted the "research location" for the interpretations presented in this book. In chapter two I invoke the response of one of Anna's high school students to a novel read by her in class to investigate the idea of the "literary imagination" and the way in which it has become "schooled" in modern Western education. Chapter three describes the intertextual relations readers form with literary fictions. In this chapter I suggest that it is desire that becomes the impetus for readers to develop, maintain, and sustain relations with literary texts—relations that endure and further develop long after the act of reading is accomplished. In chapter four I make connections between theories of cognition and theories of reader-text engagement and, in so doing, develop a theory of reading that I call "embodied action." Chapter five presents images that depict the experience of reading with other people. It is in this chapter that the art of hermeneutics is introduced as an interpretive framework for the discussions that appear in this and later chapters. Chapter six extends the idea of reading as embodied action to a discussion of curriculum as embodied action, focusing primarily on the way in which curricular relations, like reading relations, always co-emerge with a perceived and interpreted world of significance. In this chapter I show the importance of the teacher's interventions in curriculum and the way in which these interventions both shape and are shaped by the teacher's and students' history of interactions in the world and with one another. In the last chapter I return to my experience as a reader and a teacher in order to re-interpret the personal vignette of shared reading presented in this introductory chapter using concepts developed in preceding chapters.

Like Sylvia Ashton-Warner, who emphasized the way "selves" and "readings" are fused, I have come to understand this book as a material extension of my own sense of personal identity that has evolved through the focal reading and research practices I have been involved in over the past few years. At the same time, I acknowledge the fact that my sense of identity is completely wrapped up in the relations that I have had with others, with the books I have read, with the experiences I have had. Each time I add a new relation to my life the complex form of my remembered, lived, and projected sense of self changes. This is why I believe it is difficult for an author to allow words on a page to become "public." It is not so much that he or she does not wish the text to become orphaned; rather, it is because there is a deep understanding that there is no word, no phrase, no theory, no narrative, that can ever capture the fullness of human thought and experience. And so, for me, it is a great sense of the partiality and transience of the following pages that causes me some anxiety as I prepare to usher this text into the world. Much of this anxiety has less to do with what has been said than what has *not* been said. As Madeleine Grumet suggests:

> Think of the repugnance one often feels for a text that is recently completed. There, clinging to all the lines, are the shreds of the ideas that never quite made it to expression, fragments of the negative example, the other possibility, that the sentence, the chapter, the ideology, the deadline, the habit, the defense mechanism just could not admit. Only time and forgetfulness smooth these rough edges so that we no longer remember what has been left behind and then the text that has seemed partial, merely provisional, prevarication, becomes THE TEXT clear, complete, necessary and sufficient.[25]

For me, this text has not yet become THE TEXT and perhaps it never will. My inquiries into the experience of reading continue. I offer this book as a literary location—as what Roland Barthes[26] would call a "writerly" text. I have not attempted to "say everything" in this text. And so, there will likely be times when the reader would like more information about particular readers, particular texts referenced, particular events mentioned. This book does not follow a "typical" reporting pattern where the reader is given a map in advance. Rather, the book has been written so that (hopefully) the reader is invited into a reading experience where the reader must "write" while "reading." This means that the reading experience may be, for some, more ambiguous than they might like. But, I think, if the reader is prepared to put up with some of this ambiguity, an interesting reading experience will develop. It is my hope that an engagement with this book will generate a reading experience which is also a "focal practice."

II

Schooling the Literary Imagination

The fictive brings about the presence of the imaginary by transgressing language itself.

Wolfgang Iser[1]

15 April, 12:15 a.m.
 Everybody—Dad, Eddie, Lao Xu—has been busy tonight. I can hear them working in the office.
 There were rumours that a Party bigwig named Hu Yao-bang is really sick and may die at any time. Also that when he does there will be a big student demonstration in Tian An Men Square. Apparently Hu had lost his position in the government a couple of years ago because he had been too lenient with student demonstrators at that time. The big boss, Deng Xiao-ping dumped him. Eddie was pretty excited, puffing away like an old steam engine, and Lao Xu looked a little bit nervous.

William Bell, *Forbidden City*[2]

Although this excerpt from *Forbidden City* contains verifiable details (the leader of China *is* Deng Xiao-ping, there *is* a place in Beijing called Tian An Men Square) and is written *as if* it were an actual journal entry, most experienced readers would have no difficulty identifying it as a fictionalized account of an historical event. This may not immediately be clear from the excerpt presented here since, removed from its original context, it alone may not announce itself as fiction. Experienced readers, however, by looking at the book's cover, publisher's notes, and overall structure would quickly identify it as a work of literary fiction. Even from this brief passage, we have a sense of "literariness." In an actual journal entry, for example, the writer may not feel the need to include the parenthetical details outlining specifically who "everybody" was, or to describe Eddie as "puffing away like an old steam engine." Expository and descriptive details, together with figurative devices and particular textual structures, become what Peter Rabinowitz has called "rules of signification and notice" which not only point to the literariness of a text, but which also help us to complete the act of making meaning from our engagement with that text.[3]

But is the difference between a literary fiction and non-fiction really as simple and straightforward as I have presented here? Or could it be that fiction has less to do with what we call "literary" and more to do with the something we might call imaginary? Are there not journal entries that are indeed very literary, interwoven with figurative language, metaphoric allusions, and unusual syntactic re-positionings? Is Susanna Moodie's book *Roughing it in the Bush*, for example, a factual account or literary presentation of a pioneer woman's life in the Ontario bush?[4] Is *The Diary of Anne Frank*[5] an actual account of a young Jewish girl's day-to-day life in hiding during the Holocaust, or are the real-life events woven through with her own yearnings, imaginings, dreams, and illusions? Will I, as a reader of *Forbidden City*, ever be able to visit Tian An Men Square without thinking of my experience of reading about the fictionalized characters' lives in that place?[6] It seems that the line between fact and fiction cannot be neatly drawn. Without references to elements of the real world, a literary fiction would be totally meaningless, and a daily life without imaginings would be at best dull—likely intolerable.

However, what seems obviously fictional to most experienced readers and to English teachers may not be as apparent to student-readers in the school classroom. Sixteen-year-old Tim, for example, in the midst of a whole-class oral reading of *Forbidden City*, became confused between historical "fact" and literary "fiction." As his teacher Anna was explaining some of the characteristics of historical fiction in relation to their reading of the novel, Tim became visibly uneasy. After a moment of alternating between attending to the teacher's lecture and flipping through his copy of the novel, he interrupted Anna. "I don't believe that this is fiction! I think that it's real! I think that this really did happen!" Several other students in the class immediately joined in with "Yeah, I think so too!" "Me too!" Anna was surprised by this outburst. Although she knew that many of these non-academic stream students were not avid readers of fiction (hence her decision to orally read the novel with the class), she felt that they would easily distinguish between fact and fiction.

In response to Tim and his classmates, Anna asked why they so strongly believed that the narrated events were true and that the characters were real people. "It's the journal entries, Mrs. Powell!" explained Tim. "They have the dates at the top—which means they must be true!" Tim went on to explain that because the student revolution in Beijing actually happened during that period of time, the naming of dates by the author was convincing proof that the journal entries were more factual than fictional. Although Anna carefully explained the difference between an historically verifiable fact and an invented fictional detail, it was clear that Tim was unconvinced.

Tim's challenge of the conventionally understood fact-fiction dichotomy for the classification of literary fiction and non-fiction points to the need in English language arts education to develop a deeper understanding of the taken-for-granted beliefs about what might constitute "literature." For although our first reaction to Tim might be of exasperation—"Why can't he see the difference!"—it is his apparent ignorance about the distinction between historical fact and literary fiction that can serve as a location for a re-excavation of what might constitute the experience of reading texts of literary fiction in schools. And so, in this chapter, I would like to take up the question, "What is literature?" More specifically, I would like to explore what we might mean when we talk about fact and fiction, literary and non-literary, imaginative and real, aesthetic and pragmatic. Because libraries could be filled with discussions on any of these issues, the discussion that follows is meant address them in relation to Tim's confusion about fact and fiction during a whole-class reading of *Forbidden City*. Furthermore, because my intention is to be provocative, rather than exhaustive, it is important for me to acknowledge that these discussions merely skim the surface of the massive literature that addresses this topic. These "provocations" are meant to lead into the next chapter which focuses on the *relationship* established between reader and the literary work of art.

Fact or Fiction?

It is conventionally understood, within the discipline of the English language arts at least, that what we call a literary fiction has something to do with something that we call "literature"; however, whether all literature is comprised of works that are fictional is less clear. Although most English language arts teachers understand the category "literature" to include novels, short stories, plays and poetry, there are a number of English language arts

textbooks, resource books and curriculum guides that include expository
texts, biographies, autobiographies, and historical texts in their list of what
constitutes literature. Given the difficulty of ascribing the status of fact or
fiction to any of these, it would seem appropriate that the category "literature" might include all forms of written expression, including those which
we do not conventionally consider literary fictions.[7] However, because we
generally do have a sense that there is something different between texts
identified as literary fictions and other written works and because "literary"
is generally used to describe a quality of "literature," this possibility must be
abandoned.

In response to the question "What is literature?" Terry Eagleton[8]
suggests that it is not possible to make the distinction between literature and
non-literature on the basis of fact and fiction. Is philosophy fact or fiction?
Can historical writing that excludes the experience of women, gays and
lesbians, and children (to name a few) be considered historically factual?
Alternatively, can historical fiction that includes invented characters acting
within historically verifiable events be considered entirely fictional? It
seems that categories such as fact/fiction, verifiable/invented cannot account
for the distinction between literature and not-literature.

Eagleton wonders further whether literature might be defined in terms
of its particular function. Might a non-fictional text have a more pragmatic
function than a fictional text? This distinction must be quickly abandoned,
for it excludes the possibility that the effect of texts often depends upon the
ways in which they are read and the purposes for which they are read.
Anthropologists, for example, in their reporting of cultures, have resorted to
"literary" devices in favor of "literal" ones in order to communicate a
particular idea.[9] And it is generally accepted, that *all* reports of cultural
events, traditions, and/or rituals are particular selections that when represented in a text are "fictions."[10] As a cultural artifact, the boundaries
between what is considered a literary fiction and what is not have been
blurred considerably.

At the same time, what is generally agreed to be a literary fiction, like
all cultural objects, is subject to the evaluative gaze of those who define the
literary canon—and, of course, to the authorship of the texts included (and
excluded) from this canonical body of work. For example, I. A. Richard's
famous experiment with undergraduate students who were asked to analyze

and evaluate a set of poems from which had been withheld the titles and authors' names clearly shows the literary fiction is culturally defined and ranked. As might have been predicted, the students' resulting judgments were highly variable: well-known and respected poets were ranked poorly, while obscure poets were given high scores.[11] It seems that the culturally determined quality of the literary fiction has as much to do with knowledge about "who is speaking" as it does with the text itself.

Because any written work depends upon the reading of the text by a reader for the generation of any literary meanings, the question of the quality and effect of this reading experience presents itself. Does a literary fiction distinguish itself from non-fiction by the *effect* it has on the reader's experiences? It is well-documented that readers derive pragmatic information from their readings of literary texts.[12] When I asked seventeen-year-old Gina what she values in her reading of literary fictions she explained

> *It helps me to understand my own life better. When I read those books I get ideas about how to solve my own problems. When I read Forbidden City, I thought of how difficult it was for Alex to have divorced parents, because I'm in that situation too. I wish I could deal with my parents like he did with his.*

For many readers the situation in the novel serves a pragmatic purpose in their lives. Even when the fictional quality of the text is acknowledged, its function in the real world seems as important as any expository or descriptive text. Given this, it seems that what we consider a literary fiction may not really be characterized as having some non-utilitarian, non-pragmatic function. Because the literary text becomes part of the reader's lived world, it begins to function as a material extension of that world. This certainly seemed to be the case with Tim and many of his classmates. As they read and discussed *Forbidden City*, it became clear that this novel, even though it announced itself as a "fiction," provided an interpretive location within which the student-readers could re-perceive and re-interpret their lived experiences in relation to those of the characters presented in the book. What words might we find to describe the specific experience of juxtaposing engagements with a literary fiction with experiences in our lives?

The Formulative and the Communicative

Susanne Langer suggests that although the literary text refers and/or alludes to elements of the material world, it does not have a real world correspondence. Although Langer wrote prior to the post-structural critique of this sort of correspondence between word and world, because her work focuses upon the *experience* of the engagement between reader and text, it bears revisiting. Langer suggests that regardless of how closely the details in a literary fiction correspond to the historically verifiable, the experience readers have with a work of literary work of art is virtual.[13] In part this is because the author has deliberately created characters to "speak" and "act" the historical events portrayed. Although there were certainly persons who participated in the actual historical events at Tian An Men Square in 1989, they were not the same as the characters presented in the novel *Forbidden City*. According to Langer, the meaning generated by the reading of a literary work of art becomes a virtual experience because it is conditioned by a text that has opened up a new interpretive location. Virtual, then, does not mean that the experience is not "real" for the reader; rather, virtual means that the experience is a wholly original production. The interaction between the reader and the text that generates the virtual reading experience.

Langer makes a further distinction between what she calls the "communicative" function of the literary text and the "formulative" function of other texts. She explains that the former is a type of written discourse that is meant to tell, to explain; the latter is a reconfiguration of this discourse into a form that does not *give* the experience but rather invites the reader into a *potential* experience. Langer makes this distinction by suggesting that

> It is the communicative office of language that makes the actual world's appearance public and reasonably fixed. The formulative power of words is the source and support of our imagination; before there can be more than animal communication, there has to be envisagement, and a means of developing perception in keeping with conception.[14]

She suggests that this formulative function of words is marginalized in schools where discourse is generally instrumental. This is largely because the reading experience conditioned by the formulative power of words cannot be predicted and, therefore, betrays the largely technocratic ranking and sorting function of schools. As a result, the process of schooling marginalizes the experience of engagement with the literary work of fiction. Asking students to locate particular meanings in the text belies the opaque quality of formulative thinking that the literary fiction is meant to condition.

Langer explains that although literary fictions are derived from the same linguistic material as discursive speech, what is created is not actual discourse, but rather "a composed and shaped apparition of a new human experience."[15] It is only in this formulated space, which is less determined than the communicative space, that the imagination is invoked and the aesthetic experience realized. The formulative, then, as related to the experience of the virtual, blurs the boundaries between the textual images presented by the author and the interpretations of these images made by the reader. The idea of the formulative announces the importance for the experience of reading a literary fiction to transgress the conventional, culturally determined boundaries of language. The text announced as "formulative" is meant to provide what one might call a liberating constraint[16]—a location that conditions, but does not constrict the imaginative experience of the reader.

In my conversations with Tim, however, it became obvious to me that although *Forbidden City* was announced as an historical fiction—a text that was meant to condition a formulative *and* a communicative response—it was not perceived in this way by him. Although Tim was able to articulate the textual differences between the novel and other "non-fiction" texts depicting the events at Tian An Men Square, he was not able to perceive the novel as anything other than communicative. For Tim, the characters Alex and Xin Hua were providing autobiographical testimony to actual experiences that were lived. Although part of the confusion may be traced to the textual structure, which suggested that the novel was an actual journal written by a participant of the depicted events, it seems also that Tim's (and other students') resistance to engage in the enlarging possibilities of the formulative function of the literary text had something to do with the *location* of reading and of the lived *situation* of the reader. Could it be that reading a novel in a school setting that emphasized the importance of the truthful and verifiable response created a reader who resisted the possibilities of a text announced as literary?

The Paradigmatic and the Narrative

In his book *Actual Minds, Possible Worlds,* Jerome Bruner[17] suggests that the difference between the literary and the non-literary is to be located in the distinction between the paradigmatic mode of thought and the narrative mode. The former "makes use of procedures to assure verifiable reference and to test for empirical truth"[18] and, generally speaking, is driven by various hypotheses whose truth value must be tested in order to be verified. Paradigmatic thinking, on the whole, attempts to banish the particular in favor of the general—to name overarching theories as a way to understand, predict, and often to control the unfolding of events. This mode of thinking is generally ascribed status as a vehicle for the determination of truth, method, and universal understanding. It is meant to demonstrate a logic which we are to believe is natural because it is verifiable. The most valued feature of paradigmatic thought is its avoidance and/or elimination of ambiguity and contradiction, for these stand in the way of its predictive powers. Although the paradigmatic mode is, in some ways, imaginative in that the generation of hypotheses requires a prediction, it is not imaginative in the same way as the narrative mode employed by the poet, the playwright, or the novelist.

Bruner suggests that when given imaginative applications, the narrative mode "leads to good stories, gripping drama, believable (though not necessarily true) historical accounts."[19] Although the literary text must draw from the same language and experiential pool as the paradigmatic, it derives its difference through a process which Bruner calls a "subjunctivizing of reality."[20] According to Bruner, to be in the subjunctive mode is to be situated in an "as if" state, where possibilities are considered over certainties. Bruner cites from the work of literary theorist Tzvetan Todorov,[21] who describes six simple transformations that transform the action of the verb from being overly determined to being psychologically in process, and, as a result, contingent or subjunctive. These transformations are 1. Mode (Inserting modal auxiliaries such as *must, might, could, would*), 2. intention (embeds act directly in its intention: *John plans to commit a crime.*), 3. Result (presupposes intent but leaves open the question of how: *John succeeds in committing a crime.*), 4. Manner (subjectifies the act and creates an attitude that modifies the action's intention: *John is anxious to commit a crime.*), 5. Aspect (a form of time marking that points to the progress of the task: *John is beginning to commit a crime.*), and 6. Status (opens the possibility that there was a wish to, a possibility, an accusation that could have led to a crime: *John is not committing a crime.*).

According to Bruner, Todorov's analysis of the structure of the text of a prose literary fiction helps us to understand that literariness has a great deal to do with the way in which some syntactic formulations invoke our imagination more than others. When the phrase "Dahlia took the money" is transformed into "Dahlia *must* take the money" or "Dahlia *intends* to take the money," a question—an intriguing space of indeterminacy—is left for the reader. Furthermore, the reader is invited into an experience that is always and forever in the process of being lived through. Although our lived experiences have beginnings and endings, the literary text is always in process. It waits for the reader to become engaged with it.

It is not surprising, then, that Tim should feel convinced that *Forbidden City* was factual. Not only does the format of the narrative with its dated journal entries closely resemble an actual journal, its plot evolves within an historically verifiable set of circumstances. Paradoxically, it likely was not the "realistic" aspects of the text that made it seem like a non-fiction text for Tim since in interviews with me he communicated a greater alienation from the factual material than the fictional. For example, Tim had difficulty understanding Chinese culture, particularly as it existed under the constraints of the Communist regime. Therefore, although he was able to discuss the relationships among characters in this novel, and his own relationship with them, he seemed, at times, unable to make connections between their actions and the political "reality" of that historical period in China. It could be argued that it was the subjunctivizing of language that allowed Tim to interact, in a generative and imaginative way, with the text and, as a result, to make him feel as though the action were real. For of course, Tim's reading experience *was* real. Furthermore, because the reading was situated within the school classroom where video-clips of the actual events at Tian An Men Square as well as historical texts with documentation of actual events were juxtaposed with the reading of the literary text, Tim became immersed in extra-textual information that supported his belief in the truth of the story. The *content* of the novel cannot, it seems, be considered in the absence of its reading *context*.

With the concept of the subjunctive, Bruner takes up Langer's theory of the formulative function of language offered by the literary text and re-describes it as an understanding of the way in which the actual structure of the text contributes to the literariness that we experience when reading it. Drawing from Wolfgang Iser's formulation of the need for "gaps" in the literary text,[22] complemented by Roland Barthes' belief that the reader needs to "write" the text that is read,[23] Bruner suggests that the "literariness" of a text is closely linked to the way in which the text is able to formulate discourse systems which "recruit the reader's imagination"[24] facilitating the kind of performance that leads to meaning-making activities.

But is it really as straightforward as Bruner has suggested? Is the difference between texts announced as literary fictions and texts announced as non-fiction merely a matter of syntactic transformations that encourage readers to subjunctivize? Is the distinction between fiction and non-fiction really hinged on things such as the formulative or the subjunctive, or is it possible that there is absolutely nothing inherent in the work of literary fiction that distinguishes it from other works? "Of course there is a difference!" might be our immediate response. Most of us have felt a "difference" in our reading of a poem by Robert Frost, a novel by Margaret Atwood, or a short story by Edgar Allen Poe. The experience of reading these is not the same as our reading of a newspaper or the instructions for programming our VCR. The question remains: "How might we characterize this differential reading experience?"

The Efferent and the Aesthetic

Louise Rosenblatt has made a distinction between "efferent" and "aesthetic" reading that is useful in this discussion. For her, the efferent is related to the instrumentally communicative function of language, while the aesthetic emerges from the experience of being drawn into language which fulfills a formulative function.[25] Her two major works *Literature as Exploration*[26] and *The Reader, the Text, the Poem*[27] have demonstrated an immense scholarship and deep understanding of the transactional relation-ship between reader and literary text. Rosenblatt has been most influential in acknowledging the importance of the relationship developed between reader and literary text. Implicit within her theory is the importance of re-symbolization on a variety of different levels. As the reader interacts with the literary text, she or he goes through a transactive process of re-symbolizing his or her own thoughts with those presented in the text. In this sense, for Rosenblatt, reading is a form of cultural rewriting—a purposeful construction and reconstruction of thoughts and ideas that emerge from the transaction between reader and text.

Positing the relationship between reader and text as an exploration of possible worlds, Rosenblatt was prophetic in shifting authority from the author and the text and moving it into the interaction between reader and text. Theorizing that reading literature is a way in which young persons can learn to better understand and deal with an ever-changing and progressive world, Rosenblatt states that its purposes must be "To supply youth with the tools and knowledge necessary for a scientifically objective, critical appraisal of accepted opinion" and "to predispose the individual toward working out a basis for a more fruitful living"[28] Rosenblatt's understanding of the reading of a work of literature as convergence of reader and text was so antithetical to the New Criticism of the day that it remained largely ignored by literary and curriculum theorists until its reprinting in 1968. It seems more than coincidental that this reprinting followed closely on the heels of the Anglo-American seminar on the teaching of English held in Dartmouth, New Hampshire in 1966, and the publication of John Dixon's[29] report of this conference where a "growth" model vs. "skills" or "cultural transmission" model of English teaching was endorsed, authorizing an approach to literature reading and teaching which was more interactive than that promoted by the New Criticism and more compatible with Rosenblatt's theorizing.

For the purposes announced in this chapter, it seems fruitful to ask whether Tim's experience with *Forbidden City* was an aesthetic experience or an efferent one. Rosenblatt coined the world "efferent" from the Latin *effere* meaning "to carry away" in order to distinguish between reading for conceptual knowledge and reading as a lived experience. She suggests that the literary work of art invites readers into an experience that leads to a transaction that is more aesthetic than efferent and suggests that it is the structure of the text and the intentions of the reader which produce this effect. Therefore, it is possible that Tim's inability to distinguish the historically verifiable from the invented fictive led to a reading that was largely efferent rather than aesthetic. Of course, given the fact efferent reading is valued in most other school subjects (and, it could be argued in many English classrooms), it is not surprising that Tim resisted the aesthetic reading within the context of the classroom.[30]

Rosenblatt makes it clear that any text may be read efferently *or* aesthetically. It is not necessarily the quality of the text that distinguishes the experiences but, rather, the conditions of reading and the intentions of the reader. As Appleyard suggests, for example, young adult readers tend to choose realistic fiction because they wish to identify with characters and to think about their own lives in relation to those presented in the text.[31] Therefore, although the adolescent's engagement with the literary text is, indeed, one that may be aesthetic, it is often one that is also efferent. It is not so much, then, the way in which the text is *structured*; it is the way in which the text is *perceived* and *interpreted* by the reader that determines the quality of the reading engagement. And, if this is so, then it does not at all seem unusual that Tim would resist believing in the "invented" features of *Forbidden City*. In my discussions with him, he told me that he appreciated the fact that Alex, the seventeen year-old protagonist, demonstrated a high level of maturity and intellectual and emotional development. "He reminds me of me and many of my friends," suggested Tim. "And I know that this is not the way that most adults think of teenagers."

Tim's comment about the similarity between his interpretation of the character Alex and his perceptions of himself and his peers most clearly illustrates his preoccupation with the efferent reading. Not only does it seem important for him to "carry away" information from the text, but it is important for him to acknowledge, through his interactions with the novel, the maturity and capabilities of teenagers his age. It is the need for identification, we might say, that conditions the efferent rather than the aesthetic response. At the same time, this formulation itself calls into question the distinction between efferent and aesthetic. Are these two terms really distinct from one another? Or might we say that one depends upon the other in the playful interaction between reader and text?

Playing the Game

In *Truth and Method* Hans-Georg Gadamer[32] explains that our present situation and consciousness are always at the end-point of the world that has preceded us. By acting within the present moment we are simultaneously affected by and affect this historical presence. Precisely this idea of the "historically-effected" nature of our consciousness comes into play when reading, for in the act of reading, the reader must work to initiate a fusion of the text as the end-point of its own history, her or his own history of past interactions in the world, and the present moment of the act of reading.[33]

By tracing the history of aesthetics, Gadamer explains that the work of art (including the literary work of art) is a coincidence of form and meaning that cannot be reduced to a generalizable concept. Human interaction with art form is an *experience* and, as such, has a subjective function. Because art must be perceived in some way (seen, heard, felt), it can never be reduced to an essence since perception itself can never be pure. Gadamer suggests that "to do justice to art, aesthetics must go beyond itself and abandon the 'purity' of the aesthetic," which means that what we know as art can never be reduced to an essence of art.[34] Like perception itself, art, in order to exist at all, must always be imbued with meaning.[35]

For Gadamer, then, the literary work of fiction, like any art form, only exists in the experiencing of it. This does not mean that anything can be deemed art. Gadamer believes that any art form is an historical interpretation—an artifact—which, like the human subjects who produce it, and later interact with it, is the product of a set of historical circumstances. Art, like all other historical artifacts, carries with it the *trace* of the culture of origin—the trace of the human minds, intentions, and conditions that shaped it. The literary work of art, then, like any art form, must be culturally announced as such. When it is *announced* as an art form, the reader knows she or he is to interact with it as such. Does this mean, then, that *anything* can be considered a literary work of art? Gadamer suggests not:

> The difference between a literary work of art and any other texts is not ... fundamental. It is true that there is a difference between the language of poetry and the language of prose, and again between the language of poetic prose and that of "scientific" or "scholarly" prose. These differences can certainly also be considered from the point of view of literary form. But the essential difference

between these various "languages" obviously lies elsewhere: namely in the
distinction between the claims to truth that each makes.[36]

Gadamer explains that whereas non-literary forms of writing are meant
to instrumentally convey a truth that has some verifiable correspondence, the
literary fiction does not. Instead, it invites the reader into an experience of
reading which is like the playing of a game. Therefore, the experience in the
work of art emerges from the reader's participation in the game.[37] For
Gadamer, the literary fiction only exists in the reader's participation with
it—in the playing of the "game" that is framed by the literary text, but
dependent on the reader (player) for the work to be realized.

This formulation suggests that the literary fiction must have the capacity
to allow various players (readers) to engage with it at various times. It is the
detachability of a work of art from any particular subject (author, reader,
spectator) that Gadamer suggests transforms a text into a form or structure
that has the quality of being repeatable. The possibility for repeatability of
the literary work of art is not to be found in the actual words which comprise
it, but rather the way in which these are structured that allows the readers to
keep changing while the text is still the same. This structural quality means
that the "play" (i.e., game between text and reader) is able to be repeated by
various readers and various contexts. The truth value of the experience of
reading a literary fiction does not lie in the ability of the reader to extract
meaning from the text (which corresponds to verifiable aspects in the world),
but rather to generate an interpretation of the text (which simultaneously
involves an interpretation of the reader). Gadamer helps us to understand
that "when we interpret the artwork, we interpret ourselves; and as the work
comes into interpretation, so we come to be also."[38]

Can looking at the interaction between reader and text as a game that is
played help us to understand Tim's confusion about the literariness of
Forbidden City? Is it possible that Tim simply does not understand that his
interaction is meant to be playful and game-like? Could it be that the book
does not clearly announce itself as a work of fiction? Perhaps the most
interesting question might be concerned with what Tim would have thought
had he *not* known of the events of Tian An Men Square and had read the
book "as if" all of the events had been concocted by the author. Would he
still have been confused? Would the reading have been more playful?

Likely some of Tim's confusion emerges from the extra-textual information provided by his teacher. Although the book was "announced" as fiction, and certainly conformed to well-known, culturally established conventions of a literary fiction, it was read alongside videotapes and written accounts of the actual events at Tian An Men Square. It could be argued that these extra-textual experiences prevented Tim from "playing" in the text, and from being "played by" the text in the same way that he might have had there not been these influences. Because texts are always read alongside other texts, other experiences, and overlapping contextual details of location and circumstance, the interpretation that Tim brings to bear on *Forbidden City* cannot be limited to his interaction with this one text. Rather, the "play" of reading must be understood to exist within the overlapping and intertwining relations of reading. Reading a text for school purposes is not the same as reading a text for non-school purposes. Tim's reading of this novel, then, is not only caught up in an interaction between a particular text and a particular reader, it is situated within a culturally and historically-effected and conditioned space that we call "public schooling." The "rules" that conditioned Tim's reading of *Forbidden City* are not merely governed by his prior experiences, the structure of the text, or the announced function of the text; the reading was also conditioned by the historically-effected conditions of public schooling. When Tim responded to *Forbidden City*, he was not merely responding to a reading of a text, he was responding to the cultural and social situation in which that reading occurs.

Iterability and Re-Marking

Jacques Derrida[39] suggests that the work of literary fiction is not a location for meaning but, rather, is a form that empties out meaning while, at the same time, remaining potentially meaningful. In other words, the work of literary fiction does not contain a transcendent core of meaning, but rather has a repeatable singularity that depends on a structural openness to new contexts. Derrida writes:

> There is no essence or existence of literature. If you proceed to analyze all the elements of a literary work, you will never come across literature itself, only some traits which it shares or borrows, which you can find elsewhere too, in other texts, be it a matter of the language, the meanings, or the referents.... And even the

convention which allows a community to come to an agreement about the literary status of this or that phenomenon remains precarious, unstable and always subject to revision.[40]

Derrida suggests that the concept of a literary work of fiction "implies that license is given to the writer to say everything he wants to or everything he can, while remaining shielded, safe from all censorship, be it religious or political."[41] The cultural value of the text of literary fiction, for Derrida, is related to the valuing of the concept of democracy since both call for a space for the voices of participants in either democratic or literary processes. As such, there is not a text which is literary fiction in itself but, rather, there are in the texts "features which call for a literary reading and recall the convention, institution, or history of literature."[42] There is, therefore, a culturally pre-determined literary *functioning* of an experience of "literariness" rather than anything essentially intrinsic to the literary fiction. Attempts to reduce the literary fiction to an essence in terms of meaning, content, form, signifier, truth, or representation Derrida refers to as "reductions and misconstruings" of literature as "thematism, sociologism, historicism, psychologism."[43]

Derrida suggests, however, that in order for work of literary fiction to be interpretable it must in some way conform to a genre as well as a set of generalized conventions which guide the reader. However, this does not mean that meaning is directed by the conventionalized form the text takes. Like Gadamer, Derrida suggests that the meaning can only occur when the reader becomes purposefully engaged with the text. The text, however, must be "marked" in advance by what Derrida calls the "re-mark" which is not a feature of the text itself, but rather the ability for the text, along with the reader, to evoke a rupture—a breaking free of the boundaries of language and experience. The literary work of fiction, at its most powerful, is able to move beyond the mark on the page, or the act of marking (adding to) the experience of reader: it has the ability to re-mark—to transform. In other words, in re-marking, both the reader and the text are altered for having been involved the act of reading. According to Attridge, re-marking is

a permanent possibility in all texts, all signs, but literature has the capacity to stage its operation with unusual forcefulness and to produce unusual pleasure in doing so.... A text in which the re-mark, and the relation between singularity and generality, are staged with haunting power is, to that extent, "literary."[44]

It is the ability for the literary text to evoke in the reader a singular meaning from the common text which Derrida names the "iterability" of the literary text. Although iterability occurs elsewhere besides literary texts,[45] according to Derrida, it is most powerfully evoked within the well-wrought literary fiction. The idea of iterability explains the ability for the literary fiction to be read by various readers over various contexts and temporal periods in a way that is "singular" to each reader (i.e. they are able to derive personal meaning from it) and, at the same time, retain the historical trace of its origins. Iterability means, for example, that although I will never be able to retrieve an original, intentional meaning of the literary text (as promoted by theorists such as E. D. Hirsch[46]), I will be able to generate a singular meaning which is, at the same, inextricable from historical traces. Derrida writes:

> To say that marks or texts are originally iterable is to say that without a simple origin, and so without a pure originarity, they divide and repeat themselves immediately. They thus become capable of being rooted out at the very place of their roots. Transplantable into a different context, they continue to have meaning and effectiveness.[47]

For Derrida, the reader does not exist before the work, but is invented by the work through her or his engagement with the work. It is the iterable character, the ability to mark and re-mark that permits this invention. However, this is not to be understood as a "natural" phenomenon. Derrida suggests that this continual invention and re-invention of the reader will only occur "if s/he is willing to countersign,"[48] for it is in the countersigning that the reader agrees to become part of the re-marking process. Derrida's descriptions of re-marking and iterability point to the need for us, as human subjects, to engage with texts that permit some sort of self-interpretation, some form of re-invention—a process of interpretation that Heidegger believes is the essence of human existence.[49]

Interestingly, in interviews with a number of students after their class reading of *Forbidden City,* I discovered that it was only when they were able to forget the historicity of the text and engage in the experience of the plot with the invented characters could they articulate their own re-invention process. Although the concept of democracy and freedom was addressed in extra-textual information provided by their teacher, they seemed to become more powerful concepts when students discussed them in terms of their experience of living alongside the characters in the novel.[50] This became particularly evident in my conversations with Tim, for even though he remained reluctant to admit the invented fictionality of the characters presented in the novel, it became evident that his "relationship" with the lives of these characters had helped him to more deeply understand the lived experience of another culture:

> *I can understand how Alex would seem so different to his friends after he came back home. I mean, even I feel different after reading the book, and I didn't go anywhere!*

It seems that even though Tim was unsure about the book's status as a work of fiction, he was still able to become re-marked. The question remains, however, of whether it was the book itself that facilitated the experience of feeling different, or whether it was the extra-textual and post-reading activities in the classroom which facilitated it.

Derrida would likely suggest that is not possible, nor even desirable to attempt to make this distinction since, like all action in the world, the reading of the literary text is always an historically-effected act that must occur within a lived context. Therefore, the interactions that Tim has in the classroom, like any other interactions he might have, will affect how he feels about his relationship with any text. And so, although concepts like *play, game, re-mark,* and *iterability* do not, in the end, nail down once and for all what might constitute a text of literary fiction, they can help us to understand the complexity of the relation between the reader and these texts.

The Real, the Fictive, and the Imaginary

Wolfgang Iser has, over the past twenty years, provided detailed and insightful phenomenological descriptions of the reader's engagement with works of literary fiction.[51] Like Langer, Iser suggests that the author of the literary text takes elements from a familiar world and puts them together in an unfamiliar way. In part, the unfamiliarity is derived from the fact that literary fictions offer less determinacy than other texts. The intention of the authors of such texts is not to present a seamless real-world correspondence through the language selected but, rather, to present a disrupted world—a world that depends upon the active participation of the reader in order to be made meaningful. This, Iser suggests, is what constitutes the aesthetic response in the act of reading a literary fiction, for it is in the process of "indeterminacy filling" that the reader becomes removed from his or her real world into a world constructed through the reader-text interaction. A structural feature of the literary fiction, then, is the deliberate insertion of indeterminacy by the author. Iser suggests that

> Texts with ... minimal indeterminacy tend to be tedious, for it is only when the reader is given the chance to participate actively that he will regard the text, whose intention he himself has helped to compose as real. *For we generally tend to regard things that we have made ourselves as real.* And so, it can be said that indeterminacy is the fundamental precondition for reader participation.[52]

Upon examination, it is clear that the novel *Forbidden City* is not overly-determined. Because the first half of the book is composed solely of journal entries written from the point of view of the main character, Alex, it is, at times, highly indeterminate and ambiguous. Since readers must rely upon these entries for information about past and present events, there is a great deal that the reader needs to "fill in" for him or herself. Why, for example, are Alex's parents divorced? Why is Alex living with his father? Although more information about Alex's family situation is given later in the novel, it becomes up to the reader to engage in a great deal of "indeterminacy filling" in the first half and, generally speaking, throughout the book. This is certainly not the way an historical account of one person's experience of Tian An Men Square might have been written. It is unlikely, first of all, that "personal" details about family relationships would have been related and, even if they were, they would likely have been mentioned only to illuminate a particular historical event. In the historical text, the author attempts to "fill in" any gaps. Details, dates, times, and witnesses' accounts all serve to make the text appear "seamless." Why, then, did Tim and some of his classmates, feel that this text was so "real" for them? Is Iser correct in suggesting that the act of indeterminacy filling, because it is something that we construct ourselves, makes the fiction seem real? He writes:

[T]he indeterminate elements of literary prose ... represent a vital link between text and reader. They are the switch that activates the reader into using his own ideas in order to fulfill the intentions of the text. This means that they are the basis for a textual structure in which the reader's part is already incorporated. In this respect, literary texts differ from those that formulate a concrete meaning or truth. Texts of the latter kinds are, by their very nature, independent of any individual reader, for the meaning or truth that they express exists independently of any reader participation. But when a vital element of a text is reader participation, it is forced to rely on the individual reader for the realization of a possible meaning or truth. The meaning is conditioned by the text itself, but only in a form that allows the reader himself to bring it out.[53]

In order for *Forbidden City* to become meaningful for Tim, it was necessary for his imagination to be invoked. For it is only by invoking the imagination, that indeterminacy filling is possible. For Tim, indeterminacy filling meant imagining what it would be like to live with a father, for his father had died when he was a baby. For his classmate, Gina, indeterminacy filling meant imagining what it would be like to live with her divorced father and his new wife instead of her mother. It seems, then, that Iser has identified the most important structural aspect of the literary text: the spaces of indeterminacy, as opened up by selections and combinations from the "real" world by the author, allow the imagination to be invoked. This imaginative response is not diffuse; it is conditioned by what is given in the literary fiction.

The reader, however, *must be notified* about how she or he is to interact with the text, for it is not only the literary fiction which contains indeterminacy. The directions to my VCR machine, for example, seem to contain many indeterminacies, as did the calculus problems which I encountered in my high school mathematics class. However, these kinds of indeterminacies are not dealt with in the same way as those found in the literary fiction, for I do not feel that I can simply "imagine" what might occur in these spaces. I do not feel that I can "invent" information that is not given in the VCR directions or in the calculus problem. These differential responses, Iser suggests, are culturally conditioned. Sets of directions and math problems are meant to "tell" not to "invite," therefore it is important for us to become more attentive to the differences between these texts and literary fictions.

According to Iser, it is essential that the literary fiction announces itself as such. The fictive that has been created must be unmasked as a fictive, for without the unmasking, the fictional text may be mistaken for the non-fictional text which, of course, would dramatically alter the way in which the reader engages with it. This unmasking might occur in the culturally agreed-upon forms that literature may take, or, if these are not clear, they might be publicly announced by the author as a literary art form.[54] In any case, the most significant difference between the fictive of the literary fiction and other fictives in our lives (images of sports heroes, political figures, rock stars, for example) is that the former must be unmasked as a fictive in order for it to function while the latter must not be.

Furthermore, although the literary fiction appears to resist the course of time, this is not because it represents transcendent, eternal values but because its structure continually allows the reader to place himself or herself within the world of the announced fictive. The deliberate repositioning of selected aspects of the world by the author amid deliberate structures of indeterminacy allows the *play*, the *re-mark*, and/or the *iterability* that characterizes the reader's engagement with literary fictions. These structures, over the course of history, have been developed in order to live alongside, yet separate from, other forms of discourse.

It is apparent, then, that texts of literary fiction cannot be simply determined by features or functions of the text alone. Rather, the form "literary fiction" is largely conditioned by the historically specific intentions of the author's selections of the real world as represented within the contextually specific conditions of the reader's engagement with these. Iser helps us to understand that

> Literary texts contain a range of signals to denote that they are fictive. These have become significant through particular, historically varying conventions shared by author and public. Thus the signals do not invoke fictionality as such, but conventions which form the basis of a kind of contract between author and reader the terms of which identify the text not as discourse but as enacted discourse.[55]

As opposed to interactions with the real world, however, the reader's engagement with the literary fiction cannot be perceived through the senses but only through imaginative interpretations of sensory perceptions. When the fictive nature of a text is unmasked, and the reader understands that she or he must work to overcome indeterminacy that has been conditioned by the author, the imagination is invoked. It is the conditioned imagination that leads to the experience of "boundary crossing" where the reader, through his or her engagement with the literary text, experiences a world which outstrips any real-world correspondence that she may know.

It is important, therefore, to understand that what we perceive as literary emerges from a recursive relationship—through the act of reading—among the *real*, the *fictive*, and the *imaginary*. As a product of the author's selections and re-combinations of details from the real world, embedded within culturally agreed-upon fictive forms, the imaginary is invoked. The reader, then, is able to participate in these mutually intended imaginings without becoming committed to the consequences of a real-world engagement with them. Even so, because these engagements are experiences, they become woven into the fabric of the reader's world, and thus we see how the imaginary weaves itself back into the real. Given this understanding, it becomes clear why we often value our engagements with literary fictions, for although they are not the same as encounters with expository texts, or with more tacit face-to-face experiences in the world, they are significant.

The Hermeneutic Imagination

By asking the question "What *is* the character of literary work of fiction?" I have demonstrated my complicity in the modern philosophical project to determine an absolute, a foundation, an essence for what could be called "literary." This desire to *locate*, to determine *once and for all*, is precisely what eludes us in the project of defining literary fictions, for these do not live within the words, within the text, or within the reader. The literary, as Gadamer, Derrida and Iser have suggested can only be found in the imaginative play that exists between a culturally situated text and reader. And although the forms and conventions that help us to distinguish texts of literary fiction from other texts are always and already historically-effected, they are also always and forever altered through the functions they serve, the interpretations they are given, and the specific ways in which they are enacted. The question, then, of what reading literary fictions reveals *to* us is not nearly so interesting as the question of what reading them reveals *about* us. As Gadamer suggests:

There are no purely formal criteria that can claim to judge and sanction the
formative level [of art] simply on the basis of its artistic virtuosity. Rather, our
sensitive-spiritual existence is an aesthetic resonance chamber that resonates with
the voices that are constantly reaching us, preceding all explicit aesthetic
judgment.[56]

It is significant that Gadamer does not locate aesthetic consciousness in
the "mind" but rather in the relational aspects of our existence in the world.[57]
David Smith explains that, in the Western world at least, we have been
trapped into believing that the mind is "the locale and arbiter of knowledge
and experience"[58] and that it is through perception that the human subject is
able to grasp reality and legitimate it through language. This valorization of
consciousness, Smith suggests, "shapes curriculum decision-making as
fundamentally a form of arbitration over the correctness or appropriateness
of ideas ... as a judgment of the degree to which they 're-present' reality, and
the truth of things as defined according to standards of orthodoxy such as
science or communal tradition."[59] It is not surprising, then, that I would seek
to name the textual essence of a literary fiction, since the value of things in
the modern Western world is often dependent upon determining the strength
of their foundations.

Gadamer, however, reminds us that "The real power of hermeneutical
consciousness is our ability to see what is questionable." [60] And so, perhaps
the question, "What *is* the character of the literary text?" can be considered
an appropriate beginning for an hermeneutic investigation into the pedagogical meaning of our relationships with literary fictions. Perhaps it has been
by traveling through the journey initiated by *this* question that I have come
to understand that it is probably not the right question, since "what *is*"
implies something fixed, something foundational. Curiously, however, it
seems that the hermeneutic question—the question to which there is not an
absolute, pre-determined, or a fixed answer—can be found within this
question, for the word *is* announces a state of being. Therefore, through a
simple syntactic maneuver we might ask instead: "What is the cultural *state
of being* of a work of literary fiction?" It seems that this is a question which
can be answered, for a literary fiction is an historically-effected form—a set
of conventions that signals a contract between author and reader—which,
when unmasked as such, invites the reader into a particular kind of
relationship. The existence of a literary fiction, then, can never be defined

by particular, fixed, pre-determined features, but can only be understood historically, culturally, referentially, and relationally.

The existential character of a literary fiction, as Iser has helped us to understand, is inextricable from the human being's capacity for the imaginative. However, in our commodified and technologized culture we have marginalized the imaginative to the "daydream," to something that is always secondary to the "real" business of day-to-day life. Nowhere is this more evident than in schools where the mark of a good student is her or his ability to keep his/her mind on task, to keep from daydreaming. Similarly, an effective teacher is able to promote this work ethic through a rigorous program of studies coupled with well-honed management skills. The imaginary is often relegated to the wasteland of arts and crafts classes, the Christmas play, the creative writing period; whereas, real work is represented by problems of algebra, science experiments, and close readings of texts.

We have a deep sense, however, of the importance of the imaginary and of the imagination. The *Oxford English Dictionary* suggests that to *imagine* is to "consider, ponder, meditate, bethink oneself"; while *imagination* is "the creative faculty of the mind in its highest aspect, the power of framing new and striking intellectual conceptions; poetic genius." Plato understood the power of the imagination, the power of poetic genius. Hence, his warning about poetics and poets.[61] The power of the imagination invoked by the poetic—the literary fiction—is well-known by political dictators who understand the subversiveness and danger of the poetically conditioned imagination. For to imagine, within the spaces opened up by the literary fiction, is not merely to imagine what might fill those spaces, but to imagine oneself as well. To imagine is to "bethink oneself," to meditate, to picture oneself in imagination. It is this human ability that leads to interpretation, to self-interpretation. This need for self-interpretation, in relation to our historically-effected conscious presence in the world, is hermeneutic. It is the kind of questioning that emerges from our continual need to define and re-define ourselves in relation to our world and each other. And because hermeneutic interpretations of our lived experience always includes thinking ahead to a future existence (what will happen tomorrow?), it becomes clear that hermeneutic understanding depends upon the imagination, for *all* prediction is a form of imaginative work. As David Smith suggests:

The hermeneutic imagination works from a commitment to generativity and rejuvenation and to the question of how we can go on together in the midst of constraints and difficulties that constantly threaten to foreclose on the future.[62]

It is the hermeneutic imagination that makes possible the experience of engagement with a work of literary fiction. It could be said, then, that literary fictions are culturally agreed-upon forms that allow the human imagination to be invoked. These forms are marginalized and valorized at the same time; although we value the form and value our engagement with them, we have had some difficulty accounting for their empirical value in our daily lives. What is understood and recognized (announced) as a literary fiction gives permission for the human subject to imagine herself or himself differently. The immersion into a constructed fictive, composed of re-positioned elements of the "real," allows the imaginary to be conditioned in such a way that the world remains unfixable, undetermined. The reader's engagement with a literary work, then, calls into question the existence of "the real."

And so, if we think back to Tim's insistence that *Forbidden City* is real and not fictional, we should be concerned. Not concerned about why he *thinks* that it is real but rather with why he should *want* it to be real. If we can agree that the retreat to the imaginary, through the constructed fictive of the literary text, is indeed a generative, hermeneutically important state of being, then why is it that Tim is not eager to enter into that realm? Why is it that he resists when his teacher insists that he must read this as a literary fiction? Moreover, why does his teacher feel that the reading of this literary text, in order to be understood, must occur amid her presentation of extra-textual material? Is it possible that the schooled context of reading is preventing Tim from accepting and accessing the fictive, and at the same time, the imaginative? Is it even possible for the *imaginative, subjunctive, aesthetic, formulative, iterable* reading to exist in a setting that valorizes and validates the *real, paradigmatic, efferent, communicative* one? Is it possible for the culturally announced forms of the literary fiction to function in school settings in the way in which they must in order to perform their transforma-tive work?

These are difficult, important questions, for they begin to address the issue of what it means for the literary imagination and the school curriculum to co-exist. Before they can be fully taken up, however, the nature of the reader's relationship with the literary text must be explored. This shall be the task undertaken in the next chapter.

III

Tracing Intertextual Desire

She entered the story knowing she would emerge from it feeling she had been immersed in the lives of others, in plots that stretched back twenty years, her body full of sentences and moments, as if awaking from sleep with a heaviness caused by unremembered dreams.

Michael Ondaatje, *The English Patient*[1]

In this passage from *The English Patient*, the character Hana enters the novel knowing that her commitment to it will be rewarded. She will leave "full of sentences and moments" that become woven into her body. This is the experience of immersion into the literary fiction, particularly works of prose fiction such as novels that have the capacity to sweep the reader into a web of experiences unlike those she or he might have in everyday life. As suggested in the last chapter, the literary fiction has the ability to invoke and condition the imagination of the reader, creating possible worlds that become part of the reader's experience of living.

Clearly, these experiences must be pleasurable, and the desire for one's children, friends, or students to have them supersedes the belief that reading is good for them. Although the reading of literary fiction is used in schools as a location to improve reading skills, to experience a particular cultural heritage, or to learn particular facts, it seems to me that all of these could be just as effectively learned through other experiences. So why read fiction? I have come to believe that those of us who have experienced what it is like to be relationally bound to works of fiction have found these experiences pleasurable—desirable, we might say. And, because we desire it ourselves, and because pleasure is meant to be shared, we wish others to participate in similar experiences.

In this chapter I will explore the reader's developing relationship with a work of literary fiction. These explorations are developed around a novel read by our teacher reading group—Michael Ondaatje's *The English Patient*. Not only was the shared reading of this novel a transformative experience for us, but it is also worth noting that the novel itself has been critically acclaimed as one of the finest works in the literary world.[2] As a valued cultural art form, it has particular relevance in a discussion of the reading relationship. As well, the plot of this novel is developed around themes of reading, writing, and literary relationality that will function as interpretive locations for some of the theoretical work that needs to be accomplished in this chapter. For me, one of the most interesting aspects of the novel is the way in which the Greek writer Herodotus' work, *The Histories*,[3] becomes a mediating text for relations among the characters in the novel. Because this provides important theoretical scaffolding for my own ideas about the reading relationship, I will start with a brief discussion of Herodotus and his writings, followed by an exploration of the significance of reading relationships within the ecology of human lived experience.

Marking Boundaries

> *In this book, the result of my inquiries into history, I hope to do two things: to preserve the memory of the past by putting on record the astonishing achievements both of our own and of the Asiatic peoples; secondly, and more particularly, to show how the two races came into conflict.*
>
> Herodotus, *The Histories*[4]

It is well known that the idea of writing books, particularly stories, appeared only recently in the history of humanity. Before that, people had developed spoken language and had come to use it for telling stories which, in large part, were meant to preserve knowledge. Stories, as kept alive by an oral tradition, became *commonplaces* for cultural knowledge. Gradually, this mode of storytelling adopted various specific syntactic devices that served two functions: first, they allowed "stories" to remain separate from everyday discourse; second, they provided structures that helped persons memorize the stories so that they might be passed from generation to generation.

In his book *Orality and Literacy*, Walter Ong[5] makes important distinctions between literate and oral cultures, suggesting that print literacy significantly alters the way cultures are organized. He explains that in pre-print cultures, knowledge, beliefs, and traditions are located in narrative stories that are passed from generation to generation. Interpretation and revision of cultural knowledge is continual and occurs naturally in the modifications made to songs, poetry, myths and legends that are passed on through an oral tradition. By conceptualizing cultures as interactive systems that are organized around the use and structure of language, Ong suggests that situating important cultural knowledge within orally transmitted stories profoundly affects the manner of interaction among people.

Ong's formulations suggest that within oral cultures, shared storytelling facilitates continued intergenerational dialogue. One could say, then, that in such cultures storytelling supports an important pedagogical relation that is critical to the coherence of the cultural fabric. Inscribed within oral cultures is an ethic of pedagogical caring for which all adults assume some responsibility. One might also say that, because the stories are continually updated, each storytelling is hermeneutic; each is an interpretation of what has been told by one's forebears.[6] It seems, then, that the pedagogy of storytelling simultaneously supports ongoing cultural preservation and cultural revision.

In Ancient Greece some stories of this type became highly rhythmic, taking on a form that Aristotle called "poetics" and which we still refer to as poetry.[7] In Greece, as elsewhere, poets were those who were known as specially gifted and were trained in reciting the traditional stories in the traditional ways. An important quality of the effective storyteller was her or his ability to add new "verses" or new interpretations. Stories and poems were always memorized and passed on through the oral tradition even though the advent of writing in Greece occurred some centuries prior (as early as 1400 B.C.). However, because record keeping was not necessary for most of the centuries prior to the ninth century B.C., writing was not extensively used. It was only with the growth of trade that more systematic and formal systems of recording were required, rekindling an interest in the use and development of written forms of expression. Soon after, the Greeks began to extend their use of writing from commerce to the recording of poems and stories. At the same time, they began keeping records of the events and winners at Olympic games, and of descriptions of the geographic features of towns and waterways of particular regions. Because these seemed to have little to do with the traditional topics of epic or narrative poetry and stories, they were recorded differently, in a more prosaic style. In the middle of this transition, from a largely oral culture into an emerging literate one, Herodotus can be located.

Herodotus lived in the fifth century B.C. Although the exact dates are not known, sometime between 480–425 seems most likely.[8] This means that he was a boy at the time of the Persian Wars—an event he used as the main theme for his book, which, in one of its first translations printed in 1584, was entitled *The Famous Hystory of Herodotus.* Although in later translations the title was changed to *The Histories*, the way in which these "histories" of the war between the Greeks and the Persians were written would suggest that the first title was perhaps more apt than the second, for it has been generally agreed that in addition to being an historian Herodotus provided one of the first models of prose literature. The general confusion about whether Herodotus' texts were historical facts or literary fictions emerged from the fact that unlike previous attempts at keeping written historical records, which largely took the form of lists of dates, locations, and specific occurrences, Herodotus attempted a more full-bodied history. Rather than merely chronicling specific facts, he was more interested in the human relationships that led to particular events and the way particular events influenced human behavior and relationships.

It is significant that in Herodotus' time the Greek word *historie* signified all intellectual pursuits—scientific, mathematical, aesthetic and historical. For Herodotus, to be an historian was to be an inquirer. Inquiry meant an active pursuit of data, gathering of stories, learning about causes of events, and rendering visible and explicit the relationships between them. His "history," then, of the events leading to and including the Persian Wars was meant to be an interpretation of his inquiries. It could be argued that Herodotus' *Histories* is a hermeneutic study in its most philosophically contemporary form, for he sought not merely facts, but an understanding of the conditions that made possible the interpretation of emerging events. Most of all, Herodotus sought understanding of the human relationships that circumscribed historical events. As a cultural interpreter, he gathered the narratives told by people, along with descriptions of their lands, their observable actions, their customs and traditions, their inventions, myths, and romantic tales, and wove this information into a highly complex story of a civilization. We could say that as a researcher, Herodotus was really a "bricoleur"—one who uses a wide variety of methods to gather various forms of data pertaining to a topic of research interest.[9]

Why would Herodotus become famous as one of the first historians? Surely "history" is meant to be a recording of the facts, not some literary embellishment of them! According to his explicators,[10] it is precisely the embellishment for which he is recognized, for it was Herodotus who was the first to go beyond the citing of facts to the important excavating of the social, political, cultural, interpersonal and relational conditions that supported any identified fact. Although not formally recognized as such, it may be argued that Herodotus was the first to understand that all human events are the result of what Husserl has called "intentionality"; that is, that all human consciousness and action *aims* at something.[11]

Therefore, although *The Histories* are not thought of as chronicles of events exactly as they happened, they have been valued for the richness of detail about Greek culture that they suggest. Like epic poems, *The Histories* became a collecting place for important cultural knowledge. Situated within a constructed sequence of events by characters selected by Herodotus, *The Histories* shows more than any other known text before the human importance ascribed to hermeneutic interpretation. From Herodotus we learn that history is embodied within the relationships among human subjects acting in (and remembering) the particularities of their historicized, politicized cultural experience. For Herodotus, compiling a history meant rendering visible the largely invisible features of humanity—the desires and relations that bind human subjects. History became an investigation into boundaries, and the way these are simultaneously held and transgressed.

Contemporary versions of *The Histories* can be found in historical fiction made famous by authors such as James Michener. Like readers of *The Histories*, readers of novels by Michener learn something of the historical events depicted in the novel. I can remember, for example, after my reading of Michener's *Poland*[12] how delighted my step-father was that I finally seemed to know enough about the turbulent history of his native Poland for us to have conversations on the subject. Somehow, during these conversations, however, I forgot that what I knew about Polish history I had learned from a literary fiction. Although I had never shared the confusion that Tim had about reading *Forbidden City*, my body had certainly been "filled with sentences." The reading of this literary fiction had altered the boundaries of my own knowledge about a country to which I was relationally bound. Did it matter that many of the characters, the specific events, the particular situations were invented, imagined by Michener? Not at all. And, of course, the experience of reading *Poland* has left a trace in me—a body-memory of reading that forms part of the collective memory of my lived experience.

Commonplaces for the Self

> *She picks up the notebook that lies on the small table beside his bed. It is the book he brought with him through the fire—a copy of* The Histories *by Herodotus that he has added to, cutting and gluing pages from other books or writing in his own observations—so they are all cradled within the text of Herodotus.*
>   Michael Ondaatje, *The English Patient*[13]

With this passage from *The English Patient*, we learn that the burned pilot, cared for by Hana, uses Herodotus' *The Histories* as a commonplace book—a book into which he has woven aspects of his own life, and which, at the same time, has become woven into him. The book is more than an artifact, more than a collecting place for ideas and thoughts he has had; it is a prosthetic device of sorts—an extension of his sense of self-identity.[14] Through his practice of re-reading parts of the book again and again over many years—of writing notes about his understandings of these readings, of gluing in pages from other books, and clippings from newspapers—the English patient shows us two things: First, that the sense of self cannot be contained by the body, but relies, to a large extent, on "collecting" places outside of the body. Second, it helps us to understand that our engagements with books are dialogic; as readers we converse with books, and although we may not engage in the English patient's practice of writing and pasting things directly into the book, there is no doubt that as we read, we write. In this sense our interaction with books is relational.

For the English patient, *The Histories* becomes a text to which he is relationally bound. The relationship, however, is more than the absorption of "sentences" into the body, but is also the reciprocal action of the physical infusion of artifacts that represent his lived experiences into the book. The book becomes a mediating object for the English patient. But as suggested in the last chapter, the meanings readers evoke are not located in the text or the reader, but in the engagement between text and reader. Therefore, it is probably more accurate to say that the place of mediation is not really in the text of *The Histories* itself, but rather in the relationship that is formed between the reader and the text—in the interstices. After this relationship is formed, the text functions to announce a *commonplace location*—a collecting place—for ongoing interpretation.

Therefore, although the English patient calls *The Histories* his "commonplace" book, and although it is true that it forms a commonplace for ideas, thoughts, reflections and other artifacts, the actual commonplace is not to be found in the book, but rather in the *relationship* he has with the book. This is an important point, for it helps us to understand the importance of commonplaces that function as material extensions of the self. Herodotus must have known this. That is why he believed history must never be merely a recording of events, but rather a depiction of relational desire—a representation of human action and interaction as fused by the human need for interpersonal relations. History could only be understood if the conditions—the relations which circumscribed and infused historical events—could somehow be depicted. Moreover, these needed to be presented in a way that would invite readers to participate, live with, and be *in relation* with/to the historical text. And so, like in the modern novel, Herodotus filled his history with characters, dialogue, adventure and gossip made coherent by a central plot and theme. The re-enactment of the historical plot with speaking, thinking and acting characters who are depicted in relation to one another provides the semiotic space into which the reader enters.

Like the English patient who finds a commonplace location for interpretation through his relationship with *The Histories,* Anna, a high school English teacher, develops a commonplace during her experience of reading *The English Patient:*

> *I feel like I'm sitting on the bed between Hana and the English patient, listening to them reading. I'm not one of them, and I'm not really myself either. I'm like a shadow that exists in their world.*

By presenting the reader with dialogue punctuated with omniscient commentary, the author creates a text that allows the reader to be taken below the surface of action and event. This becomes the structural key allowing Anna to function as a "shadow" in the text—what Geoff Fox has called the "Dark Watcher."[15] Within this human-text relationship, readers develop a "commonplace for the self." Just as Hana and the English patient establish a relationship through the reading of novels together, Anna develops a particular relationship with a novel by reading about their experience of reading.

Once the relationship is established, it exists as part of the reader's world and sometimes functions as a mediating space within which the reader negotiates other aspects of her or his life. The relationship, then, between the reader and the literary fiction as the commonplace is something that must be examined in greater detail. What is the significance of this relationship? How do these reading relationships become positioned among interpersonal relationships? What effect does one seem to have on the other?

Searching for the Trace

> *Caravaggio watches Hana, who sits across from him looking into his eyes, trying to read him, trying to figure the flow of thought the way his wife used to do. He watches her sniffing him out, searching for the trace.*
>
> Michael Ondaatje, *The English Patient*[16]

Although Caravaggio had known Hana when she was a child, the intervening years had erased the significance of that knowledge. Hana was no longer a child. She was no longer merely an extension of her parents. "What she was now was what she herself had decided to become.... He could hardly believe his pleasure at her translation."[17] To come to know Hana again—to understand the translation—Caravaggio needed to read her. And yet, for the moment, all he can do is study her face, look into her eyes—windows into the soul. But eyes are also mirrors—two way mirrors. They are openings that allow the world to enter the body for interpretation. The surface of the eye, however, also functions as a reflector. As Hana watched Caravaggio study her, she saw not only him, but herself.

When I look into your eyes, I do not see into you. I see me. Am I reading you when I look into your eyes? Or am I reading myself? Is it possible that I am in you and you are in me? Searching for the trace, it seems, is complicated. Often, while seeking the other we locate ourselves.

Prior to the war, Caravaggio was an accomplished thief. Because these skills were useful in a war where surveillance of enemy activity was required, Caravaggio became a spy. What qualities would make one proficient as a spy? It would seem that the most important quality would be the ability to create the conditions necessary to access "secret" information while remaining unnoticed, anonymous. Paradoxically, to learn some*thing* secret, you often need to know some*one*. Locating information, therefore, often requires entering into relations with someone. In order to retain anonymity, however, an efficient entry and clean escape is required. This was Caravaggio's specialty: gaining entry to houses, to locked rooms, to other people's lives. And then disappearing. Without a trace.

Caravaggio's skill became a habit. During his time at the villa he became preoccupied with trying to gain entry to the English patient's mind. He, more than any other character, had the desire to read the other. It was the ambiguity of not knowing that Caravaggio could not stand. The ambiguity of not knowing his position *in relation to others*. Rather than peering into himself, however, he peered into the others which, disturbingly, only brought him closer to himself. In tracing he was traced.

Tracing, it seems, is also a part of reading.

As our reading group discussed our responses to this novel we came to understand how closely we had become implicated in the lives of the characters. Most interesting, however, was the way in which we were finally unable to separate our understandings of ourselves from our understandings of the characters. Throughout our discussions we remarked on the similarities between the way the characters in the book were "thrown" together at the villa and the way we had ended up together in the reading group. Ingrid was the first to notice:

> *It's quite remarkable how quickly, as a group of strangers, we have gotten to know each other by reading and talking about this book together. We seem so much closer than I would ever have imagined. Just like the characters in the novel. It's like we have opened our minds to each other.*

But had we really? Was it our "minds" that were opened? Or, like Caravaggio, did we, in our relations with the novel and our relations with each other, experience "being traced" during our shared reading experience?

"What's on your mind?"

"I can't read minds, you know!"

"You've been on my mind all day."

What we say about minds suggests a contradiction about what we believe about the mind and the body. On the one hand, there seems to be general agreement that the mind and the body are two separate things. This severing of mind and body was heralded in the writings of the ancient Greeks and formally announced in the seventeenth century through the philosophy of Descartes,[18] whose famous maxim *cogito ergo sum* has underwritten the modern era. More commonly known as Cartesian Dualism, it has contributed to ongoing debates about the "problem" of the mind. And it really is a problem. For if the mind and body are considered separate entities, one cannot validly infer, on the basis of knowledge about one, anything about the other.

On the other hand, *seeing is believing*. Modern science has generally valued that which can be perceived and measured. Hunches, intuitions, dreams and the imagination remain marginal to the empirical and rational because they often have little verifiable correspondence to the natural world and generally do not subscribe to some formal system of logic. Hence the fundamental contradiction: If we are to believe that minds and bodies are really separate, how are we to learn about other minds? Are our relations with others really only based on getting to know their bodies? Or does the body somehow give us access to the mind?

One way to resolve this dilemma is to assume that there *is* some correspondence between what is going on in the mind and what the body is "saying." Reading the body, then, would be the same as reading the mind. But, of course, there is often little correspondence between mind and body. We sometimes look interested when we're not, innocent when we're guilty, calm when we're troubled. In fact, our relations with others would be continually tumultuous if our mind could be read through our body. How difficult life would be if our body betrayed every trace of our thoughts! Furthermore, it would eliminate the need to "search for the trace" since there would be no need to search. Everything on the *inside* would somehow be marked on the *outside*.

It is the inside/outside split that becomes most interesting, for it is generally assumed that the mind is in the brain, that it is *inside*—contained in a body that can be seen from the outside. The problem of knowing the mind of the other is the problem of getting in. But is it really true that the mind is contained entirely in the brain? Is it true that the self is contained entirely in one's body? Or is it possible that the mind is not only distributed throughout the body, but also outside of the body? Is it possible that a mind can be shared by two or more persons? Can a collective mind and a collective self exist?[19]

In *The English Patient*, four characters are thrown together into a bombed out villa in northern Italy at the end of the second World War. As the days and weeks slip by, they gradually come to know one another. This is accomplished through conversation, shared responsibilities, what they say to each other about one another, and from what they *do not* say (since silence is a form of communication). The English patient says little about himself or others and is not able to participate in the sharing of responsibilities. Hana comes to know him, in part, by reading parts of his "commonplace book." In addition, she reads novels to him and, in the midst of those readings, talks about what has been read. And so, even though Hana cannot read the English patient's mind, nor does he tell her what is on his mind, they come to know one another. She, by reading his commonplace book and by listening to responses he has to shared readings of other books; he, by noticing her habit of reading too quickly, noticing the kinds of books she selects, listening to the sound of her voice, and interpreting her touch. But most of all each of them watches and is watched. They study one other. They try to read one another's face, eyes, hands, body. They *search for the trace* that will permit them some understanding of the other. All this is accomplished within the conditions of their thrown-ness—the condition of being together in a particular place at a particular time.

There are consequences to not locating the trace, to not being able to locate oneself amid relations with others. It is the experience of being othered, of being excluded, of being an outsider. There are those who are more used to or more willing to live with these feelings of exclusion. In *The English Patient*, Kirphal Singh (Kip), the East Indian working in the British army as a bomb-disposal expert (a sapper), is accustomed to being an outsider. In fact, although he enters into relations with all of the other characters, he keeps his bed in a tent outside the villa, on the margins of the property. He retains a space around himself. For both Hana and Kip, it is *desire* that brings them together, and yet, at the same time, desire that keeps them apart. They each like this. They have found the trace of the other yet do not feel that they must appropriate it.

During a discussion of *The English Patient,* I confessed that unlike Kip and Hana, I disliked the feeling of being an "outsider," and this included my experiences of reading novels. As a consequence, I always felt a great deal of anxiety during the initial stages of reading. I was afraid that I might never be able to "get in." Mena concurred, adding that when she had difficulty "getting in" she not only felt like a "stranger," but felt like an inadequate reader. She believed that the fault for not "getting in" must be related to some reading deficiency. Ruth's experience was very different. For her, "getting in" was part of the excitement, part of the sensual experience of reading:

> *I loved the first chapters of this book, especially because it was not clear what was going on. It was a delicious mystery. Having to really listen to the text—to have to work to get into it—was part of the wonderful experience of reading it.*

What is the significance of remaining outside of relations with other people and outside relations with literary fictions? Do these experiences intersect in any way? Are they related to our search for the trace?

The phenomenon of establishing relations with others is discussed by Sartre[20] who suggests that often when in the presence of another person we experience ourselves as viewed from the perspective of the other. According to Sartre, this is the experience of being judged, of being endowed with a meaning which is not of our own making. We are no longer a being for ourselves but, instead, a being for the other. The other is finding meaning in us and interpreting it. Being watched means being interpreted. At the same time, we can become the subject which interprets the other. We can also be the author of our own interpretations of ourselves. These interpretations, however, cannot be separated from each other. They occur within situations and, because of this, they overlap and intertwine. Their beginnings, endings, and intersections are invisible.

As we watch others operating in the world we do not merely learn about them, but about the way they perceive world. We see through others aspects of the world that we are unable to experience ourselves. The relations among ourselves, others, and the world that we share are of being and not knowing. The way we *are* with each other is more fundamental than what we *know* about each other. At the same time, in order to be with one another, we need to know something about them. Knowing, however, can never precede being. It is an endless circle, but not necessarily a vicious one.

Entering into relations with others sometimes means that we must move more slowly than we are accustomed. The English patient, for example, knew that Hana was deeply troubled, yet he did not *know* the trouble. He also did not *ask* her about the trouble, just as she did not inquire into his. Instead, he taught her about reading:

> Read him slowly, dear girl, you must read Kipling slowly. Watch carefully where the commas fall so you can discover the natural pauses.[21]

Did he intend a double entendre? Did he wish her to know that it was also important in life to move slowly? Was it a lesson he had learned in his own relations with others? This was Anna's interpretation:

> *It really helped me when he gave us those "reading directions." I did slow down, and by slowing down I relaxed and began to see much more in the book. It's how I eventually really got into it. By slowing down enough to notice things that I had not noticed before. I think that maybe sometimes we move too quickly—not just as readers—but as persons. And when we move too quickly we don't really notice other people. We don't get to know who they really are.*

Hana, the English patient, the others in the villa, Anna, the rest of the reading group—all became implicated in a complex web or relations that required ongoing interpretation. As we were immersed in these emerging relations we were all trying to discern traces of ourselves and of the others. We soon learned, however, that not all interpretation was formulated around the visible.

By perceiving a presence of others we also perceive an absence. We experience others as conscious, but we do not experience their consciousness. At the same time, however, these absences refer to a presence—an experience one could have of others' consciousness. This means that the solution to the "other minds" problem involves finding some direct experience of the presence of another consciousness. Being watched by the other is such an instance. Sartre explains:

> If the other-as-object is defined in connection with the world as the object which *sees* what I see, then my fundamental connection with the other-as-subject must be able to be referred back to my permanent possibility of *being seen by* the other.[22]

The experience of being watched gives us the experience of ourselves as object. We come to see ourselves as we are seen in the world by others. At the same time, we experience the other as a subject: the subject who perceives us as the object. Sartre suggests that our defense against being the object of the other-as-subject, is to engage in the same behaviour—to become a subject of the other-as-object. These are not relations based on what is known, but rather on relations of being with others that result in a sense of self as well as a sense-of-self-as-known-by-the-other. These are eventually fused into a sense of self that allows one to become functional in the world. It helps us to understand our position among other *seemingly* autonomous selves. This points to the importance of developing relations with others since it is only through these relations that we are able to assess our location in the ecology of any situation. Sense of location is important to understanding our self, for we can only understand ourselves *in relation to* others.

These formulations suggest that the sense of self-identity cannot be contained within the body or the mind, but emerges rather from our symbiotic relations with others.[23] In coming to know others we learn about ourselves. It is important to note, however, that it is not a static or unified self that we come to know, for in the coming-to-know—in the understanding of the other's perception of the world—we are changed. We evolve through our relations with others. This means that relations with others are essentially unstable in the sense that they are always fluctuating between our being-an-object to the other's subject and our being-a-subject to the other's object. Since it is the mind that is commonly believed to be the storage place for knowledge, it would follow that knowledge about the self must be somehow part of the mind. According to Sartre, however, the self (and by implication, the mind), does not really exist only in the body, for a sense of self emerges from our perceptions of, and relations with, others in the world. Just as these relations remain unfixed, so does our own sense of location amid the fabric of relations in which we are immersed. This is likely why our spatial and temporal location greatly influences our sense of self and our relations with others. It is impossible to maintain the same relation with the other when the context changes.[24]

Herodotus seemed to understand this. His method of inquiring into past events suggests that he believed that the truth of history was not to be located in particular events, in particular perceptions of events, or in particular interpretations of events by witnesses. Like a sense of self, the trace of history could only be located in the dynamic among persons, events and the location of these. And so, in order to convey an understanding of this, he needed to create a narrative that could somehow re-present, re-perform these human/world/event interactions. Michael Ondaatje also seems to understand this since his depiction of the relational dynamic among the four characters in *The English Patient* emerges from the continually evolving interaction of selves, events, memories of events, and texts, as contained within a particular place. All of these exist at the end-point of an historically-effected consciousness which, as Sartre suggests, is not really located in each of us, but exists in the world.[25] The consciousness that we have of ourselves, of each other, of our relations with each other does not belong to us. It belongs to the situations that we share with others in the places that contain us. This is not only true in our lived interactions with others in the world, it is true of our imaginative ones such as those we have with literary fictions. As readers of *The English Patient*, for example, our reading group became immersed in the thrown-ness of the world-as-experienced by four characters over a particular temporal period, and, as we engaged ourselves as both subject and object in that world, we came to simultaneously know about those characters and about ourselves and our relations to one another.

In *Phenomenology of Perception*, Maurice Merleau-Ponty[26] discusses the importance of the conditions which contain our developing relations with others. By reminding us that we are not placed in a natural world but a world that has been shaped by preceding generations of human interactions, he points to the importance of the artifacts that condition our actions in the world. Human-made artifacts (such as tools, dwellings, texts) bear the imprint of human behaviour and, as a consequence, in their very being-there participate in the constitution of the evolving sense of self. He writes:

> Just as nature finds its way to the core of my personal life and becomes inextrica-
> bly linked with it, so behavior patterns settle into that nature, being deposited in
> the form of a cultural world. Not only have I a physical world, not only do I live

in the midst of earth, air and water, I have around me roads, plantations, villages, streets, churches, implements, a bell, a spoon, a pipe. Each of these objects is moulded to the human action which it serves.... In the cultural object, I feel the close presence of others beneath a veil of anonymity. *Someone* uses the pipe for smoking, the spoon for eating, the bell for summoning, and it is through the perception of a human act and another person that the perception of a cultural world could be verified.[27]

The relations that we form with others are always mediated by the cultural objects that surround ourselves and others—cultural objects that carry a trace of human history. Getting to know others depends upon understanding the way in which their experience and their actions are mediated by cultural objects. It is impossible to make clear distinctions between persons and the things that surround them. Nor is it possible to understand things in the absence of knowledge about how they are used. Heidegger suggests that one cannot know about "things" by merely looking at them; knowing about them means having an understanding of how they are used—an understanding that can only occur in the relationship developed when subject and object became engaged in use:

The less we just stare at the hammer-Thing, and the more we seize hold of it and use it, the more primordial does our relationship to it become, and the more unwieldy is it encountered as that which it is—as tool.[28]

Knowing about "things" means knowing about how they are used, and, at the same time, being aware of their history of having been used by human subjects. It follows, then, that forming relations with others—getting to know them—always occurs in cultural situations within which are placed artifacts that are not only immediately useful but which carry the "trace" of their history.

According to Merleau-Ponty, we do not first come to know ourselves and our situation *before* we come to know the other. We do not come to know others by watching them and making comparisons to ourselves. Rather, our sense of self co-emerges with our interactions with others and things within the experience of living with them. He writes:

In the experience of dialogue, there is constituted between the other person and myself a common ground; my thoughts and his are inter-woven into a single fabric, my words and those of my interlocutor are called forth by the state of the discussion, and they are inserted into a shared operation of which neither of us is the creator.[29]

Only later, as one or the other speaker reflects on the conversation, does it appear as one's personal activity, and only then does it become part of a personal history. Only later, do these events come to be understood as comprising some aspect of one's sense of self. It is this personalizing of our interactions and relations with others that forms the trace that marks the body. The English patient understood the importance of such relational marking:

> We die containing a richness of lovers and tribes, tastes we have swallowed, bodies we have plunged into and swum up as if rivers of wisdom, characters we have climbed into as if trees, fears we have hidden in as if caves. I wish for all this to be marked on my body when I am dead. I believe in such cartography—to be marked by nature, not just to label ourselves on a map like the names of rich men and women on buildings. We are communal histories, communal books. We are not owned or monogamous in our experience.[30]

Intuitively, we know that we do not really have exclusive possession of our self. But then, neither do others have exclusive possession of it for us. In fact, in light of the formulations just presented, it seems that our sense of self becomes part of a world consciousness, part of the ecology of being-in-the-world. Although we may at times be unwilling, we are always and already participants. And just as we enter a world which is already marked with the historical trace of all those who have come before us, we leave having marked. A trace of us is left in the world.

But even while we still live, as the English patient reminds us, we feel the need to mark and be marked. Our bodies bear the mark of life. We have scars, stretch marks, wrinkles. An attempt to erase these markings (through cosmetic surgery, for example) seems a violation, a refusal to acknowledge the importance of having "been there" in the world, an attempt at anonymous interaction in the world. But of course we know that none of this anonymity is really possible, for no matter how hard we try we will always, in some way, wear our life on our sleeve. The trace is always there, although often it is invisible. The trace represents our history of interactions in the world.

It is the thread that runs through our bodies and connects us to an historical, contemporary, and future world and, at the same time, to all of the relational ties that bind us to these worlds. The trace is a binding, a boundary, and a map, for it is by tracing the sense of self in relation to others, to the artifacts that surround us, and the conditions of these relations, that we are able to reflect upon our own life in an interpretive way.

This helps us to understand why it was so important for each of the four characters in *The English Patient* to "sniff out" the trace of the others. By searching for the trace, they engaged in the kinds of interactions that led to established relations among them and provoked them to inquire into themselves and their own situations. Even though, as Merleau-Ponty reminds us, we can never experience what the other experiences—we can only have our own experience—we can never really *own* that experience. It is always more than us and more than we can ever say:

> As soon as existence collects itself together and commits itself in some line of conduct, it falls beneath perception. Like every other perception, this one asserts more things than it grasps.... [W]hen I say that I know and like someone, I aim, beyond his qualities, at an inexhaustible ground which may one day shatter the image that I have formed of him. This is the price for there being things and 'other people' for us, not as the result of some illusion, but as the result of a violent act which is perception itself.[31]

Relationality is always and forever based on acts of perception and interpretation. Once we locate the trace, we begin to try to understand. It is only through these intersubjective relations—these acts of reading others and being read by them—that we can have any individual experience of self. In order to experience a sense of self, we need to experience some relation between self and others. This helps us to understand three things: First, that the self can never be imprisoned in the body. It exists in the largely invisible relations among others, within the culturally-made artifacts that emerge from the natural world, out of the conditions of our "thrown-ness" in the world, and from the historically-effected conditions of all of these. Second, it helps to explain the phenomenon of intersubjective desire, for it is clear that without relations with others, we cannot really have a sense of self. The sense of self simply will not emerge on its own. It is not given; only the potential is given. Without relations with others we would never learn language; the world would have no meaning. As adults, we realize that the continual evolution of the self requires intersubjective relations that facilitate these ongoing re-readings and re-writings of the self. Finally, the importance of historical "collecting" places for the knowledge which has emerged from the interaction of selves, can be more clearly understood. Things like *The Histories* do not merely chronicle human events, they chronicle human-world-human relations, and the desire that infuses these. Novels such as *The English Patient* are also collecting places for knowledge. Unlike non-literary fictions, however, these require more than the participatory gaze of the reader. They require more than an objectified interest. Because of their structural features, culturally announced as fictions that are to be read in a particular way, they require the reader to imagine, for it is only through the imagining that a deep relation with the literary fiction can be established. Summoning the imagination shifts the gaze from one of appropriation to one of relational participation.

Looking for the Joke

> *He picked up the fuze-pocket tube and peered down into it again. He saw nothing. He was about to lay it on the grass when he hesitated and brought it back up to the light. He wouldn't have noticed anything wrong except for the weight. And he would never have thought about the weight if he wasn't looking for the joke.*
>
> Michael Ondaatje, *The English Patient*[32]

Kip did not know he would become a bomb-defusing expert. His potential was recognized by his commanding officer, Lord Suffolk, who understood that, like many creative tasks, bomb disposal required more than skill. The successful defusing of a bomb meant the ability to imagine the character of the bomb maker—the mind of the enemy. Kip, it seemed to Lord Suffolk, had this ability.

Soon after Kip joins the ranks of the "sappers" Lord Suffolk is killed while defusing a bomb that has been re-configured—re-mapped—so that the detonation device was altered. Survival meant not merely searching for the trace, but *looking for the joke*. The joke in the bomb was the trick, the game being played between the bomb's author and its reader. Kip was a good reader. He always seemed to locate the joke. Not only did this help him stay alive, but each time he learned the trick he was able to tell others. Similar to the experience of understanding jokes that are meant to be funny, learning the joke of the bomb ("getting it") depended on perceiving what was strange. One of the reasons that Kip was successful was that, for him, the familiar was never transparent. His ability to see the familiar as strange allowed him to see and understand the unusual—the trick. By being able to trace the way in which familiar and strange were configured (mapped), Kip was able to find the joke.

Roland Barthes uses the word "jouissance" to describe the pleasure one feels when engaged with a literary fiction. The Old English cognates for jouissance shared similar meanings to those from Old French. In both languages jouissance had explicit sexual connotations: pleasure, eroticism, orgasm. Interestingly, the English form eventually lost all of these meanings while the French retained them. By describing the relation between reader and text as one of jouissance, Barthes pointed to the sensuality and sexuality of reading relationships. Unfortunately, many of the erotic allusions were lost in the 1975 translation (entitled *The Pleasure of the Text*) where jouissance was translated as "pleasure, bliss." For Barthes, however, jouissance is simultaneously sexual, spiritual, physical and conceptual.[33] Jouissance means more than pleasure, for jouissance implies not a state, but an action—a playful eroticism.

There is an interesting connection between the words "joke" and "jouissance." Joke originates with the Latin "jocus" meaning jest, joke, game. A joke is a game that we play and which plays us. The word "game" originates from the old Norse word "gaman" meaning pleasure. "Play" has a variety of meanings, including to rejoice, to dance, to play for stakes, to make sport or jest of, to engage in amorous activities, or to be sexually indulgent.

"She's playing with his affections."

"He's playing around on her."

"Quit playing games with me!"

What we say about our relationships with others—sexual or other-wise—demonstrates how we are mapped by desire. Like the word "jouissance" which simultaneously announces the sexual, spiritual, physical and conceptual, the language we use announces our complicity in the joke (game). Derrida has helped us to understand that words are not transparent.

Their meanings are not self-evident, but rather, are always in a state of being fixed and unfixed in their "différance."[34] Words simultaneously point to and defer meanings. We can only understand significations in relation to other ones. Following Wittgenstein, Lyotard pointed to the consequences of these "language games,"[35] reminding us that, in the modern, Western world at least, we have become overly enamored with the "metanarrative," the "grand theory." Grand theories, although they are gamelike, are not necessarily playful.[36] It is the playfulness, the relational quality implied by this playfulness, that is pleasurable—desirable.

For Kip, locating the joke of the bomb—identifying the map—was jouissance. The experience of defusing the bomb was not unlike exhibitionism: much of the pleasure is derived from the possibility of being caught. Jouissance is being in the midst of what Foucault would call a "limit-experience" where the juxtaposition of usually contrary experiences such as pain and pleasure announce a commonplace for new understanding.[37] This is the experience of being caught by the joke.

"I just about died laughing."

"I was so embarrassed I could have died."

"I was frightened to death."

Laughing, being embarrassed or frightened, dying—all bring us closer to some sense of being that is pre-linguistic. Like an orgasm, it is something that can be planned, but when it arrives, is always surprising, always a form of boundary crossing. Such is the experience of jouissance. Like the joke, it defies theorizing.

Reading bombs, reading novels, reading persons. Are all these mapped by desire, inscribed by the joke, the game, the jouissance of living through life? Does a novel have a joke? Readers who are quickly able to discern the map of the story—the story grammar—are thought to be good readers. In schools, the ability to predict what will happen next in a story is considered the mark of a proficient reader. Similarly, persons who are able to quickly read the character of the other are said to be perceptive, to be good judges of character. ("She read him like a book!") This is a quality that is admired and desired, for the ability to read the other means being able to adapt one's manner and approach to suit the other's character. Establishing quick relations with a book or another person, then, seems to be dependent on "reading the signs." But is this really a reading of what is present or is it a reading of what is absent—something only present in its possibility? Is it not the ability to notice the *presence of an absence* that we really value?

For Kip, finding the joke in the bomb meant looking for the absence. It meant looking for what lay between the configuration of wires and metal comprising the bomb. It meant reading the subtext. Locating the joke meant thinking about the "possible" history of the bomb's construction. This was not a question of intention, for the bomb maker's intention was clear. It went beyond intention to the realm of the imaginative. What did Kip imagine the bomb-maker was thinking when making the bomb? What did Kip know about bombs and their makers that would help him to "read" each of them, to decode and interpret the complex grammar of the relation between bomb and bomb-maker in order to find the trick, to unweave the knot of the mystery? It might be said that Kip's success lay in his ability to "not see" a predicted grammar, but rather to see an imagined grammar, for too-quickly predicting the probable grammar—the probable character of the bomb—would mean certain death. The joke was *never* to be found in the familiar, but always in some re-organization of the familiar. Therefore, it might be said that Kip's talent lay in his ability to make predictions that emerged from his imagination rather than from empirical evidence, for it was by imagining the joke that he was able to locate it—to get it.

Gadamer makes it clear that our "pre-judgments" make possible new understandings.[38] We need "old understandings" in order to generate new ones. Just as Kip's history of interactions with other bombs formed the foundation for his skill at finding the "joke" in new ones, so too does our history of interactions with other people help us to form new relations. We know, for example, that when we meet and try to get to know others who interest us, we desire information about them that extends beyond what can be retrieved by watching them. We need to allow them to tell us things about themselves. We ask them about their occupation, their interests, their "situation." We try to locate them within our map of understanding and, at the same time, begin the process of constructing a map of our understanding that includes them. As this is going on they are doing the same. As these relationships develop, the simultaneous mapping continues, each becoming more elaborate as the history of their interactions with one another becomes more involved and complex.

Is there a joke to be located in the relationships between persons? It seems that it is not a requirement. However, it could be argued that the joke is the mystery, the absence. It is the game which must be played in the forming of the relationship. Often it is a sense of the "presence of an absence" that fuels emotional and physical desire in a relationship. The excitement of knowing *something* about the other, but not *everything*. If everything were known, there would be no need to work to form a relationship; when the world is totally given, it is no longer challenging. There is no game to be played, for the playing depends upon some resistance. It is the resistance that we often like. It is not surprising that lovers of many years sometimes find their relationships monotonous; the text of it is too familiar, too predictable. Desire has been squeezed out by presence. Too much has been revealed. Jouissance has evaporated.

It was absence, not presence, to which both Hana and Kip were attracted in each other. Hana has a deep sense of all of this:

> He will sit up and flip his hair forward, and begin to rub the length of it with a towel. She imagines all of Asia through the gestures of this one man.[39]

As does Kip:

> When he looks at Hana he sees a fragment of her lean cheek in relation to the landscape behind it.[40]

Things not said, but known. The way in which the body is marked by the civilization that precedes it. Seeing a cheek "in relation to" the landscape behind it. Unlike in the bomb, the importance of the joke amid human relations is to know that it is there, but not to locate it. For once the joke is located it must be told—it must be given. Someone has to *get it*. Locating the joke of the bomb allows the bomb to be defused. With bombs this is desirable. With relationships it is not. So, it seems, that perceiving the presence of the joke is important in relationships with others, but locating, telling, saying *once and for all* what the punch line, the bottom line, the truth might be is not so desirable. In order to maintain jouissance the play must continue. The game must not end.

And what of the relation with a work of literary fiction?

It is significant that when talking about our relations with novels we often speak of getting "lost." There is a sense that it is only by becoming lost will we be found. There is something hidden which is sought. "Hide and Seek" is a game that can be associated with forming relationships with the literary fiction. Playing Hide and Seek is a delicious combination of excitement, joy, nervousness. Jouissance.

Hiding in the furthest corner of the closet, scarcely breathing, aware of the heartbeat, the breath, the rustle of clothing tucked into garment bags. You—the hidden one—wait. Hoping to be found ... but not too quickly. The other senses you are near, hesitates in front of the closet door. You hear the other's breath. Then, a moment of silence—hesitation. The sudden rush of adrenaline when the closet door is whipped open. The other, not sure you are there, finding you. Screams of capture, joy, delight. "Got you, I got you!"

Jouissance. To be hidden, sought, then found. One requires the others. There is no game without being hidden, no game without being sought and found, no game without playing and being played by the game. It requires a "losing and finding" amid a dedicated playing. There is no joy, no game, when one partner does not "play" properly. Hide and seek, losing, finding, the joke, the trick, *got you.* It's all in the playing.

As mentioned in the previous chapter, Gadamer equates the fusing of self and literary work of art to a game where the player simultaneously plays and is played by the game. Although constrained by the rules of the game, these rules do not determine the meaning of the game; only the playing can do that. Similarly, although the literary fiction is constrained by a set of linguistic conventions and stylistic structures that are produced by the author, the meaning can only be realized in the evocation of the text by the reader. In a well-constructed and evocative literary fiction we find ourselves immersed in the midst of the performance that is the text (the play), and if we read well (play well), we find ourselves being immersed in (played by) the game that is formed between ourselves and the text. Gadamer tells us that

> Play fulfills its purpose only if the player loses himself in play. Seriousness is not merely something that calls us away from play; rather, seriousness in playing is necessary to make the play wholly play. Someone who doesn't take the game seriously is a spoilsport.[41]

He also suggests that

> The movement of playing has no goal that brings it to an end; rather, it renews itself in constant repetition.[42]

Becoming lost (or hidden) in the literary fiction, then, is not a disorientation, a loss of direction, but rather a losing of the "given path" (the lived world) in order that a "possible" path (an imagined world that includes the reader's engagement with a literary fiction) may be found. Finding depends on something being hidden, sought, located. Hide and seek, lost and found is jouissance. It is through this playing that one "finds oneself" in a relationship with a literary fiction. As Gadamer suggests, "In spending oneself on the task of the game, one is in fact playing oneself out."[43]

Playing oneself out in the relation between self and literary fiction, however, means living in between submission to and dominance over the text. The game is not well played if the reader is overly domineering or overly submissive. As Ingrid read *The English Patient*, she was determined to control the text until she found that this made playing the game impossible:

> *I can remember fighting and fighting. Fighting for control. Fighting so that I could control the book. Because that's what I normally do when I'm reading a book. I feel like I've got to have control over where I'm going with this thing. But with this book I didn't feel like I had any control and I really found that frustrating. But the minute I surrendered to the book and said "Okay, I'm going to stop fighting. I'm just going to read!" was when it started to have some meaning for me.*

In order for Ingrid to play well she needed to try not to fight the text, for fighting is not playing. Playing involves a to-and-fro movement—a play of movement rather than a coercion. Mena, on the other hand, found that submission to the text excluded her from the game:

> *The characters all seem so detached for me. I don't see the connections. I keep waiting for the author to put it together for me, and he's not. So I'm stuck. Stuck waiting for some connections to be made. I can't seem to finish this book.*

Being stuck stops the play. In discussions of our involvement with *The English Patient*, we all agreed that the development of a relationship between the reader and this text depended upon a playing that demanded an equal commitment from both reader and author/text. Each needed to "play well" in order for a meaningful relation to be established. This meant that the reader could neither dominate the text, nor be dominated by it. The forming of the relationship that would lead to the evocation of meaning between reader and text depended instead on an attentive and committed playing between reader and text.

Playing as a metaphor for reading the literary fiction becomes an important way to help understand the importance of "the joke" in the relationship between reader and text. The joke is not to be found in the author, the text or the reader. Unlike in the bomb, the joke is not meant to be "found" to be "defused" (decoded) in order for the "trick" to be neutralized. The joke in the relationship between the reader and the literary fiction is the vanishing horizon. Although it exists, it can never be reached; it can never be grasped. The joke is the ever-evolving relation that exists with the playing of the game. No matter how often we engage in the game of hide and seek—even if we hide in the same closet each time—there is the excitement of what the "finding" will bring: an eruption of excitement and pleasure. Jouissance.

As Iser has helped us to understand in the last chapter, the relation between reader and literary fiction depends upon a conditioned imagination, the reader's ability to imagine a possible world in his or her engagement with the literary fiction. That which is signified by a word or an image in the lived world may become ambiguous in a lived world that includes the reading of a literary fiction. The signifier becomes split. Words become symbols for things other than what they represent in the non-fictional world. It is important for the reader to know that they are to see and understand all words, images, characters, situations in the literary fiction *as if* they were real. It is the *as if* relationship that contains the joke, for it is within the space of this relationship that the reader's own world as well as his or her own self, must also become re-configured.

In order to "get into the text," the reader must become committed to the playing of the game. The reader must assume that there is a difference between the literary fiction and other texts. It is in assuming the difference and becoming committed to playing that the reader will become played. Being *lost* in the text, then, is *finding* oneself hidden in the play of the text. Paradoxically, it is the playing, the hiding, the losing that allows one to be sought and eventually found. If the reader is never "found," the relation between the text and the reader has not been meaningful, for only in the evocation of meaning between reader and text does the reader learn something about herself that was not known before the reading. Locating the joke in the relation between reader and text, then, means arriving at something meaningful. Locating the joke is finding oneself in interpretation.

Unlike relations with other texts, however, this interpretation is not pre-determined. It is not the thesis of an essay or the answer to a mathematics problem. It is what has been learned through the playing of "hide and seek" in the relational space between reader and text. Locating the joke is the playing of the game. Iser helps us to understand that the game of the text is made possible by the gaps—the spaces deliberately left by author between that which is given and that which must be formulated by the reader:

> Communication in literature ... is a process set in motion and regulated not by a given code but by a mutually restrictive and magnifying interaction between the explicit and the implicit, between revelation and concealment. What is concealed spurs the reader into action, but this action is also controlled by what is revealed: the explicit in turn is transformed when the implicit has been brought to light. Whenever the reader bridges the gaps, communication begins. The gaps function as a kind of pivot on which the whole text-reader relationship revolves.[44]

If the reader is not able (or not willing) to engage in the construction of meaning, there will be no relation formed between reader and text. It is within these "working relations," which paradoxically must occur in the to-and-fro motion of the play between author, text and reader, that the joke may be located. But, unlike the joke that is meant to be funny or the joke in the bomb, the "getting it" does not depend on some pre-determined intention. The joke in the literary fiction, like the relations we have with other persons, is never found once and for all, for like our relations with others, we do not want our relations with the literary fiction to be defused or neutralized. The game—the evocation of meaning—does not end when the last page has been read. For like all relational experiences, those between reader and literary fiction become part of the fabric of the reader's world. It becomes a referential memory.

Looking for the joke can be understood as a metaphor for the constant search for meaning in our relationships with others and with literary fictions. It is a game of hide and seek that we are always and forever in the process of playing. We sometimes hide in the other in order to be found; the other hides in us in order to find her/himself. We can only know our selves in relation to the other. Just as our sense of self, of mind, or of consciousness is not to be found inside of our bodies, but rather in the ecology of our intertextual relations in the world, neither can the meaning of the literary fiction and reader be considered in isolation. Like *The Histories*, the meaning between reader and literary fiction is located in that which is evoked in the historically-effected interactions that locate us in a present moment. Just as the meaning of history is not to be located in particular events, but rather in the relationships that circumscribe those events, the meanings that we evoke in our relations with literary fictions are always evoked within a complex fabric of other historically-effected relationships.

Jouissance, in our relationships with others, is simultaneously sexual, spiritual, physical and conceptual. This is true of our relationships with literary fictions. Playing a game well is always an interesting set of paradoxes: submitting and dominating, predicting and reflecting, playing and being played. Playing well means knowing more than the "rules of the game"; playing well depends upon a commitment to the game and to a desire to give oneself up to the game. It requires, in some sense, learning to be uncomfortable; learning to live with ambiguity; learning to tolerate the resistance of the literary fiction itself. Ambiguity precedes the relation with the literary fiction. Like any relationship, the one between reader and text demands a tolerance for not knowing. This is because any relationship (human or otherwise) is primarily ontological, not epistemological. The relationship between Kip and Hana was not based upon what they knew about one another but on who they were to one another. The relationship between the English patient and his copy of *The Histories* was not contained in what was written but rather in the relationship of the writer(s) (both he and Herodotus) and the written. The relationship between Ingrid and *The English Patient* and the failed relationship between Mena and the same book can only be discussed in the way they were with the book, not who they were or what they knew about the book.

The relations between self-other and self-literary fiction exist in an ecology of lived experience. Just as we are really unable to separate our sense of self from our body and our senses of self from our relations with others, we are unable to extricate ourselves from the relation that we form with the literary fiction. Nor can the literary fiction extricate itself from us. Just as we are altered for having read, the text is altered for having been read. Although it may be argued that the marks on the page remain the same, the significance of the marks are always unstable. Because significance must exist within ever-evolving meanings as constituted relationally, it is clear that *The English Patient* is altered for having been read. The question again becomes one of location. Are our human-text-literary relationships always and forever formed in the realm of the *symbolic?* Or is it possible that there are some relationships or some significations that move us into another realm? Is it this other place that marks the particular relation between reader and literary fiction?

Transgressing the Symbolic

> *Hours later we were in the sandstorm that hit us out of clear morning, coming from nowhere.... We had to keep moving. If you pause sand builds up as it would around anything stationary, and locks you in. You are lost forever.*
> Michael Ondaatje, *The English Patient*[45]

For the English patient, the desert had been a place to play hide and seek, for with its ever-shifting sands, history was quickly covered. Too much covering, however, such as would occur if one remained stationary during a sandstorm, meant suffocation. The desert was both liberating and restricting; one could feel confined and exposed at the same time.

Unlike the European cities the English patient had known, for the English patient, the desert had an elusive history. For him, like many other explorers who roamed the deserts of Northern Africa during the two decades prior to the Second World War, the desert became a place of enticement and mystery. But the ever-shifting sands—the covering, re-covering, uncovering—permitted no mapping of the desert. There were few landmarks, few points of reference. The desert resisted containment by a map-maker. It resisted the language of maps, the choreography of place. The desert, and the historical secrets/places/events that it held, would not be pinned down to particular places on a scrap of paper. For the English patient it became a constant reminder of the excess of life, the excess of meaning, and the fact that words could never contain the fullness of experience. The desert defied categories. The English patient eventually discovered what centuries of nomadic desert people had always known: There *is* a truth in the desert, but it is never fixed. Like sand it shifts suddenly—circling, rising, settling in re-configured patterns, which although familiar, are always original.

Living within an ever-shifting landscape has its consequences. If a sense of self is known in relation to others and to a sense of place, existing in a place that is always on the move, and where all inhabitants move, means that the sense of self feels less fixed. The self, like the dwellers of the desert, becomes nomadic. It defies boundaries, categories, names:

> [A]fter ten years in the desert, it was easy for me to slip across borders, not to belong to anyone, to any nation.[46]

In order for the self to function, however, it must have a sense of stability, of being centered. Being decentered means madness, psychosis, what psychotherapists call "borderline syndrome." Jane Flax explains that borderline syndrome occurs when the subject lacks a coherent, unified core-self. [47] The lack of a core-self leads to a psychosis emerging from the lack of a self-referent through which the subject is able to enter into and negotiate the transitional spaces between self and other, inner and outer, reality and illusion. Most of us have learned strategies for escaping this condition. We find "collecting" places for our sense of self. For many of us, these are located in things around us: our possessions, homes, stories and rituals. Our self is mapped, so to speak, in the historical, cultural, and personal conditions of our living through life. These become boundaries, markers, and signifying systems that help us to locate our self.[48]

What happens when one is placed in the desert, away from one's own historical, cultural, and familial borders, markers and signifying systems? What become the "collecting places" that facilitate the continued revitalization of the self? For the English patient, his commonplace book—his annotated copy of *The Histories*—serves this function. And it was Katharine Clifton's desire to know more about him that provoked her to ask him for it:

'That book you look at in the evenings?' 'Herodotus. Ahh. You want that?' 'I don't presume. If it is private.' 'I have my notes within it. And cuttings. I need it with me.' 'It was forward of me, excuse me.' 'When I return I shall show it to you. It is unusual for me to travel without it.'[49]

For a short period of time before the war, during their explorations of the Northern African desert, the English patient and Katharine become lovers. The relationship, Katharine knew, depended on a transgression of boundaries—not just boundaries of friendship and marriage (for her husband was the English patient's friend and colleague), but a transgression of her known and interpreted sense of self. Asking for the English patient's commonplace book meant asking for the self of an other. Offering to show it meant an offering of the self.

Even in the desert where boundaries shift, where things cannot be contained, the nomads who live there must maintain a sense of self. But the desert teaches the nomads that the truth of the self is no more fixed than the truth of the desert. Surviving in the desert means knowing that yesterday's truth about the location of the oasis is not today's, for the oasis is contingent upon ever-shifting conditions. Insisting that water might be found where it had been located by previous explorers usually meant death. The truth of the desert is a contingent truth. Truth telling is important, but the telling of truth does not mean the fixing of it. When truth is fixed it becomes dogma.

In coming to know the other, we often become simultaneously consumed with wanting to envelop the other, and to be enveloped. There is a sense that in order for the relationship to work, there needs to be some reconstruction of the self and so, to enable that reconstruction, the infrastructure of the self (its history, its character) must be excavated. Katharine and the English patient have a stormy relationship. Although they were consumed with knowing the other, they could not rewrite the truth of their individual senses of self and like many who become involved in a secret relationship, they became victims of their own fixed truth. This, of course, created stasis between them. And, for Katharine this leads to mistrust: "If I gave you my life, you would drop it. Wouldn't you?"[50] Keeping their affair secret meant standing still; allowing the sands to gather over them, smothering life. They could not be true to themselves, true to each other, or true to their relationship.

Post-structural theorists have rejected the possibility of such "truth-telling" insisting that truth, as something stable and fixed, does not really exist.[51] Derrida suggests that "There is no such thing as truth in itself. But only a surfeit of it. Even if it should be for me, about me, truth is plural."[52] As a product of hierarchically organized relations of power, normalized discursive practices, and inevitable processes of marginalization and silencing, the relationship between the signified and the signifier is always and already problematic. There is no universal truth, no fixed meaning, no bottom line, no last word. Like the truth of the desert, all truth is conditional, contingent, shifting, and elusive. This understanding means, of course, that there is no single author of truth, no single reader, no single interpreter. Truth always, already, forever, depends upon everything.

How does our existence in an endless chain/play of signifiers—an unfixable truth—allow us to maintain a sense of identity and an ability to engage in relationships with others? Do we need some sense of borderline, of boundary, of category, of "map" in order to function? Does meaning require a sites of collection and containment?

Even in the desert there are meeting places—places to find food and water, shelter and companionship. Collecting places. Places that have a name, a purpose, a function, a history, and a meaning. We have names for these places: we call them routines, rituals, artifacts. There are mealtimes, Saturday evenings out, photograph albums, Grandma's brooch, movies we see over and over, songs that mark the passages in our lives. Like *The Histories*, these become collecting places for "truths"—the truth of having marked and having been marked; the truth of having lived; the truth of having moved through the world. All of these exist within the realm of the symbolic; all of them present and re-present signifying systems. Without these traces and maps to keep track of the choreography of our selves and our relations with others, we feel alienated from our own lives.[53] For although we have a sense that the truth of our situation may be constantly changing, just as the truth of the world around us is changing, we have the urge—the desire—to keep track of it.

Julia Kristeva suggests that even though our signifying practices are always in a state of flux, this flux must always occur in a rhythm of the fixing and unfixing of meaning.[54] As a psychoanalyst who is ethically bound to help her patients, Kristeva believes that insisting that there is no truth is irresponsible. In psychoanalytic practice there are some responses and actions that are more appropriate and effective than others; some actions and interventions will lead to a "cure" while others won't. *The cure is the truth.* It is not a generalizable truth, but a particular truth. A truth for this person, in this situation, in this place. But a truth nonetheless. It is a relational truth. Toril Moi explains:

> The modern, unstable and empty subject, [Kristeva] argues, ought not to be fixed and stabilized, but to be turned into a *work in progress*. This means that psychoanalytic patients must be left, at the end of analysis, in a position which enables them to express themselves.[55]

But this expression, of course, requires a sense of self-identity—a subjectivity—governed by the immersion of the speaking subject in discursive practices. This is problematic, since it is precisely these discursive sites which the borderline patient is trying to escape. Kristeva argues that the kind of speaking or writing most appropriate for such patients is imaginative, for it is only in the realm of the imaginative that the subject is able to grasp a sense of self or identity, but not be required to fix it into a rigid self. Kristeva writes:

> I think that in the imaginary, maternal continuity is what guarantees identity.... The imaginary of the work of art, that is really the most extraordinary and the most unsettling imitation of the mother-child dependence. [It is] its substitution and its displacement towards a limit which is fascinating because inhuman. The work of art is independence conquered through inhumanity.[56]

It is within the realm of the imaginary that the "borderline" patient and the analyst are most purely able to engage in the discourse of transference. For Kristeva, transference becomes a psychoanalytic situation in which love (transference love) is allowed to establish itself, allowing the subject to find a location for her/himself within the symbolic order, to move from chaos to a subject-position that permits speaking—truth telling. This is not a universal truth, an absolute truth or a generalizable truth, but a truth that emerges from a *relation* between two speaking subjects held within a particular situation.

For Kristeva the move to the imaginary and the symbolic are dialectically involved in the speaking subject's production of language. In *Revolution in Poetic Language* [57] she theorizes that all signifying processes are dependent upon symbolic and semiotic processes. The semiotic process is related to the "chora"—a word she defines as

> an essentially mobile and extremely provisional articulation constituted by movements and ephemeral stases.... The *chora*, as rupture and articulations (rhythm), precedes evidence, verisimilitude, spatiality and temporality. Our discourse—all discourse—moves with and against the *chora* in the sense that is simultaneously depends upon and refuses it. Although the *chora* can be designated and regulated, it can never be definitely posited: as a result, one can situate the *chora* and, if necessary, lend it a topology, but one can never give it axiomatic form.[58]

The semiotic as "discrete quantities of energy [that] move throughout the body of the subject who is not yet constituted as such"[59] eventually becomes arranged according to the conditions of the speaking subject's historical thrown-ness, genetic make-up, biochemical state, family and social structures, cultural conditions, and so on. The ecology of the body-mind-world system, then, contributes to the semiotic system—the chora—from which the various symbolic systems at once depend upon and refuse (for much of the chora *must* be refused in order for a core-self to become developed).   The process of signification (which for Kristeva is the jouissance experienced when there is meaning between signifier and signified) is an articulation of two processes—the semiotic and the symbolic.

Although any symbolic system is dependent upon the semiotic system, it is not true that the semiotic precedes the symbolic. Rather, the two co-specify one another. Although the chora is ever-evolving, in order for signification to occur, it must be split. It is the splitting of the chora that allows the subject to speak. The chora may be thought of as the "excess" of language—the drives, the pulsions, the infinite heterogeneous possibility of language—while the symbolic is that from the chora which has been claimed, mapped—choreographed—by the symbolic system(s). This is an important point, for if the chora is understood as that which is simultaneously needed and refused by the symbolic system, then acts of signification both depend upon and repress the semiotic chora. For Kristeva, conceptualizing of the two systems meant a reconceptualizing of the importance of the imaginary as invoked by poetic language, for it is in the literary fiction that the subject (reader) is able to transgress the symbolic to the semiotic. In Kristeva's words:

> [I]t is a transgression of the thetic when truth is no longer a reference to an object that is identifiable outside language; it refers instead to an object that can be constructed through the semiotic network but is nevertheless posited in the symbolic and is, from then on, always verisimilar.[60]

Because it has the capacity to transgress the symbolic, the realm of the imaginative is able to rupture the symbolic, altering it forever. In its capacity to invoke the imaginative, the literary fiction facilitates transgressions of the symbolic into the semiotic chora, thus changing the processes of signification.

For the English patient, the desert was, metaphorically speaking, the semiotic chora—a largely unformulated, motile, ever-shifting space which resisted mapping. The few reference places—the villages, towns, oases—were part of the symbolic system (the signifying system) of place. Like any symbolic system, these points of reference both depended upon and refused the desert. They existed with and against one another. The English patient, like the other desert nomads, existed with and against the desert. Because the symbolic system of place within the desert was vague, ambiguous, and difficult to map, it was like an open text—it ruptured the symbolic more than other geographical locations he had known. The symbolic system of place in the desert demanded more of its inhabitants. It demanded a greater tolerance for resistance, for difficulty and for the ambiguity of not knowing whether or not there would indeed be an oases or a town the next day. Or would the oasis be dry? Would the direction to the town be lost in a sandstorm? One did not stand still in the desert. To survive one had to keep moving.

It was this perpetual motion with/in/against the symbolic and the semiotic of their own sense of selves that the English patient and Katharine located their relationship, but because there was no fixing of their relation with one another, no fixing in the symbolic order (it remained secret), there could be no rupture by the semiotic. For something new to be formed there must be a simultaneous fusing and rupturing of something old. This is a lesson of hermeneutics. By trying to fix a pre-formulated sense of self, neither the English patient nor Katharine was able to engage the semiotic in order to transform the symbolic (their own selves) into a relation between the two. Closed systems eventually stagnate; they become suffocated with their own debris.

> We had to keep moving. If you pause sand builds up as it would around anything stationary, and locks you in. You are lost forever.[61]

The truth of the interaction of symbolic systems, whether in the desert, or in the relations between self and other, depends upon perpetual motion. Not frantic motion, but motion represented by the dialectic between the semiotic and the symbolic orders. It is within this co-emergent fabric of relations that the reading of the literary fiction can be located. Reading requires moving, locating, and relocating one's self in relation to a co-emergent world. It is a continual bridging of newly opened spaces—gaps—that make themselves present in the ever-emerging intertextual fabric of lived experience. In her essay, "Bodyreading," Madeleine Grumet suggests that the act of reading is a bridging of the gap between public and private worlds. This move from the private to the public is often difficult, for in the journey we are confronted with the ambiguity of the traveling. She writes:

> If reading is a passage between the public and the private world, the journey is fraught with danger. To give oneself up to the text is to relinquish the world in order to have the world; it is a birth and a death. And so it should not surprise us to find a child wary of reading, reluctant to follow that line across the page without knowing where it leads.[62]

In order for meaning to be evoked, however, the passage *must* be made. This passage (reading) like all signifying practices, becomes what Kristeva calls "transposition"—"the ability to pass from one sign-system to another, to exchange and permutate them."[63] It is the intertextuality of sign systems—the transposition—that allows reading to occur, for it is through the process of transposition that a new signifying practice (i.e., deriving meaning from reading) is able to occur. Without transposition reading is meaningless. Formulating a relationship with a literary fiction, in addition to invoking a series of intertextual transpositions within the realm of the symbolic order, also means transgressing the symbolic—rupturing these orderly transpositions—in order to permit the imaginative. It is the invocation of the imaginative that the boundary-crossing possibility of the literary is hinged, and why, as Grumet suggests, the child (or any reader for that matter) should be wary of following the line which is likely to lead to transpositions that dip into the semiotic chora. For this is a journey to the unknown and the unexpected. Following the line means playing the game, it means searching for the trace, looking for the joke, transgressing the symbolic order and anticipating the jouissance that occurs when the relation between reader and literary fiction is established.

Locating Transformative Spaces

The multiplicity of consciousness appears to us as a synthesis and not as a collection, but it is a synthesis where totality is inconceivable.

Jean-Paul Sartre[64]

As our reading group continued to read and discuss *The English Patient*, our relations with the book and with one another became more intricate and complex. Each of us, the characters in the book, the author, Herodotus's *The Histories,* the English patient's relationship with his commonplace book, Hana's relationship with Kip, Kip's with Hana, Ingrid's frustration with the book, Mena's inability to finish it, my concern that she would/could not, the excursions into the realm of the imaginative as conditioned by *The English Patient*—all of these became fused into a complex fabric of relations.

And now, with this text, I have attempted to bring together, into a symbolic system, a sense of the complexity of this web of intertextual desire. Although all of our lived experience occurs within a tightly woven fabric of relations, it seems that the inclusion of the relation with literary fiction (whether it becomes publicly shared or not) significantly alters the texture of that experiential fabric. The act of reading is not something that is merely added to a collection of experiences. As Sartre suggests, it becomes synthesized into our consciousness. I have tried to show, however, that a conscious sense of self is not something contained within us, but rather is something that is located in the collecting places of particular relations we establish with others within an experienced world of significance. The relation that we establish with the literary fiction announces a commonplace for self-interpretation.

Although we form reading relations with all texts read, the relationship between the reader and the literary fiction often becomes more generative, more transformative than our relations with other texts. Because the evocation of meaning with the literary fiction depends upon an imaginative engagement by the reader, the developed relationship sometimes requires that the reader transgress the boundaries of the symbolic system. This is the place of jouissance—the transformational space opened up through the relation between reader and literary fiction. It is within this relational space that the reader's world becomes re-woven, and it is this re-weaving of the reader's self that alters the reader's interactions with the world. It is an infinite chain of significance. The relationship with a literary fiction, then, is not merely an *escape* from the reader's lived world; it is a relationship, which, through the space opened up by the conditioned imagination of the reader, becomes a *transformative* space.

Of course transformational spaces—transgressions of the symbolic order—do not necessarily depend upon the literary fiction. They can occur any time images or emotions are aroused that escape any language at hand. Viewing Van Gogh's "Sunflowers," attending an Elton John concert, falling in love, feeling a sexual stirring for a passing stranger, are all experiences that make us more aware of the semiotic chora and are experiences that can create transformational spaces that alter, more profoundly than other experiences, the conscious fabric of our lived experience. The particular significance of the literary fiction, however, lies in its power to simulta- neously *use language* in order to *transgress language.* The well-constructed literary fiction asks that the reader become more nomadic than usual, searching for the trace of meaning by moving through the often ambiguous landscape of the text. This movement, through an uncharted landscape, becomes the choreography of reading leading ultimately to the evocation of the artwork: the relation between reader and text. Because the literary fiction does not demand a fixed truth, the reader can continue to be nomadic. Because the "truth" of the text depends as much on the reader as the text, each reading (even repeated readings) brings the reader to a newly formu- lated truth and, in turn, to a newly woven fabric of relations and experiences.

It is important to remember, however, that these relations between individual readers and texts, although generally developed amid *private* relations between one reader and one text, are never really private, since the significance of the reading depends upon the public context of reading while, at the same time, it alters the very context in which it is situated. Therefore, the significance of the reading relationship is a continually evolving significance; it can never be located within fixed systems, but rather emerges from the interaction of systems that are always in a state of interdependent flux. Any intervention into the reading process, then, must be considered within an explication of the significance of the relation between reader and literary fiction. The English patient's reading directions to Hana—which, in turn, became reading directions for our reading group—is an example of the way in which meaning and the sense of self-identity of the reader co-emerge within the interpretive space of intertextual transposition.

As English teachers reading and discussing this book, we became increasingly aware of the interrelational dynamic that occurred within the context of our reading group, and more particularly how this dynamic, as it was evoked by our individual readings of *The English Patient,* helped us to more clearly understand that reading, teaching, and curriculum were inextricably woven together. It seemed so complex, in fact, that several group members felt overwhelmed. What was the relationship between what we had learned about reading and our role as teachers who used literary fictions in our classrooms? How can the *significance* of the reader-text relation contribute to a deeper understanding of the complex fabric of interpersonal relations in the classroom? The next chapter will begin the process of excavating these questions by providing a discussion of reading as embodied action.

IV

Reading as Embodied Action

This is a story of how I fell in love with a woman, who read me a specific story from Herodotus. I heard the words she spoke across the fire, never looking up, even when she teased her husband. Perhaps she was just reading it to him. Perhaps there was no ulterior motive in the selection except for themselves. It was simply a story that had jarred her in its familiarity of situation. But a path suddenly revealed itself in real life.

Michael Ondaatje, *The English Patient*[1]

A Reading of a Reading

The chapter from which the preceding passage was taken is written from the point of view of the English patient, and begins with the line "I promised to tell you how one falls in love."[2] With this line readers of the novel become part of the collective at the villa; they listen with Caravaggio, Hana, and Kip as the English patient tells his story. And, as usual, this story of the English patient's past life is bound up in layers of stories. This one is about his former lover Katharine, who, during a celebration marking their return from a week-long expedition in the desert, recites a story from the English patient's copy of *The Histories*. The story is about the barbarian king Candaules who was so obsessed with his wife that he continually described her remarkable beauty to his friends. Concerned that he is not believed, Candaules urges one of his favored spearmen, Gyges, to hide in his bedroom in a place where he would be able to observe the Queen undressing. Gyges does so but is seen by her. Because she immediately suspects that this has been arranged by her husband, she remains silent. The next day she calls Gyges before her and insists that he either kill the King, take over the kingdom and marry her, or be slain himself. Gyges rules Lydia for twenty-eight years.

As Katharine reads this story to the group of explorers, the English patient wonders if it is for her husband's or for his benefit. Is she trying to communicate a message through this story? Because the English patient is recounting from memory Katharine's reading of Candaules, he has information that was not known during the original event. He knows, for example, that he and Katharine will later become lovers. He knows that Katharine's husband Clifton will soon die. Was the telling of the story of Candaules and the Queen a foreshadowing of what would eventually occur between the English patient and Katharine? Or was this re-telling a re-interpretation of events by the English patient that made the relationship between the story of Candaules and his own experience more coincidental than they really were? Is the truth in the event or in the re-telling of the event? Is it in the doing or in the telling? Or is it only in the remembering?

As our reading group discussed this chapter we wondered about the importance of shared stories and the particular significance of reading and talking about literary fictions together. Did our reading and discussion of *The English Patient* mediate our relations with each other, or did our relations with each other mediate our reading and discussion of *The English Patient*? During our discussion, I suggested that Katharine was drawn to the story of Candaules because she was feeling suffocated by her husband's attentions. Anna agreed and also suggested that Katharine's oral reading was a way of demonstrating, for all present, that the Katharine who had arrived on the plane from England some weeks prior did not exist anymore; living in the desert had changed who she was. Ruth believed that Katharine's oral reading was an acknowledgment (to herself and to the others) of her sense of sexual power—that her new situation and her new knowledge had given her a greater sense of her own desire and desirability. Ingrid wondered if the reading had not been more innocent—less contrived—but once accomplished, created a prophecy that became self-fulfilling. As we puzzled over this chapter we could not help but wonder if we were learning more about the characters in the novel, about our personal reactions to our reading of it, or about ourselves and each other.

Remembering the Body

> *Moments before sleep are when she feels most alive, leaping across fragments of the day, bringing each moment into the bed with her like a child with schoolbooks and pencils. The day seems to have no order until these times, which are like a ledger for her, her body full of stories and situations.*
> Michael Ondaatje, *The English Patient*[3]

The stories that we tell about ourselves and our experiences reflect our history of interactions with others in the world. It is the arrangement of language into narrative forms that gives us a sense of self and allows others a point of access to that self. Telling stories, listening to them, and reading them (to oneself or to others) opens a window to other worlds, other persons, and other experiences. Interpreting the way in which our interactions with literary fictions alters our lived experience helps us to more deeply understand what it is like to exist relationally amid texts and among other readers. It is an act of hermeneutics.

In the last two chapters I commented on the experience of reading literary fictions. I suggested that the culturally agreed-upon forms of the literary fiction give readers permission to situate themselves amid such texts in a way which invokes and conditions an imaginative response to the text. It is through these imaginative experiences that the reader is able to move beyond her or his daily lived experience into another lived experience as conditioned by the literary fiction. I proposed that these imaginative spaces help the reader to understand that lived truth is slippery and contingent, for by imagining a situational possibility during the act of reading, there simultaneously occurs a questioning of what exists. Readers cannot imagine what it is like to be in another situation unless they can somehow blur the presence of their existing situation. At the same time, the relationship with the literary fiction must be considered a "real" experience that contributes to an individual's history of interactions in the world. I explained that the relationships we develop with literary fictions become collecting places for various experiences we have had (including our imaginative experiences) and, therefore, become important narrative and conceptual reference points for our evolving sense of self-identity. Tapping into these commonplaces becomes a way to trace and locate the way in which we and others are situated in relation to our histories and our present circumstances. Although the character of these commonplaces may vary widely, they all hold the potential to immerse us in the experience of finding significance for our selves through our marked relationship with the literary fiction. I also suggested that it is "jouissance" that signals the transgression from known symbolic systems into those which have, in some way, dipped below the surface of the symbolic to the place where we are able to find new ways to express old thoughts. This, of course, often leads to new thoughts, new interpretations, and new experiences. Finally, I attempted to present the complexity of what it is like to establish and maintain relations with others, especially as these are mediated by readings and discussions of literary fictions. I developed an extended metaphor of tracing, mapping, and weaving to show how our relationships with each other and the books we read become woven together into an intricate fabric of lived experience.

At this point the sufficiency of this conception of lived reading experiences must be called into question. Can the image of "weaving" adequately account for the complexity of these lived relationships? Or is it possible that the relationships that readers develop with literary fictions and with each other are not merely "woven together" into a fabric of experience? If the stories told at the beginning of this chapter are any indication of the complexity of the interrelationships among readers, texts, and each other, it seems that the weaving metaphor is not able to account for the way in which readers are continually resituated among reinterpretations of historical, cultural, literary and experiential narratives. Thinking of these intertextual relations as a fabric is like thinking of them as a jigsaw puzzle in which various experiences are made to fit together. It implies some pre-determined plan, rather than the contingent, often serendipitous nature of each of these experiences. It further implies that each thread in the fabric of these intertextual relations can be removed from the whole largely unaltered. This is a misleading image, for we know that once we have had an experience with another person or with a literary fiction, we cannot leave that experience unchanged. Furthermore, the metaphor of weaving implies that there is a causal relationship among components of lived experiences. There is a sense, for example, that reading a literary fiction has the ability to *cause* a particular response, action, or experience. Did the reading of Candaules to the group of explorers cause Katharine to think of her husband and the English patient differently? Or was it merely coincidental that at some point following this reading that she and the English patient became lovers? Can we, in any way, locate the beginnings and endings of the way in which our lives become co-implicated with one another and with the literary fictions we read?

Readers of *The English Patient* bear witness to the way in which the English patient's identity is caught up in his relationship with his common-place book. Neither the book nor he remain the same for having continued a relationship. First Katharine, and later the others at the villa, learn about him by reading this book. *The book matters.* If he had chosen a different book, a different identity would have emerged. Had Katharine and her husband Clifton flown into the Amazon rain forest instead of the Northern African desert, their relationship would have evolved differently. Had our reading group read Margaret Atwood's *Cat's Eye*[4] instead of *The English Patient*, our relationships with each other would have evolved differently.

It seems that we are transformed by our interactions with texts and with each other. If we imagine that we are a thread in a fabric of a complex web of intertextual experience, we are a thread that cannot remain the same for having been in the fabric. Unlike the silk thread in a tapestry which, generally speaking, retains its original form when pulled from the fabric, we cannot be pulled out of our current relations unchanged. Nor can the literary fictions that are read. They, like us, are different for having been involved in a literary relationship. If this is so, then reading must be understood as more than a transaction between reader and text, more than a fusion of horizons, more than a transposition of symbolic systems. Reading, whether it is done for private or public purposes, must be understood as not only the re-creation of the self, but of the various systems to which that self is relationally bound.

This chapter is meant to function like a hinge, linking the first three with the last three chapters. It is like the spine of a book which, at the same time, functions to bind, to identify, and to separate, for although the first three and the last three chapters are related, they are also distinct from each other. The first three chapters develop the idea of intertextuality around the metaphor of weaving, while the last three depart from this metaphor, developing instead the ideas of "co-specification" and "co-emergence." It is in this chapter that I make the transition from weaving to co-emergence by re-describing the development of the human cognitive system in terms of a reconceptualized theory of biological evolution. Finally, the concept of reading as embodied action is presented to re-describe the complexity of intertextual relations that include readings of literary fictions.

During this writing there were times when there did not seem to be words or images to depict some of the theory that was to be presented. Because of this, the language that has been chosen may occasionally seem somewhat cumbersome. However, I believe that although changes in language are often awkward, they are necessary. Following Richard Rorty, I feel that an understanding of our situation as human subjects can only change if we consciously endeavor to use our existing language in new and imaginative ways.[5] If our language is, as Rorty suggests, a collection of metaphors that have eventually become "literalized" through common usage, it seems that the only way to begin to understand any phenomenon differently is to invent new metaphors. This shall be my task in this chapter: to create new images to depict what it is like to be relationally involved with a world that includes the reading of literary fictions.

The Importance of Skin

> *In the Pisa hospital she had seen the English patient for the first time. A man with no face. An ebony pool. All identification consumed in a fire. Parts of his burned body and face had been sprayed with tannic acid, that hardened into a protective shell over his raw skin.*
>
> Michael Ondaatje, *The English Patient*[6]

Skin is a paradox. It must contain a body and, at the same time, allow the body to engage with its environment. Skin reminds us that we are, simultaneously, autonomous and dependent. Most of the time, however, we fail to notice the extraordinary qualities of skin. It is usually only when it is cut, burned, itchy, or ruptured by a sore that we realize that our skin is what separates our inside from the outside. Therefore, more than any other organ, it is skin that reminds us that all of our interactions in the world are embodied.

Of course, it is not only human flesh and bone which are contained by skin. During one of our early discussions of *The English Patient*, our reading group was struck by the image of "unskinning." Each day Hana picks plums from the trees outside the villa and "unskins the plum with her

teeth, withdraws the stone and passes the flesh of the fruit into his mouth."[7]
She unskins the plum. This phrase provoked a lengthy conversation among
us about the unusual syntax Ondaatje had chosen. Why the verb "unskins?"
Anna found it most provocative:

> *I found it interesting that she "unskinned," not "skinned" the plum. I wondered
> if it was meant to suggest something ominous about this situation, or if it was
> meant to be a direct link to the fact that the English patient is so badly burned
> that he too is unskinned.*

What could unskinned really mean? As a descriptor skinned announces
what remains when the skin of something is removed. Could the action
"unskinning" suggest a removal and a simultaneous rejuvenation of skin?
Or was unskinning simply used to catch the reader's attention? In the end
we could not decide. However, with this unusual reconfiguration of a
common word, a literary location had been announced. A space of
indeterminacy had been identified that we individually and collectively
interpreted. For us, the paradox of skin became the ambiguity of unskinned.
Eventually, we began to wonder about the significance of skin as a
boundary, a locator, and an identifier. For, of course, it was not only living
things that required skins. Books also needed skins (covers) in order to be
readily identified. This is the outer skin. This outer skin serves as clothing,
covering for the many pages, each of which seems to have a "skin" of its
own. The feel of the book, we agreed, (the skin of the paper) was just as
important as the content of the book. We also agreed that the tendency that
some of us had to mark the skin of books by writing on the pages was a
deliberate inscribing of experience on skin, not unlike the tattooing of human
skin. Ingrid reacted quite strongly to the idea of "marking" the skin of
books:

> *I hate to see books marked up. For me, it's a desecration.*

Is marking the skin of a book the same as unskinning? We decided that
it was not, for marking allowed the integrity of the entity to remain intact
whereas unskinning meant some significant transformation of that entity.
We also agreed, however, that sometimes unskinning was necessary. It
became necessary for Hana to unskin the plum in order for it to become

integrated into the English patient's digestive system. For the English patient, the skin of the plum was a barrier, imprisoning the nourishment he needed. With the unskinning, the plum's insides were now on the outside—simultaneously liberated and exposed—not unlike the English patient himself. It could be said that marking the skin (of books or people) allows the trace of experience to become visible and shows the way identity evolves with experience, whereas the unskinning of the plum and the burning of the English patient's skin remind us that we are simultaneously autonomous and dependent. It is only the thinness of skin that makes the body seem distinct from the world. Once the skin is removed, the body dissipates into its surroundings. Unskinning repudiates the idea that the human body is other to the world.

In the Western world we have not been very successful at understanding the way in which our bodies are ecologically caught up in and with our environment. More specifically, we do not seem to really believe that our body *is* an environment in itself. Although many of us believe that the body houses something we might call the mind and/or the soul, we usually forget that it is always part of the environment with which others must interact. As discussed in the previous chapter, our bodies, and the bodies of others with whom we form relations, are necessarily changed through and with our worldly interactions. Unfortunately, modernity has taught us to ignore the body, to believe that our bodies are something which *live in* but are not really *part of* various locations. But, of course, as Merleau-Ponty has suggested, we are an inextricable part of the unity of the world. And, as such, the very ecology of our lived experiences bears examination.

This is precisely what Humberto Maturana and Francisco Varela have attempted in reporting their studies in evolutionary biology and human cognition. In their book, *The Tree of Knowledge*,[8] they investigate the way in which human subjects have come to know, arguing that popular theories of the way in which human cognitive systems develop have largely ignored biological history and the way in which this history is embedded in our current physiological, ecological, social, political and cultural structures. Beginning with a reconceptualization of Darwin's theories of evolution, they develop a theory of cognition which suggests that our current condition as human subjects emerges from our biological and ecological history of interactions in earth. At the same time, what we call our "environment" is always co-implicated in human action and, therefore, bears the mark of human interactions. In order to help us to understand the applications of this post-Darwinian theory of evolutionary biology to human cognition, they have defined several theoretical principles that serve as conceptual collectors for this new thinking. The language used to describe these concepts has been further elaborated in Francisco Varela, Evan Thompson, and Eleanor Rosch's book *The Embodied Mind*[9] where the phenomenology of Maurice Merleau-Ponty, the hermeneutics of Martin Heidegger and Hans-Georg Gadamer, and traditional zen Buddhist philosophy have been integrated.

My decision to incorporate this work into a discussion of the experience of shared reading in schools emerges principally from the fact that I read these texts alongside our group's reading of *The English Patient*. As I continued to think about skin as a boundary that both separates and identifies us as individuals interacting in an ecological world, I became more interested in the significance of the studies in perception that guided Maturana and Varela and Varela, Thompson, and Rosch's work.[10] At the same time, I was involved in another reading group where we were painstakingly working our way through Gadamer's *Truth and Method*.[11] And so, like Hana, I was situated in a horizontal reading of texts that continued to co-evolve with my relations with others in the world. Although I was having an individual experience with each text, I was also experiencing the reading of one text *in relation to* the others and *with other readers*. In a sense, all of these readings became one. It could be said that the various texts, readings, and interpersonal relations around these readings had become *unskinned*. And so, it is not unusual that with this writing I continue my reading and interpretation of these texts as part of my project of developing a deeper understanding of what it means to read literary fictions with other persons.

Re-Reading Darwin

Maturana and Varela help us to understand that all of our experience of the world is inextricable from our physiological structure. The organizational structure of our bodies fundamentally affects the way that we are in the world. Moreover, our own history of actions in the world (biological, social, cultural), as well as those of our forebears, affects how the world appears to us. In order to better understand what we call our cognitive system—our way of knowing—we need to understand not only how we function biologically in the world, but how the biological structure we call our body and the place we call our world co-evolve.

Although this may already sound quite logical, it is not generally the way that we think about our human/world relations. In fact, much of the language that we use to discuss any changing relationship among persons and/or things indicates that we have trouble understanding that learning always co-emerges with living. When thinking about close human relationships, for example, we tend to talk about the way in which these might ideally evolve. What we say about the initiation of these relationships betrays this belief: "You need to get to *know* your partner before you make a commitment!" We say this as if the person's identity is somehow something static that we can learn about in the absence of our shared lived experience. In reading theory we talk about schematic learning where teachers are encouraged to help students develop scaffolding structures based on their own experience in order to more effectively learn new material. Again, there seems to be a deliberate forgetting of the way in which all of these previous memories and experiences are altered by the ongoing action among persons and texts in the school classroom. Educational discourse generally speaks in terms of states, learning, and efficiency, all of which are often defined in the absence of discussions of the human/world relations that necessarily circumscribe all cognitive development.

According to Maturana and Varela, much of our disembodied talk about the process of learning arises from our belief that we can actually subtract ourselves from our world. Furthermore, they suggest that there is a deeply embedded cultural belief in the idea of survival of the fittest. In part, this is a consequence of the cultural internalization of a particular interpretation of Charles Darwin's theory of natural selection. It is conventionally believed, for example, that evolution is a process through which the environment chooses some organisms for survival over others because those organisms have more optimal traits. Given this view, it is not surprising that the environment is understood as "giving directions" for particular paths of evolution.

In *The Tree of Knowledge*, Maturana and Varela outline a view of evolution which they suggest is better able to account for the complexity, diversity, and tangled interrelationships among organisms and between organisms and the environments in which they are contained. They suggest that in order for any living organism to survive, it must successfully co-exist with an environment through a process called "structural coupling." When a living entity is structurally coupled with the medium that contains it, it may *seem* to the observer that the entity is functioning according to directions given by the environment, but it is actually functioning within a choreography of congruent disturbances in which one is influenced by the other. Only when the mutual disturbances from each entity and its environment become congruent can they be said to be structurally coupled. Thus, the very structure of any entity and the environment that contains it are always affected by the way in which they disturb each other.

Of course, this all becomes incredibly complex since structural coupling between entities and environments occurs at various levels and is continuous. The important point for this discussion is that, biologically speaking, it is inaccurate to suggest that living entities are determined by their environments—that is, they do not develop in order to optimally fit their environment. Rather, structural coupling is contingent upon whatever conditions happen to be present. A living entity survives not because it has developed an ideal form but, rather, because it has developed an adequate form to allow structural coupling to continue. Structural coupling, then, can be understood as an ongoing dialectic between living entities and their environment where each simultaneously determines the other.

The idea of structural coupling (or mutual specification) is a dramatic shift from our conventional understanding of Darwinian theory, for it rejects the idea that living forms are determined or adapted by some process of ideal trait selection. Rather, it presents structural change as a necessary function of a complex mutual relationship between living entities and their environment. This leads to several important conclusions: First, whether or not an environmental disturbance will prompt a response from an organism is a function of the organism's structure (as determined by its history, biology, and context). Although changes are triggered by the environment, the structural adaptation is determined by the previous history and current structure in the living unity. Second, although living entities trigger changes in the environment, it is the structure of the environment, as determined by its prior history of mutual specification that will determine the structural changes that this disturbance triggers. Changes in the environment are not determined by a living entity that lives in it but, instead, the environment reacts according to what is possible because of its history of structural coupling. In other words, we could say that both living entities and the environments are *structure determined:* they are limited by their previous history of interactions with each other. Third, this continual process of structural coupling has no discernible beginning or end points. One cannot say whether the environment or the entity has made the first or the last disturbance. Like the hermeneutic circle of understanding, the structural changes between organism and environment exist in a continual circle of evolution.

This process of evolution is what Maturana and Varela call "natural drift." For them, natural drift signifies the serendipitous path of evolution. They suggest that

> Evolution is somewhat like a sculptor with wanderlust: he (sic) goes through the world collecting a thread here, a hunk of tin there, a piece of wood here, and he combines them in a way that their structure and circumstance allow, with no reason other than what is able to combine them.[12]

Understanding evolution as natural drift simply means that living entities are neither determined by their environment nor do they determine their environment. Rather, through the necessary process of structural coupling, which is required to maintain equilibrium between the two, each specifies the other. Using the word "drift" helps to signify the variability of this evolution. Although always constrained by each other, (living entity and environment), the direction that evolution may take greatly varies depending upon the particular conditions at any given time in the history of ongoing structural coupling. Maturana and Varela equate natural drift to the many possible paths drops of water may take if hundreds of handfuls are thrown from the summit of a hill. Although each handful of droplets will fall depending upon the particular relationship that it has with infinite environmental contingencies, particular lines or patterns will become evident after some time. These patterns are never pre-determined or selected by the environment but, instead, represent the number of possible variants emerging from ongoing structural coupling. The most important point for this discussion is that "what an environment is cannot be separated from what organisms are and what they do."[13] The environment is as much a reflection of the biology of the species as the species is a reflection of the environment.

Contrary to popular interpretations of Darwinian evolutionary theory, Varela et al. suggest that the evolution of living beings is more the result of a process of satisfying the conditions necessary for the integrity of the living entity to be maintained. Put simply, biological evolution does not wait for an optimal solution—a best fit. It accepts whatever allows life to go on. Varela et al. use the metaphor of "bricolage" to account for this phenomenon, where bricolage is understood as "the putting together of parts and items in complicated arrays, not because they fulfill some ideal design but simply because they are possible."[14] "Good enough" forms, not ideal ones, are all that are necessary for the maintenance of structural coupling.

This, I believe, is an important point, for it means that living entities do not remain viable because optimal genetic structures are selected but, instead, because they maintain a structure which is possible. This means that the process of evolutionary drift is more about *discarding* those traits that would compromise the viability of the living entity than of selecting traits that would ensure its viability. By thinking of evolution as a process of discarding, rather than selecting, it becomes clear that what remains after discarding allows for greater diversity than what remains after optimal selection, especially when the goal of evolution is understood in terms of "good enough" rather than optimal processes. "Good enough" must not be seen as something that is less desirable or mediocre, but rather as a process that encourages variation by maintaining as much diversity as possible. "Good enough" means a temporary fixing of the minimal conditions for the necessary while maintaining a broad range of resources in anticipation of the possible.

Re-Reading The Joke

What implications do structural coupling and evolutionary drift have for understanding the development of human intelligence and human action in the world? How are what we perceive, what we learn (know) and what we do caught up in each other? How can a "good enough" theory of evolution help us to understand the human cognitive system?

In chapter three a description of Kip's talent for bomb disposal was presented. It was suggested that this talent was largely a result of his ability to see what others could not see, to perceive differently. And, of course, seeing a usually invisible choreography, (or looking for the joke of the bomb) meant imagining the possible, rather than the probable. Kip seemed to be able to see what others could not see. Or, we could say that he somehow saw things differently. It was this capacity to see things differently that allowed him success at bomb disposal. How can we explain Kip's remarkable talent in terms of what is believed about human cognition?

Varela, Thompson, and Rosch[15] carefully detail two commonly accepted theories of human cognition: cognition as "representation" and cognition as an "emergent system." They then carefully outline a theory of cognition as "embodied action" that is largely developed around the ideas of structural coupling and natural drift. The following three re-readings of Kip's ability to locate the "joke" in a bomb demonstrate the significant differences between these three views of cognition.

Cognition as Representation

Emerging from a metaphor of mind as computer or information processing device, this view of cognition suggests that the formulation of meaning by human subjects is the result of a process of learning how to effectively use symbols that represent a world that is independent of the knower. The central idea is that intelligence so resembles computation in its essential characteristics that human cognition can be characterized in terms of computation of symbolic processes in much the same way as the operation of computers is defined. From this point of view, intelligent behavior presupposes the ability to develop an accurate internal representation of an external world. This has become our "commonsense" view of cognition where thought consists of physical, symbolic computations leading to successful action and interaction in a pre-given world. Similar to Darwinian evolutionary theory, the subject is "determined" by the environment and is seen as more or less successful depending upon the suitability of the response to particular conditions. Improving cognitive capacity or functioning is seen as achieving a more "optimal fit" between what is needed for successful action and what is possible (cognitively) by the subject.

The popularity of this view can be discerned in our metaphorical descriptions of cognition as information processing, solving problems as computing data, and the act of remembering as retrieving information. Words are thought of as locations for meaning; meaning, in turn, is transmitted from one cognizing agent to another in order for communication to occur.[16] For cognitivists the mind is located in the brain which, in turn, is understood as a storage place and processing centre for knowledge.

If we believe that our cognition is a process of symbolically representing a reality that exists independent of our perception of it, we might say that Kip has been educated to see differently, and that any person who is sufficiently capable and motivated should be able to learn the skills necessary to engage in this sort of behavior. Noticing a different choreography of place might be understood as the result of having experienced an alternate symbolization of the world. Kip's talent, then, could be understood as a combination of experience and direct instruction that has altered his perceptual schema in ways that would prepare him to receive and process information differently. Kip could be described as having been programmed to be able to locate and process information leading to accurate location of well-hidden bombs.

Hermeneutically, we might situate ourselves with the early hermeneuts who believed that interpretation was largely a process of getting the meaning of a text right in order to promote a deeper understanding of it.[17] From this perspective, "getting it right" for Kip would mean decoding the joke. This would have been made possible by his familiarity with particular symbolic formulations that he was able to manipulate in creative ways in order to solve the problem presented to him. Speaking behaviouristically, his reward could be positive reinforcement (self-satisfaction or admiration of peers) or negative reinforcement (not getting blown up). Basically, then, Kip's ability could be interpreted as an act of creative symbolic decoding and processing in order to meet particular contextual challenges.

For me, it is interesting how natural this interpretation sounds. Although words like "processing" emerge from a mind as computer metaphor, they no longer function as figurative devices but, instead, as literalized truths. Most of us would not question this usage since our conception of learning is now well-entrenched in this once-metaphorical thinking. But can this view of cognition as the processing of symbolic representations of a world really account for this complex act of creative interpretation? If this is the way in which learning really occurs, why is it that only a very few soldiers who were trained in the same way as Kip were able to demonstrate his proficiency? Was their deficiency merely due to a lack of interest and motivation? Not likely, since failure to find the joke of the bomb meant certain death. Perhaps, then, they lacked talent. Could it be that the interpretation required of an effective sapper was not something that could be simply learned, but required talent? If so, what is this mystical thing that we call "talent" or "innate ability" to which we refer when the computer metaphor fails us. Is talent a genetic pre-disposition or is it a culturally acquired one? Nature or nurture?

Cognition as an Emergent System

Rather than understanding the brain as a central processing device, thinking about cognition as an emergent system means understanding intelligent action as the product of the interaction of various neuronal networks in the brain. These neuronal networks are thought of as presymbolic, meaning that they do not depend upon symbolic representation of a world in order to exist. Through their evolving interaction with one another these complex neuronal networks become self-organized into what Marvin Minsky has called "societies of the mind."[18]

This "society" metaphor is useful for describing the way genetic networks, immune systems, and ecological systems work for it suggests a process of interaction where new properties emerge from the interaction of already-existing components. From this perspective, learning is not understood as decoding a pre-given world as represented symbolically, but is understood as the product of interacting neuronal behaviour which, within each organism, self-organizes in order to create a system that is functional. This understanding of intelligence is founded upon a metaphor of construction rather than representation. The cognitive system is not thought to be a linear system whereby various levels of symbolic processing intersect in order to allow effective action in the world but, rather, a system enabling the emergence of new global properties from an evolving network of components. In other words, intelligence is more than the sum of the parts that produce it.

How might a "society of mind" view of the cognitive system explain Kip's abilities? Unlike the other sappers who are selected by Lord Suffolk to comprise the bomb disposal unit, Kip was not raised in England. Although his native India was a British colony, his history of experiences as a child and young adult differed significantly from his fellow British soldiers' experiences. We learn, for example, that in India old machinery and furniture is not discarded but, instead, is re-used in some way. Most of the citizens from Kip's village, we are told, are more likely to carry with them a screwdriver than a pencil.

If cognition is understood as an emergent system, Kip's talent might be explained as emerging from cultural circumstances that provoked a particular choreography of interaction among neuronal networks in his brain. Because mechanical innovations were desired in his native India where there was a shortage of materials, the ability to re-invent useful artifacts from old—to see a new choreography amid a pre-given one—could be described as the construction of specific abilities to meet particular environmental needs. Therefore, although his ability seems as though it is the product of innate talent, a society of mind theory of cognition would suggest that his effectiveness at discerning the joke in the bomb was possible because of his history of interactions in the world. If he is good at adapting to the challenges presented to him as a bomb defuser, he will live to utilize these new adaptations on the next bomb. Human cognition develops, we could say, to serve the world. Because this explanation represents our common-sense view of the operation of a cognitive system as something developed in the brain it seems sensible and logical. But is it really?

Although a view of cognition as an emergent system rejects the idea that human intelligence is the result of symbolic processing, it is more similar to than different from theories of cognition as representation, for like them, it also suggests that the environment and learner arise independently of one another. Although human subject and world are involved in a relationship with each other, it is the human subject who is seen as adapting (hopefully optimally) to a particular environment. It is important to understand that even though society of mind theories have helped us appreciate the complexity of the relationships that comprise the human cognitive system, they have not accounted for two things. First, the possibility that emergent properties from these self-organizing systems are not optimal solutions to environmental demands. Second, that the history of emergent global states of any organism's system of cognition fundamentally affects the way it is able to act on the world. Therefore, although these theories have more successfully accounted for the complexity of cognition, they still evolve from a fundamental belief in the optimization of forms for the purpose of adapting to the ongoing demands of particular environments.

Cognition as Embodied Action

What happens if we think of Kip's ability in terms of a theory of "embodied action" as derived from a theory of evolution as natural drift? In order to clearly distinguish their theory of cognition from other theories, Varela et al. have aligned cognition with the phrase "embodied action" to illuminate two important points:

> First, that cognition depends upon the kinds of experience that come from having a body with various sensorimotor capacities, and second, that these individual sensorimotor capacities are themselves embedded in a more encompassing biological, psychological, and cultural context. By using the term action we mean to emphasize ... that sensory and motor processes, perception and action, are fundamentally inseparable in lived cognition. Indeed the two are not merely contingently linked in individuals; they have evolved together.[19]

Cognition as embodied action is philosophically grounded in the phenomenological work of Merleau-Ponty who, in *Phenomenology of Perception* and *The Primacy of Perception*[20] insisted that all human knowledge was necessarily embodied in the world.[21] Epistemological questions for Merleau-Ponty were always questions of ontological embodiment. That is, to know something is to know through a body that exists historically, temporally, spatially in a world. Varela et al. explicitly align their theory of enaction with Merleau-Ponty's belief in the inextricability of world and subject:

> The world is inseparable from the subject, but from a subject which is nothing but a project of the world, and the subject is inseparable from the world, but from a world which the subject itself projects.[22]

It is this sense of "double embodiment" (i.e. our bodies are both biological structures and phenomenological-experiential structures) which formed the basis for Merleau-Ponty's insistence that in order to understand our lived situation we needed to more explicitly acknowledge the ongoing dialectic between our physiological structure (body) and its relationship to its surroundings in any discussion of mind or self.

Cognition as embodied action is also philosophically closely aligned with the work of Heidegger and Gadamer. It was Heidegger who insisted that philosophy must move away from a preoccupation with knowing into an ongoing reflection on "Being."[23] In *Being and Time*[24] he laid the groundwork for a philosophy which refuted the notion that philosophy was able to find some univocal truth outside lived experience. Instead, Heidegger believed human subjects could only find truth by exploring multiple understandings and orientations to truth. Heidegger believed that ontology and history are inseparable; human subjects come to understand only within ever-evolving present moments which are always the terminal point of everything that has come before. For Heidegger, truth was not something that could be fixed or located after the fact; truth was the ongoing project of coming to understanding of human existence in each present moment. Most relevant for this discussion is Heidegger's idea that the essential aspect of humanness is the ability to think about one's existence. For him, thinking is never a closed system but is the traveling of a road. Each thinker goes a way uniquely her or his own as determined by the ongoing historical relationship between her or his existence and the world into which he or she has been thrown. For Heidegger, neither the world "that is" nor the being "who knows" is determined by the other; they are co-determined through their dialectical relationship with each other.[25]

Because Gadamer's philosophical investigations emphasize the importance of interpreting the conditions necessary to make understanding possible, they provide important philosophical support for a theory of cognition as embodied action. With his concept of the "fusion of horizons," which refers to the coming-to-agreement or the arrived-at "meaning" in the process of conversation between two differently situated consciousnesses, Gadamer helps us to more clearly understand how truth does not exist *in* the world but is continually fixed and unfixed in our ongoing relationships *with* a world.[26] For Gadamer, hermeneutics is not about locating or fixing truth; it is about the ongoing process of understanding the conditions necessary for understanding to occur.

What Merleau-Ponty, Heidegger, and Gadamer share is the belief that human beings do not act on an objective world, nor that the world acts upon humans as objects. The central insight to be gained from hermeneutic and phenomenological studies is that knowledge is not something which is pre-given in the world—it is not embedded in the world waiting to be located. Nor is knowledge embedded inside some essential inner-self revealed through introspection. Instead, knowledge is viewed as emerging from our ongoing interpreted action in the world. Varela et al. suggest that in order for us to better understand our lived situation as human subjects a continuing dialogue between Continental philosophy and cognitive science must develop:

> The challenge posed by cognitive science to the Continental discussions ... is to link the study of human experience as culturally embodied with the study of human cognition in neuroscience, linguistics and cognitive psychology. In contrast, the challenge posed to cognitive science is to question one of the more entrenched assumptions of our scientific heritage—that the world is independent of the knower.[27]

This suggests that cognition must not be thought of as a process through which the human subject attempts closer and closer approximations of a received world, but as a process by which cognitive systems and the world are mutually specified. We neither determine our world nor are determined by it; we *co-emerge* with a world. Co-emergence is the pivotal concept in a theory of cognition as embodied action.

Situated as it is between post-Darwinian evolutionary theory and the Continental philosophic traditions of hermeneutics and phenomenology, cognition as embodied action asserts that cognition is a system of intelligence which brings forth a world of understanding. Simply put, human intelligence is not seen as the ability to know a fixed, stable, truthful world; rather, intelligence is understood as the ability to maintain viability with an ever-evolving world. What we call our cognitive system is not something that is innate, nor is it something that is determined by a world. It is, instead, a system that develops from our history of interactions with our world. The world co-evolves with its subjects.

The importance of historical interaction to sensory perception is described by neurologist Oliver Sacks'[28] account of Virgil who, through surgery, became sighted after nearly a lifetime of blindness. As the bandages were lifted off, Virgil did not, as we might expect, jump up and exclaim "I can see!" Although he was now aware of a profusion of light, color, shape and texture, his history of blindness meant that he was unable to draw out meaningful images. In effect, Virgil could not see. For him, seeing required months of living through a now-visual world and, in fact, even though physiologically vision was possible, it was never fully attained. His previous history of blindness prevented him from successfully living a life that included visual perception. This example helps us to understand that what we see is more a matter of what we have learned to see rather than an internal representation of the world. What we perceive is a version of the world that we have brought forth through our history of interactions with others. This ultimately has biological consequences, for as Varela et al. suggest:

> The vastly different histories of structural coupling for birds, fishes, insects, and primates have enacted or brought forth different perceived worlds of color. Therefore, our perceived world of color should not be considered to be the optimal "solution" to some evolutionarily posed "problem." Our perceived world of color is, rather, a result of one possible and viable phylogenic pathway among many others realized in the evolutionary history of living beings.[29]

This explains why all cultures do not perceive color in the same way. It is not that what is out there is different; rather, our experience of living teaches us how to see. Because our experience collects in a physiological body, which has a prior history of learning (including an inherited genetic structure), seeing color is always the product of an historically, culturally and biologically conditioned set of lived experiences. What we see is more a result of what our history of structural coupling (both as an individual and as a member of a human species which has a history of genetic evolution) allows us to see. This is why it is useful to think of perception as "bringing forth" a world of seeing, hearing, tasting, and so on, rather than "representing" the world as it "really is." In fact, the colloquial language we use about perception betrays our intuitive understanding of this theory of perception. When we say that we must acquire a "taste" for a particular food, develop an "eye" for art, an "ear" for music, a "feel" for painting, we demonstrate our sense of needing to learn to perceive in ways that allow our relations with our environment to be maintained.

At this point it becomes apparent that cognition as embodied action is most closely aligned with the post-Darwinian view of evolutionary theory presented earlier since its most important theoretical point is that the cognitive system evolves through a process of evolutionary drift which is determined by a living entity's history of structural coupling. This suggests that the cognitive system is not determined by its environment through some process of natural selection through which optimal survival traits are selected, but, instead, that the cognitive system evolves through a process of attaining a *good enough* fit. Cognition is seen as a collection of capabilities that are organized together not because they are ideal but simply because they are possible.

Aligning the development of cognitive systems with the idea of evolutionary drift is an important conceptual breakthrough in our understanding of the way in which cognitive systems function since it helps us to understand that the development of intelligence is more a process of discarding than optimizing. Varela et al. suggest that

> The task in evolutionary biology is to change the logical geography of the debate by studying the tangled, circular relations of congruence among items to be explained. The first step is to switch from a *prescriptive* logic to a *proscriptive* one, that is, from the idea that what is not allowed is forbidden to the idea that what is not forbidden is allowed.[30]

This shift in thinking helps us to understand the great diversity among various species within one habitat, among members of any one species, and among cognitive systems. The most important point for this discussion is, however, that understanding cognition as evolutionary drift—as a process of *satisfying* rather than *optimizing*—suggests that there is no "ideal form" to which a system of cognition might strive. There is no predictable or logical endpoint. If organisms (including human beings) were actually made to conform to ideal forms their long-term survival would be seriously compromised, for we know that environmental conditions are unstable and usually unpredictable. It is not the organism best suited to an existing environment that has the greatest survival potential; it is the organism with the greatest range of flexibility that will likely be able to maintain a relationship with an ever-changing environment. The physiological form needs to be "good enough" rather than "ideal." The same is true for systems of cognition. Cognitive systems are most effective and most capable of coping with unforeseen and fluctuating conditions if they have more general rather than specific traits. Understanding cognition as embodied action suggests intelligence is more a matter of developing sensory capabilities that offer a broad range of perceptions rather than narrow situationally specific ones. A "good enough" system of cognition does not mean that it is merely adequate; rather, a good enough system has developed a broad range of capabilities allowing it to function adequately in existing circumstances and, at the same time, the system has retained enough flexibility to withstand unforeseen and evolving environmental contingencies.

In order to reconceptualize Kip's ability to interpret the choreography of a bomb, we need to remember that a theory of cognition as embodied action asks that we believe that there is no direct correspondence between our perception of the world and the way that the world "really is." Because of our species-specific history of structural coupling leading to a particular path of understanding, what humans perceive is not the same as what other species perceive. Our perceptual systems have not evolved in response to a pre-given world, nor has our world been determined by our perceptually guided action. What we are able to perceive has co-emerged with the world that contains us. At the same time, individuals within our species are the product of a particular genetic biological unity, which, in turn, is the product of hundreds of generations of our forebears who have been structurally coupled with particular environments. As Varela et al. suggest, we do not merely inherit a gene pool, we inherit the environments that have been structurally coupled with a gene pool.[31] Our genetic heritage, therefore, is inscribed with previous worlds. Genetic material is not merely a blueprint; it is a collecting place for history, much like the English patient's common-place book.

When Kip walks into a room, what he sees (which of course conditions what understandings are possible) is wholly determined by the way in which he embodies a cumulative history of co-determination between his lived and species-specific histories of interaction with the world. As he surveys the room, he does not simply perceive a world of significance, he *brings forth* a world of significance. He sees and understands things that others do not.

Most important, this world he brings forth must co-exist with the worlds brought forth by those with whom he exists. There must be a convergence in order for there to be a shared world of significance. Therefore, Kip engages in what Madeleine Grumet[32] has called "pointing to the world" in order for others whom he is with to begin to understand the significance of his world and for the process of social convergence to continue.

Simply put, a theory of cognition as embodied action suggests that having a body that occupies space in a medium with which it must maintain an ongoing relationship is inextricable from the cognitive system that develops. Body and mind may never be considered apart from one another, for it is the body that takes up space in the world. Every action, every experience, every movement, matters to the development of the cognitive system. It is only when we become "harmonized" (some might say socialized) with our medium that we believe that the mind is in charge of the relationship between world and self. Any rupture or breach of this harmony—such as a broken leg, a trip to a foreign country, the sudden death of a loved one—jolts us into an awareness of how our sense of self is inextricable from our relational connections to the world and to each other.

Kip's unusual expertise at bomb disposal is not simply the result of his own history of interactions in a world requiring mechanical innovation. He does have talent emerging, in part, from his and his forebears' interactions in particular environments. What we call heredity must also be understood as the collecting point for human history in the world. Therefore, we must understand that although Kip, like any other human subject, can choose to interact with his environment in many ways, he will always be a structure-determined creature. This simply means that his own genetic and experiential histories of structural coupling with particular co-emerging environments has resulted in a particular cognitive system that becomes part of the ecological unity of the planet. Therefore, although we can say that Kip is structure-determined, we must also understand that the environment in which he exists is also structure-determined. Successful cognitive action simply means maintaining a viable, co-emerging relationship between the two. For Kip, this means successfully defusing the bomb.

Unskinning Reading

How can an understanding of cognition as embodied action help us to further interpret the "reading of a reading" presented at the beginning of this chapter?

We might say, first of all, that the Queen's immediate and accurate assessment of Gyges' motive for hiding in her bed chamber was not a lucky guess. A theory of embodied action helps us to understand that her correct interpretation was likely possible because of her history of interactions with her husband, Candaules. In fact, after years of living with him, and bringing forth a world of understanding with him, her perception of the world, and her developed intellectual capabilities were likely very much like his. We might say, that over the years, they had grown to understand together. We could also say that it was precisely this collectively held understanding that ultimately proved to be deadly for Candaules. Years of sharing a life had promoted *unskinning*.

What about Katharine's re-telling of the story? We must understand, first of all, that Katharine was not reading this story in a vacuum. Her reading of the story existed alongside other texts and other experiences. In fact, the story of Candaules was situated in various layers of contextualized narratives: it was embedded within a collection of stories called *The Histories*. This particular copy of *The Histories* was the product of many years of evolution with the English patient who had made it his common-place book. In no way could he and the book be separated. *Unskinning*. This, in turn, was being read by Katharine within the context of a particular set of human and environmental relations that co-evolved with her reading and interpretation of this story. When Katharine read this story aloud, she began to understand her relationship with her husband differently, not because of some moral in the story, but because her current relational situation required her to make decisions that were not necessarily optimal, but sufficient for her emotional well-being. In other words, Katharine was unable to read about Candaules in the absence of the evolving lived experiences she had and was having. Her reading, like any reading, was not merely a vertical reading of one text; it was a horizontal reading of multiple texts of already lived and current experience. *Unskinning*.

And what of our reading group's understanding of Katharine's reading of Candaules? It, of course, was simultaneously affected by the complex set of intertextual relations of these layered stories and our own history of interactions in the world, both in and out of the context of our reading group. In other words, it was finally impossible to say whether our experiences prior to reading and interpretation gave the story meaning, or whether our interpretations gave new meaning to our own lives. *Unskinning.* Reading was not something that was simply transposed onto existing human relations; the reading and interpretation of this passage became an inextricable part of the environment with which each of us were attempting to remain viable. This helps us to understand that reading and interpreting literary fictions, within our literate culture, is an integral part of our species specific (i.e., human) experience. In other words, reading doesn't just change the way we think and act; it affects, in every way, who we are. And if reading affects who we are, it necessarily affects what we know and what we do. We could say, then, that the experience of reading has not only altered us phenomeno-logically, it has altered us biologically.

This prompts us to wonder whether the very organization and structure of our bodies is altered because we read literary fictions. Is it possible that generations of engagement with print text has changed us biologically? A theory of reading as embodied action would tend to suggest that this is likely the case for, like anything in the world, the reading of literary fictions is not merely something added to already fixed and established relations in the world which are untouched by reading. Fictional readings become an inextricable part of our daily embodied action in the world and, therefore, fundamentally change all relations we have in the world. *Unskinning.*

It is important to remember that, like any innovation, the act of reading (particularly the reading of literary fictions) is a relatively recent human innovation. We have not always developed human relations around acts of textual engagement. Walter Ong[33] explains that with the invention of the printing press and eventual education of greater numbers of persons, the literary fiction became seen (particularly in the Western world) as a way in which to educate upcoming generations about historical facts and cultural traditions. Therefore, in addition to serving as an aesthetically pleasing art form, the literary fiction was thought to enable cultural transmission. Much of the late nineteenth and early twentieth century literary criticism attempted to explicate the "meaning" of a literary work in light of its historical circumstances of writing. Interpretation meant not only the "fixing" of meaning in the text, but fixing the text in particular historical period.[34]

In the 1930s and 40s, a group of theorists endeavored to extract literary fictions from their historical circumstances and develop a method of criticism which would enable readers to perform "close readings" of texts.[35] These "New Critics" believed meaning was embedded in the literary fiction, and this meaning could be extracted by any reader who closely attended to what the text was saying. Words were considered transparent symbols, and it was the capable reader's task to be able to interpret these symbolic structures. Attempting to discern what the author may have meant in the historical circumstances of writing was the "intentional fallacy," while describing meaning in terms of the affect of the text on the reader was the "affective fallacy."[36] The text was seen as authoritative in itself; authors no longer existed for the reader, and the reader was reduced to an excavator of already-present meaning.

The work of Saussure, [37] however, altered the landscape of literary criticism and, in some ways, many of the ideas about the significance of reading the literary fiction. For Saussure, words were no longer seen as entities that "contained" some inherent truthful meaning in themselves. Rather, words could only be known by the way in which they differed from other words. The relationship between signifier and signified depended upon the way in which this relationship was positioned within any discourse. Meaning could not be located in words, but rather in the structure of combinations of words. Literary structuralism was modeled after this and, particularly with the work of Northrop Frye,[38] literary meaning began to be defined in terms of the organization of the text—the metaphors, archetypes and tropes that provided the "form" for the text. Meaning was understood as emerging from particular structures, and so it was more important to notice the structure than the particularity of words. Again, however, the text was de-historicized, and meaning was seen to reside in the structure of the text rather than in the reader. Even so, literary structuralism was a very important conceptual shift from New Criticism for it helped to show that meaning could never be considered apart from form. Unfortunately, although form and content were now re-connected, the reader still remained subtracted from meaning-making. Meaning still existed prior to and, independent of, the reader.

Generally speaking, the post-structural theorists[39] accepted Sausurrean linguistics, with one important caveat: the meaning occurring within the relationship between signified and signifier must be understood not only in terms of its difference from other structures, but also in terms of the way in which meaning is continually deferred. As mentioned in previous chapters, Derrida has been the most influential post-structuralist, and, with his coining of the word "différance," has shown that meaning is as much a matter of what is not said as what is said. One of the projects of post-structuralism, then, has been deconstructive readings of texts which do not attempt to locate truthful meanings in words or in forms, but rather in the way each of these by their very presence announce an absence.[40]

More closely related to the social sciences (especially psychology) than linguistics and semiotics, subjective criticism has privileged the reader rather than the text. According to theorists such as Norman Holland[41] and David Bleich,[42] meaning can only be located in the reader's psychological response to a literary fiction as these are socially and culturally situated in communities of interpretation. Because persons are seen to have individually constructed sets of experiences, and because reading depends upon perception as seen through the lens of that psychology, meaning can only be a product of the reader and can never be located in the text.

As discussed in chapter two, theorists such as Louise Rosenblatt and Wolfgang Iser have promoted an understanding of reading the literary fiction that does not privilege author, historical circumstances of writing, reader or contextual circumstances of reading. By suggesting that reading evolves from the relational work (Iser's formulation) or the transaction (Rosenblatt's) between reader and text as situated in the particular circumstances of reading, they have not only re-asserted the importance of the phenomeno-logical act of reading, they have pointed to the importance of the evolving relationship among readers, texts and contexts of reading. For Iser and Rosenblatt, meaning is not something in the text or the reader, but rather in the evocation of meaning as generated by the interpretive (I would suggest "hermeneutic") work of the reader.

By using the word "transaction," Rosenblatt[43] initiated an important conceptual shift to an understanding of meaning as emerging from the interaction of reader and text. Although Iser's theories have generally been aligned with Rosenblatt's, unlike her theory, even his earliest theorizing has never really considered the meaning as something which existed between the reader and the text (as in a transactional meaning) but instead as something inextricable from the lived experience of reading. In *The Act of Reading*, he explains that the reason that we often feel that we are living another life while we read has to do with the fact that we are continually in the process of responding to our own reactions to the text so that after a time it is unclear whether it is the text or previous responses to the text which have the most influence on the kinds of meanings that are evoked. He writes: [A]s we read, we react to what we ourselves have produced, and it is this mode of reaction that, in fact, enables us to experience the text as an actual event."[44] For Iser meaning is no longer a "third thing." Instead, meaning is understood as inextricable from the intertwined relational activity between reader and text as situated within the reader's ever-evolving lived experience. However, even in his later works,[45] Iser still suggests that the reader's imagination is conditioned by the literary fiction. It is this formulation which demonstrates clearly that his theory of reading is firmly embedded within a philosophical tradition that understands our task as human subjects is to adapt to the varying conditions of a world that exists apart from our experience of it.

In order to accept a theory of reading as embodied action one must believe that human beings must retain ongoing structural coupling with an environment in order to remain viable. Unlike other living species, however, humans organize their world and their interpersonal relations through the use of a language that has the potential to retrieve and narrate histories of individuals and groups of individuals. (At least we think we're the only ones who can do this!) Language, then, becomes an important symbolic system for the development of cognition during ongoing structural coupling. It is important to note that, as human subjects, we do not interact with individuals or individual things one-by-one as they occur in an environment; rather, our environment is comprised of everything that is *not-us*. This means that coherent and meaningful action in the world depends upon ongoing structural coupling between *us/not-us*. It is most important to understand, however, that although it seems like there are *two* things (us and not-us), this is not really the case, for we are always already part of the *not-us* with which all the rest of the world relates. We are part of the environment. Our bodies exist in the integrity of the world's ecology. *Unskinning.*

If we are to reconceptualize the reading of the literary fiction as embodied action, we must understand that although literary fictions are identifiable as distinct entities, they do not exist independently from other entities in their environment. In other words, literary fictions are always read *in relation to* everything else in the environment. During the act of reading, the literary fiction becomes read with a world that includes reading. We could say, that although we have culturally imposed distinctions between a text and things that are not a text, there is fundamentally no fixed boundary between the literary fiction and anything else in our environment, for the literary fiction always exists in the not-us world with which we maintain relations.

It is at this point that the departure from the weaving metaphor becomes necessary, for just as organisms co-evolve with their environments, literary readings co-emerge with the experience of readers reading as situated in a perceived world of significance. This explains why when and where we read matters, for even if our reading is done privately (i.e., one reader, one text), the location of reading matters. If I am reading a new novel at home and I receive an unexpected call from an old friend, that telephone conversation exists with my reading of the book. It becomes part of the act of reading. Reading the same novel in another context (such as in a school classroom), means that the text exists within a different organizational structure of not-us and therefore must have an altered identity as a literary fiction. Of course, this contradicts commonsense beliefs about reading since even if we believe that the meaning is always the product of interaction between author and text, we often forget that the actual identity of the text and the reader depends upon situational location.

Understanding reading as embodied action means keeping in mind the image of unskinning. When applied to reading, unskinning asks us to understand that although there are physical differences between literary fictions and other things in the world—and differences between various readers—neither readers nor literary fictions can escape their prior histories of interaction in the world. Not only are these literally inscribed in the words that are used to comprise the literary fiction and in the cognizing body of the reader, but these histories are also inscribed in the ideological and material culture that supports reading. The meanings that are derived from reader-text interactions, however, must never be thought of as optimizations regardless of how well-written the text or how earnest the reader. Instead, reading as embodied action must always be thought of as co-emergent drift where the infinite contingencies that are part the act of reading are continually in the process of evolving. Literary fictions, then, always co-exist and co-evolve with and through readers, reading environments, and histories of interactions among these.

The very existence of literary fictions that are read contributes to the environments in which readers and non-readers exist. Therefore, it is not true that non-readers are not influenced by literary fictions. Like everything else that is part of our culture, literary fictions are involved in the ecology of relations in which all human subjects participate. Like mass media advertising, popular music, films, or television, literary fictions must be understood as cultural icons that influence our overall cultural lexicon and the way in which we embody culture. Even if the text is only read by the author who composes it, the fact that her or his literary imagination is invoked ultimately changes the ecology of world relations.

It could be said, then, that literary fictions co-emerge with a world whether they are continually read or not. Long after my initial reading of *The English Patient* I continued to re-think the text in relation to new circumstances. This is not an unusual phenomenon. Many readers who engage imaginatively with a text continue that imaginative process long after the reading has been complete. In fact, the conversations our reading group had about *The English Patient* suggested that a much deeper reading occurred weeks following the actual reading of the text. It was only when we had lived with the memory of the reading for a time were some of us were able to more usefully integrate our imaginative engagement into interpretations of our present lives. This is an important point, for it helps us to understand that the endpoint of reading can never really be defined, for once the act of imaginative literary engagement becomes part of our history of experiences, it is forever inscribed in the collective experience we bring to new situations. Literary engagement, then, becomes part of the infinite circle of understanding that co-emerges with our world. It becomes, one could say, part of a world consciousness. Again, this evokes the unskinning image, for even though the entities that comprise this global consciousness are distinct, in the end, we are finally unable to extricate one from the other.

It might also be said that a literary fiction that *I* have read exists differently in the world simply because I have read it. Although this sounds like a commonsense idea, it is not really, for most of us do not actually believe that one reader reading can change the status of a literary fiction. And perhaps, in the conventional understanding of change, this might be true. However, if we believe that readings become part of the world, then we must agree that even *one* reader completing *one* reading of *one* literary fiction will, in some way, have her or his phenomenal world affected by that imaginative encounter. And, if one person's world is affected, then, of course, her or his relations with others in the world will be affected. Even though millions of persons have purchased and read copies of *The English Patient,* my reading of it has altered, in some way, how it will come to exist relationally with and through the world. My reading, and every other person's reading of *The English Patient*, in some way is integrated into the world and, therefore, begins to co-emerge with that world. *Unskinning.*

This last point demonstrates the way in which the meanings evoked from engagements with literary fictions become part of the ongoing evolution of knowledge that exists among us/not-us. This means that literary meanings must not be thought of as "third-things" that emerge from transactions between readers and texts, but instead as a material part of the self as it is inextricably bound to a relational world. From this, we can say that the body literally carries meaning in it in the phenomenological and biological sense. This is Hana's experience of reading:

> She entered the story knowing she would emerge from it feeling she had been immersed in the lives of others, in plots that stretched back twenty years, her body full of sentences and moments, as if awaking from sleep with a heaviness caused by unremembered dreams.[46]

We could say, then, that our engagements with literary fictions become part of our physiological encounter with the world and eventually influence and shape us biologically. *Unskinning.*

Thinking of imaginative literary engagements as embodied action means understanding that the reader's lived, experiential world is actually bigger because of reading. (In much the same way in which the English patient's copy of *Herodotus* is larger than it was before it became part of his life.) It also means that one's sense of self, one's understanding of the world, one's very existence is as much caught up in the forms we call literary as in our own bodies. Just as the literary fiction begins to bodily live within our own experience of the world, we begin to live in the very body of the text. This means, of course, that if we are seeking some truth of physical existence and literary fictional practice, we will seek in vain. For, in the end, there is no fixed truth in the literary fiction, in the reader, or in any meaning that occurs through reading. Truth simply becomes understood as whatever allows successful structural coupling between a human subject and a world that allows an imaginative reading to continue. A truthful reading of a literary fiction, therefore, is one which does not compromise the evolving relationship among readers and texts in the unity of us/not-us. If confusion, misunderstanding, and irreconcilable differences in understanding occur causing a rupture in us/not-us, then truth is absent. In the end, the relations among us/not-us that includes the imaginative engagement with a literary fiction must, like any form of structural coupling, be thought of as an ever-evolving, slippery, unstable truth. *Unskinning.*

Relations in us/not-us that include readings that invoke the literary imagination are always in a state of flux. Understanding is always in the process of being fixed and unfixed. Interpretation is never merely a scrutiny of any one relational component of the act of reading; rather, it is an examination of the complexity of ongoing relationality among *us/not-us.* In the following chapter I will suggest that hermeneutic interpretation is required if we are to better understand the complexity of lived experiences that include shared readings of literary fictions.

V

Bringing Forth a World of Understanding

Hermeneutics is about creating meaning, not simply reporting on it.

David Smith[1]

In the last chapter, reading was described as a form of embodied action. Using the image "unskinning," I suggested that during and following acts of engagement with literary fictions various identity transformations occur. Not only is it impossible to identify causal relationships that might lead to these transformations, but the beginnings, endings and/or boundaries of the forms that emerge from reader-text relations are blurred and, at times, impossible to discern. To this point, I have suggested that our understanding of the character of literary fictions, our unique relationships with these texts, our sense of self-identity, and our way of bringing forth a world of understanding are all hermeneutic. In this chapter, I will elaborate on these ideas through an investigation of the practice of shared reading as informed by our reading group's discussions of *The English Patient*. Drawing primarily upon David Smith's[2] concept of "the hermeneutic imagination," this discussion is oriented around the questions: "How do teachers experience the shared reading of literary fictions?" and, "What can interpretations of these contribute to an understanding of the use of literary fictions in schools?"

Invoking the Hermeneutic Imagination

In the introduction to his essay on the subject of the hermeneutics as a form of educational inquiry, David Smith suggests that

> The aim of interpretation, it could be said, is not just another interpretation, but human freedom, which finds its light, identity, and dignity in those few brief moments when one's burdens can be shown to have their source in too limited a view of things.[3]

Understood in this way, the interpretations that human subjects bring to bear upon their lived experiences are caught up in the ecology of ever-evolving subject/world relations. Interpretation must not obstruct one's perceptions; rather, interpretation must be like the horizon of a prairie field and the vast blue sky that meets it. It must be discernible and, at the same time, must appear ungraspable in its vastness. I would suggest that the aim of interpretation must be to continue to strive for deep understandings of one's ecological relationship in the unity of the us/not-us relation.

As a form of interpretive inquiry, the contemporary project of hermeneutics can be described as the ongoing need to understand that what we know, what we do, and who we are must always be interpreted. These interpretations must occur alongside a deep awareness of our historically-effected situations within a world of significance that we bring forth with others. Hermeneutic inquiry is not a "truth-telling" phenomenon; it does not attempt to report the way things *really* are (or were). Instead, hermeneutic inquiry entails a re-collection of and meditation on some of the contingencies of life that, in Gregory Bateson's words, have resulted in "differences that make a difference."[4]

As Heidegger and Gadamer have explained, historical consciousness can only be present to us in terms of our futurity. We can only make decisions about who we are and who we might become in light of what Gadamer has called our "pre-judgments"—our prejudices.[5] Here "prejudices" is not meant in any negative sense, but simply refers to the fact that understanding depends upon having already understood. We are forever implicated in the circularity of experience and understanding. Coming to understanding is not a truth-telling phenomenon. It is not an act of abstracting our understanding from the world in order to say what the world is *really* like. Nor is understanding any sort of reproductive activity. As Gary Madison suggests, "To understand an experience, to reconstruct the past, is not to 'represent' it to ourselves; it is to transform it."[6] Just as Freire has suggested that reading the word is a reading of the world,[7] hermeneutic scholars have reminded us that these readings are always and forever interpretations. In reading the word (literally and figuratively), we simultaneously write or bring forth a world of significance.

David Jardine explains that the most important task of hermeneutics is to bring to light the "presuppositions" of our lived experience that are buried in normativity and habit. He suggests that "the task of hermeneutics is to recollect the contours and textures of the life we are already living, a life that is not secured by the methods we can wield to render such a life our object."[8] As Gadamer demonstrated in *Truth and Method,*[9] neither truth nor method can be determined by or located in the other; truth and method are forever co-implicated in the dialectical relations between them. Furthermore, these are always understood as co-emerging with the contingencies of lived experience.

In his writings, Heidegger suggests that what is announced as "truthful" is historically-effected. Truth is always caught up in forms of language used for the expression or narration of experience. For Heidegger, truth is not something that is revealed, but rather "un-concealed" (from the Greek *aletheia*). Truth as un-concealment does not emerge directly through the human subject, but through the language that is spoken.[10] Following Heidegger, Gadamer developed his philosophical hermeneutics around the maxim, "Being that can be understood is language."[11] For Gadamer, language is not a "third thing" which hangs—suspended—between persons and their world; rather, language is inextricable from these relations. Language and world are forever contained in an ever-evolving, mutually specifying, ecological existence.

The relations among language, experience, and interpretation are discussed by Richard Rorty who explains that "The suggestion that truth ... is out there is a legacy of an age in which the world was seen as the creation of a being who had a language of his own."[12] Like proponents of a theory of cognition as embodied action, Rorty rejects any notion that the world "gives directions" for our understanding of it:

> As long as we think that there is some relation called "fitting the world" or "expressing the real nature of the self" which can be possessed or lacked by vocabularies-as-wholes, we shall continue the traditional philosophical search for a criterion to tell us which vocabularies have this desirable feature. But if we could ever become reconciled to the idea that most of reality is indifferent to our descriptions of it, and that the human self is created by the use of a vocabulary rather than being adequately or inadequately expressed in a vocabulary, then we should at last have assimilated what was true in the Romantic idea that truth is made rather than found.[13]

Does language speak us or do we speak language? Contemporary hermeneutic scholars such as Smith [14] and Jardine [15] would not likely situate themselves at either end of this dichotomy but, like enactivist, evolutionary, and cognitive theorists Maturana and Varela, [16] would suggest that truth is an ontological rather than epistemological concern. Our experience of living through a world requires the maintenance of a relation with the world. This does not mean optimal adaptation according to directions given by a world (as in the formulation, "language speaks us") or through the adapting of the world through directions given by us ("we speak language"). The maintenance of relational viability to one another and to the world (the continuation of the us/not-us relation) requires continual interpretation. Each of us, those with whom we interact, the various contexts in which we act, the words and symbols we use to communicate—all of these are relationally bound together in something that we experience as "everyday life."

Madeleine Grumet suggests that "the problem with everyday life is that it is always the ground, rarely the figure." [17] Not only is the specificity of everyday life usually invisible to us, but the relations between this specificity and the interpretations we make of our lived situation (the theories, we could say) are often announced in the absence of these details. As Grumet explains: "The dailyness is hard to recover. Memory often records it only as a backdrop to the drama that interrupts it." [18] It is the function of hermeneutic inquiry to render visible this usually-invisible backdrop—to make the ground the figure. And, in so doing, hermeneutic interpretations help us to understand that it is not experience that shapes language or language that shapes experience but, rather, that these co-specify one another during events of participating in the ongoing ecology of the us/not-us relation. Engaging in hermeneutic inquiry means understanding that the maintenance of our relations to the world requires an ongoing conversation. We, the world that we identify as "not ourselves" (i.e. outside the boundary of human skin), the languages we use to mediate our relations, all co-specify one another—all co-emerge—through the process of existing simultaneously.

When we are confused, when we misunderstand, when we misinterpret, when we are excluded, silenced or marginalized, we are experiencing a rupture—a breach in the relation between ourselves and the world. Hermeneutic inquiry attempts to excavate these sites of rupture, seeking to better understand what is at work within them, endeavoring to render visible that which has become invisible to present consciousness. In this sense, hermeneutics has more to do with absence than presence for, as Derrida has reminded us, anything present to our consciousness requires that something be deferred or absent.[19] It is the presence of this absence that often causes a sense of self-doubt, confusion and, at the same time, often propels the self into self-inquiry as a way to eliminate these confusions and doubts.

This reifying of the self has led to the modern problem of isolation and alienation. The belief that the self is somehow "enclosed" inside the "mind" of an individual who is able to exist in a fully named and articulated world has led to ongoing cultural and personal neurosis. Charles Taylor[20] has described this phenomena as the result of three "malaises" of modernity: "individualism," "instrumental reason," and "loss of freedom." The primarily Western belief that one is in control of one's own life—a life which can be improved through a particular ethic of living—has, in Taylor's view, led to a type of "soft despotism" whereby individuals become so preoccupied with their own striving that they become politically inert, removed from the ongoing discourse of public life and decision-making. Similarly, Albert Borgmann[21] has suggested that much of the modern world has become a victim of what he terms "sullen indolence," which he describes as "the incapacity to be pained by things undone and challenges unmet,"[22] and as "people's inability to find meaning in suffering, and the acceptance of resentment, resentment not of people but of inalienable pain."[23] Like Taylor, Borgmann believes that much of this sullenness and indolence can be traced to the frantic, hyperactive grasping for a fuller, more perfectly defined life—a grasping that has co-evolved with the modern quest for truth and certainty. In addition to making individuals feel overly responsible for their own situation, soft despotism has removed a sense of communal responsibility for others.

The enclosing of self and self-responsibility within the individual has alienated and isolated individuals from each other and from the world with which they must maintain relations. Therefore, although there is an illusion of an autonomous and independent self which is self-knowing and self-interpreting, there is the need to maintain relations with the environment. When the self is understood as imprisoned in the body, interpretation is understood as self-narration rather than as some deeper understanding of the way in which the self is continually mutually specified with a world.

Hermeneutics seeks to reinstate the relationality of life itself and generate an understanding of self as a linguistic construction which stands in the place of the evolving focal points of our lived experience. In this view, the self is not comprised of some foundational core within which each person continually adapts to ongoing lived experience. Rather, the self exists with the narrative interpretations of our ongoing, historically-effected (but not determined) relations in the world.

As Sartre[24] and Merleau-Ponty[25] have suggested, we can only know about the self through our perceived and interpreted relations with others as contained in a world. This means that what we know and how we know it are inextricable from who we think we are in relation to each other and our inherited ways of having lived as a species. Producing hermeneutic interpretations means not only acknowledging these inextricable relations, it means continually remembering them in the midst of hermeneutic inquiries. First and foremost, this means understanding that inquiry has no definitive beginning or end points, for as a part of an ongoing conversation with the world, inquiry can only slip into what is always already there. Hermeneutic inquiry is not a process whereby sites for objective inquiry are constructed; hermeneutic inquiry is a process of interpreting one's complicity in the midst of already-existing sites of lived experience in order to come to a deeper understanding of what the experience of being-there presents to us.

Understanding the way in which we are implicated in these hermeneutic inquiries requires knowledge about the way a sense of self-identity co-emerges with situated, lived experiences. In his book *Narrative and the Self*,[26] Anthony Kerby explains how our understanding of ourselves and our relation to the world depends upon the ongoing writing and reading of identity. He describes a model of the human subject that takes narration as fundamental to the emergence and reality of that subject. Kerby suggests that the sense of self, as constituted through language, is the result of discursive praxis rather than something that has ontological or epistemologi-cal priority. For Kerby, self-narration is understood as an interpretive activity, not simply a mirroring of the past. As such, the meaning of any memories of the past that are re-presented through a language of narration are never fixed or final, but are continually re-written in light of present circumstances. The excavation of the past within the context of the present, because it is always an interpretation, is a selective and imaginative activity. Kerby's formulations about the self are properly hermeneutic since they demonstrate the way in which our perception (gaze) is always historically-effected (subject to pre-judgment) while, at the same time, continually influenced by present circumstances and interpretations. Furthermore, this ever-evolving gaze is not directed by an individual body or by a world (including others in the world) but, instead, by the discursive practices which circumscribe relations among these.[27]

The ability to respond to the world (response-ability) may be understood as the ability to remain in relation to the world. As human subjects, this means coming to a deeper understanding of the way language exists within this complex ecology of relations. Language must be understood as "essentially material,"[28]—that is, an extension of the sphere of activity of the human body. Therefore, the sense of self, although not located "in" the body (mind), is, as Merleau-Ponty would suggest, "embodied" in the physiological and phenomenological circumstances of our lived experience. Although the sense of self is understood by Kerby as the product of creative narration—a fiction; it is a fiction which must enable the human subject to remain viable with her or his environment. When this idea is aligned with Varela et al.'s theory of cognition as embodied action and Gadamer's account of the historically-effected nature of consciousness, it becomes clear that human existence is largely dependent on the ongoing interpretations of our ever-evolving situation. This suggests that hermeneutic inquiry must refrain from questions of insulation and isolation (What does this mean for me?) and strive for inquiry that demonstrates our response-ability to those with whom and with which we co-exist. This does not mean that we should engage in a hermeneutics of exhortation (What did he mean by that? What can we say about her?) or truth (What does all this *really* mean?), but that we should instead aim for continued understanding of our participation in the ecology of lived experiences. This, according to David Smith, means developing the "hermeneutic imagination."[29]

Smith[30] suggests that most research in the field of education emerges from what he calls the "tradition of consciousness" or the "critical tradition." The tradition of consciousness insists that research in education involves getting the facts of a particular case right and conveying them accurately. Whether this is research founded upon the "scientific method" or more qualitative forms of inquiry such as ethnography, the aim of research is understood as the reporting of the "truth" of what the world is really like. Although the critical traditions are more concerned with excavating what discourses of power contribute to various social evils and inequities, these share with the tradition of consciousness the idea that "the nature of reality can be decided in advance of a full experience of it."[31] Therefore, although these traditions are generally at odds with one another (one seeking to name and stabilize culture, the other seeking to emancipate disempowered individuals and groups) they share the belief that it is possible to inquire into the world by standing outside of it. Inquiry becomes commentating.

Smith suggests that philosophical hermeneutics, when applied to research in the field of education, can be a way out of the unproductive binaries between traditions of consciousness and the critical traditions. For Smith, hermeneutic inquiry is not a commentary *on* or *about* something; it does not purport to proclaim any fixed truth, nor to assist others in the elimination of a false consciousness about the way things *really* are. Instead, hermeneutic inquiry is guided by what he calls the "hermeneutic imagination." He writes:

> In educational terms, the hermeneutic imagination throws open the challenge to inquire into what we mean when we use words like curriculum, research, and pedagogy. We are challenged to ask what makes it possible for us to speak, think, and act in ways we do.[32]

The hermeneutic imagination seeks to illuminate the *conditions* that make particular interpretations possible and, further, to describe what conditions might alter our interpretations. Understood as such, it becomes clear that hermeneutic inquiry is not merely an excavation of what makes things work (as in, for example, descriptive and expository accounts of the enactment of a curriculum or the reading of a literary fiction). Further, hermeneutic inquiry involves more than an interrogation of the socio-political architecture of such events. Rather, to engage in hermeneutics is to engage in *creative* interpretations which, in themselves, hold the potential for the generation of knowledge. This does not mean that various interpretive frameworks are ignored, but rather that these are understood as tools which can help to shape the hermeneutic imagination more creatively. Therefore, although feminist, psychoanalytic, or deconstructive analysis may be used, no one of these is used exclusively. Hermeneutics avoids the isolation of a particular interpretive ideology. It is believed that interpretation should be a creative process emerging from a dedicated mindfulness of the matter of interest. As Smith suggests in the epigram used at the beginning of this chapter, "Hermeneutics is about creating meaning, not simply reporting on it."[33] Hermeneutic research, then, cannot be identified with a particular method but is a "bricolage" of methodological tools assembled by the researcher to deepen understanding of a particular situation.[34]

Although these methods may vary greatly, depending upon the researcher's interests, experiences, and intentions, what they share is an appreciation of the imaginative, creative impulse that underpins the process of inquiry. Hermeneutic research depends upon the invoking of the hermeneutic imagination. Like the literary imagination, the hermeneutic imagination does not exist apart from conditioning situations. Like any event of understanding, the hermeneutic imagination is always implicated in language and, because of this, is continually conditioned by the kinds of language events with which it co-emerges. Just as the literary imagination depends on the reader's engagement with a particular literary fiction, the hermeneutic imagination depends upon the conditioning effects of some event-structure. Although the hermeneutic imagination may be invoked in a variety of ways, Gadamer suggests it is best conditioned through events that have the character of a conversation. He writes:

> We say that we "conduct" a conversation, but the more genuine a conversation is, the less its conduct lies within the will of either partner. Thus a genuine conversation is never the one that we wanted to conduct. Rather, it is generally more correct to say that we fall into conversation, or even that we become involved in it. The way one word follows another, with the conversation taking its own twists and reaching its own conclusion, may well be conducted in some way, but the partners conversing are far less the leaders of it than the led. No one knows in advance what will "come out" of a conversation. Understanding or its failure is like an event that happens to us. Thus we can say that something was a good conversation or that it was ill fated. All this shows that a conversation has a spirit of its own, and that the language in which it is conducted bears its own truth within it — i.e., that it allows something to 'emerge' which henceforth exists.[35]

Here Gadamer does not mean to suggest that all conversations are
hermeneutic or that all hermeneutic inquiry must consist of verbal conversations. Instead, conversation is meant to be understood in a more figurative
way, showing how hermeneutic interpretations always emerge from the
middle of things. Like a good conversation, in which the speakers forget
themselves and attend instead to the topic of conversation, good hermeneutic
inquiry emerges from situations in which a matter of interest is held in
common (one could say, in a *commonplace*) among participants. Compatible with the idea of cognition as embodied action, hermeneutic inquiry
shows how meaning co-emerges with meaning-making activities (such as
reading) and, furthermore, how these ever-evolving meanings represent a
world of significance which has been brought forth by the inquirers.

Just as a good conversation does not generally proceed through pre-
established questions or methods, neither does hermeneutic research.
Instead, inquiry exists in the middle of some matter of interest. Through the
process of what Ted Aoki has called "dwelling in the middle,"[36] that
questions for inquiry will eventually present themselves and, through that
presentation, help the participants in the inquiry come to a deeper understanding of the subject that is held in the commonplace of inquiry. The
hermeneutic imagination, then, is conditioned by the ever-evolving moment-
to-moment contingencies of living through the commonplaces of inquiry
which, because of the way in which participants must exist within them,
resemble the act of conversation. What is held among those involved in the
inquiry, like the subject of a conversation, will transform and evolve as the
event of inquiry is played out. Crucial to the quality of this process of
hermeneutic inquiry, according to Gadamer, is the imagination of the
researcher:

> What [is it] that really makes the productive scholar? That he has learned the
> methods? The person who never produces anything new has also done that. It is
> imagination (*Phantasie*) that is the decisive function of the scholar. Imagination
> naturally has a hermeneutical function and serves the sense for what is question-
> able.[37]

The hermeneutic imagination of the researcher functions very much like
the literary imagination of the reader for it too is conditioned by the "textual
conditions" in which it is invoked. Additionally, like the literary imagina-

tion, the hermeneutic imagination will only be invoked if particular conditions are present or announced. Just as the literary fiction must be announced as such in order for readers to engage imaginatively with it, sites of hermeneutic inquiry must be announced as such in order to evoke the hermeneutic imagination. Even though all events hold the potential for interpretation through the hermeneutic imagination, because most events are not announced as such, they will remain uninterpreted. Furthermore, if the comparison to the literary fiction is extended, it becomes evident that not all events hold the same potential for interpretation. Like literary fictions that are overly predictable and comfortable—or as Barthes[38] would say, "readerly"—events that are like this eliminate the needed play required for the hermeneutic imagination to be invoked. Like Barthes' notion of the "writerly" text, which requires that readers engage in greater degrees of speculation and interpretation in order to maintain a meaningful reading relationship, the hermeneutic imagination is best invoked in events that are more "writerly."

As a "writerly" form of research, hermeneutic inquiry does not seek the comfort of a pre-determined scientific research method. Instead, the hermeneutic researcher seeks sites for inquiry that allow questions to emerge from shared dedication to some matter of interest. These sites, like Hana, Caravaggio, Kip and the English patient's readings and discussions of Herodotus' *Histories* become "commonplace" events. Because successful engagement within these sites cannot be founded upon pre-determined methods or fixed research structures, they are much more unpredictable and ambiguous than most research sites and, as a consequence, require that inquirers move from an approach to research as "telling" to one of "listening."[39] Just as readers of writerly literary fictions must be attentive to sudden shifts and breaches in the text, so too must be the researcher who places her/himself within the structures of the writerly research text.

In sum, educational research which supports the hermeneutic imagination may be characterized in four points. First, it seeks to locate sites for inquiry that situate interpreters in the middle of the activities related to some topic of mutual interest. Second, it seeks to situate all participants in activities that allow the path of inquiry to be "laid while walking." In hermeneutic inquiry, method depends upon interpretations given to questions which "present themselves" rather than questions which are pre-determined. Third, hermeneutic inquiry does not seek comfortable situations or solutions, but rather seeks the rupture—the breach—in order to illuminate what is silenced and deferred in the ordinary course of daily events. Finally, hermeneutic inquiry must never devolve into reports of what was done, discovered, or concluded but must, instead, show the ongoing and co-evolving relationship among what is known and coming to be known, what is done, and some sense of who the inquirers are and are becoming.

In the next part of the chapter I will present six "hermeneutic windows." The term "hermeneutic window" is used as an image to suggest the way in which hermeneutic inquiry can give us access to horizons of understanding that were not previously there—that is, to help us see what we had not been previously able or willing to see. As such, hermeneutics can become a window into new understanding. As a prelude to chapter six, which discusses the experience of teachers sharing reading with students in schools, these interpretations focus on five teachers' experiences reading and discussing *The English Patient*.

Out of Bounds

> *I wanted to erase my name and the place I had come from. By the time war arrived, after ten years in the desert, it was easy for me to slip across borders, not to belong to anyone, to any nation.*
>
>   Michael Ondaatje, *The English Patient*[40]

> *Teaching was beginning to overwhelm me. I had forgotten why I was doing it, and who I was while doing it. I needed a place to re-group—to think again about why I was teaching English.*
>
>   Ruth

As we shared responses to our readings of *The English Patient*, our reading group was struck by the frequent references to boundaries and their transgression. The villa was at once a convent, a barracks, and a hospital. The history of its shifting functions were recorded in its structure. Wrapped up in Hana's identity were child, nurse, friend, lover, daughter. Caravaggio announced himself thief, spy, soldier. The English patient was not English; the British soldier Kip was not British; Herodotus' *Histories* was at once a history and a fiction. And, as we read and discussed this novel, we came to realize that we too were crossing boundaries, re-defining borders, and wondering about the complexity of our involvement with each other as we continued to share our readings of this novel.

Because our group emerged from an open invitation from me to form a reading group, we ended up more or less "thrown" together, not really knowing one another. There were five of us: three teachers from one high school (Anna, Ingrid, and Mena) and two former junior high school teachers who were graduate students at the local university (Ruth and Dennis). None of us found our initial meetings very comfortable.[41] Later conversations with individuals in the group, plus reflections of my own feelings of discomfort in the initial stages of our process, helped me to understand that many of the feelings of discomfort had to do with feeling "out of bounds." Because I, unlike most university researchers, had not prescribed the activities of the group or asked that the group identify a problem that we could address in our meetings, we had to attempt to deal simultaneously with the uncertainty of not knowing each other and of not knowing precisely why we were gathered together. Even though we had quickly agreed that we were all interested in reading and discussing literature, our purposes for doing this were not immediately clear. One could say that the hermeneutic question had not yet presented itself. We felt at loose ends, displaced, out of bounds.

What does it mean to be out of bounds? In a sport like football "out of bounds" means being outside of the playing area in a place where the game cannot go on. It is really a "no-place" (Greek *u-topos*, "utopia"). In order for a particular demarcation of "space" to be considered a "place" there needs to be some potentially meaningful activity assigned to that place. In football, the place—the playing field—designates a space in which particular rules will be invoked in order for the game to be played. In the school classroom, particular rules about how one is to conduct oneself are understood and, from this understanding, emerges some sense of the classroom as a place. The movement from space to place requires the delineation of a set of rules that help to define the way in which interactions will occur within a particular space. When the rules and roles are defined in the absence of a space, playing cannot occur. Alternatively, when the space is defined in the absence of a sense of rules and roles, playing the game becomes a different kind of play—a back and forth exploration of the space by those present. As "rules" are defined, the space takes on the feeling of a "place."

In order for understanding of one's situation to occur, there usually needs to be an understanding of one's position and purpose in a space. Feeling "displaced" is a problem that needs to be solved in order for one to overcome feelings of being out of bounds. Such was the case for the four main characters depicted in *The English Patient*. All, in one way or another, were living in spaces that were not yet places and, at the same time, were attempting to come to an understanding of their situation with others in these spaces. Kip, for example, was thrust into the middle of a war-torn space which required that he somehow translate his past lived experiences into a set of skills that would allow space to become place. Translating his perceptual abilities and mechanical skills into those required for bomb-disposal helped to re-configure the boundaries of his own sense of self in relation to the newly inhabited space. The English patient, we learn, has spent the greater part of his lifetime negotiating ever-shifting spaces—so much so, that his own sense of self seems to be in question. It is through conversations with others at the villa that he finally seems able to locate himself. For Kip, Hana, Caravaggio, and the English patient, the villa is a space that is no-place (utopia)—an opening, a breach, a rupture in history/geography where no-longer-useful boundaries could be erased, dismantled, re-drawn. This utopic space permitted them to remain out-of-the-bounds of their own lives until each of them could develop a new interpretation of who they had been and who they were becoming.

In many ways, our experience as teachers meeting to discuss our readings of a literary fiction was similar to the experiences of the characters depicted in *The English Patient*. Although we met in a particular space (in one of the classrooms in the high school) which usually functioned as a specifically purposeful place (i.e., learning place for students), it was not immediately clear to us how we were to configure ourselves in relation to each other within this space. The classroom place had now become just another space—an opening in the middle of things. Our usually well-defined and bounded selves (teachers, university students, researchers) were called into question. Who were we in this space if we could not be teachers? Who were we if we could not be university researchers armed with a pre-determined research plan? We were missing the map. Like desert explorers, we felt the anxiety of feeling unable to map the ever-shifting dunes; we sought landmarks, conventions, habits to which we could orient, locate, and re-draw the boundaries of ourselves in relation to each other. Like explorations in the desert, however, mapping the terrain of our explorations into reading and teaching could not (did not) emerge from a pre-determined plan but, instead, co-emerged with the path which was laid as we read together. Like the inhabitants of the villa in *The English Patient*, we felt the loss of previously defined boundaries of who we were. Interestingly, for most of us the anxiety and apprehension associated with this loss was quickly transformed into the excitement of what playing together in this not-yet (utopic) place would yield.

It is important to understand that upon convening this reading group I had a particular research interest. I was interested in what it was like for teachers to move from the experience of reading literature to the experience of teaching it. This interest, however, did not drive the group since the teachers were primarily interested in reflecting upon their own reading and their current teaching practices in order to work collectively to plan new units of study. Clearly, these varying interests had points of intersection; each seemed to require that we spend some time reading and discussing our reading processes and responses. At the same time, all of us entered the shared reading space with historically-effected "selves" which were, of course, the launching pad for some of these interests. Although we played with these ideas in our first meetings together, we seemed to quickly agree that a useful starting point for any discussions would be shared responses to selected pieces of literature. This led to an initial list of short stories, which we read and discussed, followed by a series of novels beginning with *The English Patient*.

In retrospect, it seems perfectly logical and natural for English teachers to inquire into their own practices by reading literature, and it could be said that this was our intention. However, it could also be said that because we felt "out of bounds," we felt the need for some activity that could become a "commonplace location" for reflection upon our situations as these became known in relation to each other in this boundless space. Rather than attempt to negotiate which questions should be taken up, we seemed to understand that the real questions—the hermeneutic questions—would only present themselves in the midst of some activity that required a responsible dedication of ourselves to some shared task. Although our initial drifting about in the first couple of meetings left us feeling uncomfortable with the ambiguity of this no-place, it was precisely the dwelling within this difficult, boundless, ambiguous place that helped us to understand that our processes (methods) must evolve with our living together in this space. And, like the inhabitants of the villa in *The English Patient*, we found that this nomadic existence was bearable when a commonplace—our shared interaction with a work of literary fiction—was announced as an interpretive location for our inquiries.

Although we only came to understand the coincidence of our situation as readers and the situations of the characters presented in *The English Patient* after we had decided to read this novel, we came to understand the importance of the parallels. We especially came to understand the importance of the cultural object as a mediating place for human interrelations and interpretations. In the novel, it was Hana who first noticed that the English patient's copy of Herodotus had become an important cultural object—an object that announced the possibility for an interpretive location. She seemed to understand that it was not so much knowledge of the cultural object itself that was of significance, but knowledge of the relationship between it and the world. *Who* has written in this book? *Where* has this person been with this book? For the English patient his copy of *The Histories* became a commonplace for the continual re-interpretation of his sense of self-identity. The book functioned as material evidence of his ever-changing sense of self and his ever-evolving relations in the world. Each time he re-read a passage, he became involved in a complex ritual of self re-invention. At the same time, this cultural object—this commonplace book—also participated in communal interpretation. As others read from the book, as passages from the book were read aloud, the relations among the four at the villa changed. As this was occurring, their sense of self and collective identities changed. The English patient's commonplace *book* then announced a commonplace *location* for interpretation.

What I am calling the "commonplace location" is not something that can be finally pinned down to or located *in* something. The commonplace location is not in the book, nor is it in the reader. Rather, the commonplace location is the space opened up by the *relations* among readers, texts, and the contexts of reading. Now, this is not a very satisfying image because, like the act of reading itself, the relations among various readers and texts and other events of lived experience are generally invisible. As well, because these relations are always in the process of evolving they are not able to be "fixed" or "contained" into neat and tidy categories. This does not mean, however, that there are not boundaries that function to identify a commonplace location; it is simply that the boundaries are not ones that are static. Although the book and the reader exist materially, one cannot say that the relation between the two as it exists among other human-world relations is ever static. Although there are forms that emerge from the reading relationship (spoken conversation about these readings, for example), these always exist within the dynamic form of the commonplace location that collects the readers' previous experiences, present reading experiences, any new thoughts that emerge from these, and any projections of what might be. All of these become woven into one dynamic form. This dynamic form, however, consists of material forms that appear fixed to us. The English patient's commonplace book, for example, seems as though it is an unchanging form and, in fact, he does not add to it during his time at the villa. The many re-readings from it by him and others, however, alter his relation with it and the relations among others at the villa. Therefore, although the commonplace *book* does not change, the commonplace *location*—the fabric of intertextual relations that include readings and re-reading of this book are dynamic.

Like the English patient's commonplace book, our shared responses to this novel became a commonplace location for inquiry which went well beyond interpretations of our own reading processes and teaching practices. Because reading, like all action in the world, is embodied, the reading that we shared became a commonplace location for inquiry into ourselves and our learned ways of perceiving and interpreting. This did not mean that any one component of this commonplace determined any other but that all of them participated in co-specifying activities that constituted our shared reading relationships. What we might call the boundaries between us (as teachers, researchers, readers, writers, married, unmarried, straight, gay, male, female) were re-written within the commonplace location sponsored by our shared reading experiences.

As we shared our nomadic wanderings/wonderings through the literary fictions with one another, we became aware that it was not really possible to discern the "effects" of any one condition or component on any of the others. However, because we were conducting our explorations in largely uncharted spaces, we became aware of the way in which the contingencies of our experience together, through a process of natural drift (bricolage), revealed to each of us a path of inquiry which eventually led to a deeper understanding of our lived situations.

Private Readings in Public

> *When I was growing up and going to school, reading really was a private thing. We wrote essays about what we read, but we never did any personal response. I guess I'm still not used to it.*
>
> Mena

> *But here they were shedding skins. They could imitate nothing but what they were. There was no defense but to look for the truth in others.*
>
> Michael Ondaatje, *The English Patient*[42]

Discussions about the differences between reading literary fictions for personal pleasure and reading them for school purposes became common during our reading of *The English Patient*. In fact, we came to understand that because our reading this novel was meant to be discussed publicly, we were unable to have a private encounter with it. At the same time, we wondered if it were really possible to ever have a private encounter with a text. Questions of what constituted a private reading and a public reading presented themselves to us: What could we say about the boundary between something that is considered private and something public? Does doing something like reading "in private" simply mean doing it alone? Or does private mean "keeping it to oneself?" Does public mean reading with others? Among others? For a common purpose? Is private the same as personal? Is public the same as communal?

In *Acts of Meaning* Jerome Bruner[43] explains that the distinction between private and public in modern Western culture has been supported by the field of psychology which, generally speaking, has attempted to locate the sense of self inside the individual human subject. By extricating processes of cognition from the cultural, historical world in which these processes are situated and distributed, psychology has supported the now-commonsense belief that the human self can be accorded distinct status as an autonomous entity. Despite this cultural belief in the autonomous self, however, locations still exist for human subjects to explore their situated selves.

Citing results from a study he and a colleague conducted using autobiographical research methods to trace the life-histories of all six members of a mainstream, American nuclear family (parents and four adult children), Bruner explains the way in which they drew distinctions between private and public life. For the Goodhertz family "home" was considered "private"—a place where they could be "themselves"—while anything that is not-home was considered "public." It was in the move from home to not-home (not-home is my term) that these family members felt that they could make disclosures and behave in ways that was closer to their "true" selves. (Of course, as Bruner later discusses, this family unit was also a place where particular rituals were developed to defer topics and aspects of selves that might be overly disruptive. I mention this, so as not to be perceived as overly-romanticizing mainstream family units.) In any case, Bruner concludes that it is within social groupings such as family units that individuals situate and distribute memories and interpretations of past, present and projected senses of self. One cannot learn much about the individual "private" self without knowing about the way in which that self is publicly constituted and re-constituted. Furthermore, these recursive explorations of "self," as known in relation to "others," typically occur within rituals and daily routines which often include narrations of past events. Shared mealtimes, for example, provide occasions within which family members have opportunities to engage in recursive narrative events. By remembering and re-telling past events in these social groupings, both individual and collective memories of events and interpretations of those memories are re-configured to include new events.

It is within family rituals, such as those of the Goodhertz family described by Bruner, that citizens find locations to re-connect socially and culturally disparate senses of a "private" and "public" self. In his book *Crossing the Postmodern Divide*, Albert Borgmann[44] traces the historical roots of contemporary distinctions between the private and the public. These distinctions, he suggests, are relatively recent, emerging principally from the Enlightenment as announced by Francis Bacon's *New Atlantis,*[45] René Descartes *Discourse on Method*[46] and John Locke's *Second Treatise of Civil Government.*[47] Although all three are implicated in the modern quest for reason, method, and absolute truth, Borgmann singles out Locke's *Treatise* as primarily responsible for the modern idea of individualism which, he suggests, led to distinctions between the private and the public. He writes:

> Locke's *Treatise* is a celebration of the individual, the unencumbered and autonomous human being. Nature and reason are little more than indistinct backdrops for the individual. The autonomy of the single self is the new authority of last appeal. The common order arises from individuals through an agreement, and this contract remains subservient to the individual.[48]

Individualism has contributed to the belief that the human subject can (should) be the author of her or his own life. That one is not able to accomplish this in the absence of others has been acknowledged, hence the need to engage in activities that are collective has been understood. However, it is this belief in the importance of the individual's rights and freedoms that has contributed to a move away from the largely integrated lives of families and communities in the pre-modern age, to the severing of what has become known as the "private" experience from the "public" experience.

As the industrial and scientific revolutions gained momentum, there evolved an increased distinction between producers and consumers of goods and a concurrent move towards specialization of both goods and services. As well, monuments such as department stores, libraries and opera houses which supported this free-market ethos, became public places where individuals gathered. As opposed to pre-modern gatherings where goods were collectively produced, where music was commonly created, and where reading and storytelling were collaborative activities, modern public places transformed persons from participants to "consumers of commodities produced for them by experts."[49]

Borgmann suggests that unlike pre-modern public gatherings, which facilitated occasions of public celebration, these newly defined public places served largely instrumental functions. This led to a fundamental distinction between two kinds of public and private experience: the "social" and the "economic." Whereas these were indistinguishable in pre-modern times where the lines between work and recreation were less neatly drawn and the rights of the individual were generally subordinate to collective interests, modernity has produced a distinction between one's "private life" and life in the "private sector." The former is generally aligned with an idea of private as something personal—something which one owns and for which one is responsible. The latter, within a free-market economy at least, exists as free enterprise and is supported by what Borgmann calls "rugged individuals"[50] who, through their own efforts, are said to concomitantly achieve personal success and contribute economically to the community as a whole. Unlike the social public-private distinction, the economic one does not understand private as something personal and undisclosed. It is, instead, something that is privately owned, but which necessarily exists in full-view of the general public.

Of course, these two understandings of private are often conflated. Public events of leisure may be privately experienced within the private sector. A cinema, for example, may be owned by an individual. Movie-goers participate in a public spectacle (watching a movie), but are expected to have a private response to that event. Although accomplished in full-view of others (in public), this response is expected to remain private during the activity of watching the movie. It is unacceptable, for example (in Western cultures, at least), for an audience member in a movie theatre to make public announcements of her or his response. Although persons sometimes *show* their response through laughter, applause, cheers and/or tears, there is no opportunity for public disclosures of how these feelings were arrived at by the individual. The response to the film is considered private. It is thought to be owned by the individual and, although publicly constituted, it is not expected to be shared.

The ambiguity surrounding socially and economically driven under-standings of the private and the public become evident in our treatment of the literary fiction. Although always existing within the historically-effected norms and values of a culture, the author, as protected by laws of copyright, is considered the "owner" of the text. Even though the author and the text emerge from a particular public context, and the text is meant to be read by the public, both the writing and the reading of the text are considered largely private activities. Even if we believe that the reader is entitled to her or his own response[51]—there is no doubt that the author is still authoritative. As consumers of the literary fiction, we want evidence of the producer. Therefore, although the authoring of a literary fiction is considered a private process (between author and text) and reading equally so (between individual reader and text), both processes are fixed within particular transactions driven by a free-market economy in which various elements of the private sector (publishers, retail stores) as well as the public sector (teachers, the academic community) compete for public access to consumers (readers).

However, even though the exchange of literary fictions functions within a publicly constituted, commodified culture of reading, the actual reading of these texts, like the viewing of movies, whether these are accomplished alone or in public, are meant to be private experiences. As belonging to the individual, these private readings become personal (i.e., part of the person) which, unlike other reading activities done in public (menus, business correspondence, contracts, invoices), are not generally shared in public. Because modern readers of literary fictions have become accustomed to understanding the reading of literary fictions as something private, the experience of reading the text has largely become a vehicle for self-interpretation rather than an opportunity for public discourse. And since the self, in the modern age, is considered contained within the individual, the reading of literary fictions becomes another self-centered activity for which the individual reader is primarily responsible. Because the reader is thought to own the text, she is believed to be able to "produce" a response that is wholly her own and that she is entitled to either keep to herself or, under certain circumstances, share with others. A private reading, then, is something that is personal (enacted for one's own benefit) rather than communal (enacted for a common good).

What happens, then, when this personal reading and response is located in a communal setting? As apparent from the quotes from Anna, Ingrid and Mena which appeared earlier in this section, the experience of reading for public purposes is somewhat different than the experience of reading for oneself. Even though each of us performed our readings of *The English Patient* privately (we read silently to ourselves), the experience was one of reading publicly. The readings that we usually kept personal—those which we believed constituted our "individual" experience of the world—were suddenly being enacted in the presence of a projected public experience in the world. Knowing that we would be expected to verbalize our experience of reading profoundly changed that experience for each of us. Although we understood that we were participants in what Bleich[52] and Fish[53] have called "interpretive communities," which affected our meaning-making activities in reading, fore-knowledge about the need to disclose these meanings in a public forum (our reading group) transformed the private experience of solitary reading into a more public one.

This is particularly significant, for in our culture what is private is closely aligned with what is secret. Although many things that are private are kept to ourselves (like some thoughts, feelings, diaries), others (such as love letters, conversations) are meant to be shared. What is private and secret depends on particular circumstances and conditions, not upon whether these are solitary or shared. A private thought (fantasy) can be had in a public place, a secret can be kept in a public place, a response to a literary fiction can be kept private (secret), or it might be shared. If the private response is shared "in confidence" (to a confidante), it retains its status as a "secret." Public announcements, however, transform what was secret to what is now disclosed. Through disclosure, a secret becomes a material extension of the self for once it becomes public, it becomes embodied within the publicly constituted narrative knowledge about an individual.

The move from private to public in reading may be understood as the disclosure that is required in the move from the personal to the communal. Of significance here is the idea that the self is in no way extricable from communal relations in the world. Therefore, although a solitary engagement with a literary fiction seems private, the activity is always situated in an interpretive community that arises from everything that is not the reader. Therefore, even if the meaning evoked between private reader and text is never disclosed (i.e. remains secret), because it becomes an inextricable part of the reader's sense of self, the "secret meaning" does, in fact, become part of the world. However, this private meaning, because it has been silenced, does not become part of the economy of knowledge; it remains excluded from participation in the private sector. It is only when private meaning is disclosed publicly that it functions as a material extension of the self, one that is able to become concretely used in the continual generation of knowledge.

Although the silencing of private responses alters life in the public sphere—since what is not present is as vital as what is present in the shaping of culture—it more clearly and obviously alters public events that have been designated communal. As opposed to "making something public," which generally means "making it available for community use," making some-thing communal implies participation in a more explicit and deliberate contract among individuals. Not sharing my personal feelings about doing sit-ups to members of my health club is not the same as withholding my personal response to literary fictions from my reading group. Although both are public, the latter has been constituted on the understanding that disclosed responses to literary fiction comprise the function of the group. Furthermore, the reading group does not merely have an instrumental function. Unlike my experience of exercise at the health club—which, although public, does not depend upon others—my experience in the reading group is a public event that is formulated around human relationships. As a member of the group—of the commune(ity) —I have a responsibility to fulfill the contractual obligations of membership, the most important of which is disclosure of my interpretations of literary fictions that have arisen from personal engagements with them. Because I can in no way extricate my involvement with this text from my entire history of experiences, my actual response always includes *all* of those experiences, including those which I would prefer to not disclose publicly to the community of readers of which I am a member.

Because we feel that we "own" our personal response to a text and are free to either keep it secret or disclose it in a public or communal setting, it begins to function as a "third thing" between us and the world. This "third thing" is illusory, in that it is inextricable from our relations in the world. But our belief in its existence makes possible activities like public disclosures of a response to a text in the absence of public disclosures of aspects of our historically-effected selves which contributed to that response. It was possible, for example, for me to understand the tumultuous relationship between the English patient and his lover Katharine because of my own experience in this sort of entanglement. However, because I did not care to reveal this private (secret) aspect of my life, I excluded the contribution it made to the interpretation of my reading to the reading group. Therefore, the personal response that I shared in our community was actually not the response which I had, but rather was an reconstruction of that response. Essentially, the reported response was a fiction.

It seems, then, that the boundaries between what we consider private and public in our experience of reading the literary fiction cannot be neatly drawn. The different experiences of reading personally and reading publicly became not only an issue for our reading group, but certainly remains an issue for the uses of literary fictions in school classrooms. As teachers who were responding to our reading of literature in the public place of the reading group, we wondered if it was significant that our reading experiences were altered by the knowledge of the need for public disclosure. Further, we wondered how much disclosure was necessary. What was the relationship between disclosures of personal readings and the development of our reading community?

Communal Commitment

As I read and re-read the book, trying to lift stuff off the page, I sometimes became angry with myself. I should have said, "Not knowing everything doesn't matter!" But I couldn't do that. I felt responsible for knowing.

Anna

He had suddenly a map of responsibility.

Michael Ondaatje, *The English Patient* [54]

Like Anna, all of us in the reading group claimed to feel responsible for knowing. As teachers socialized in a culture that believes that teachers should know, it is not surprising that we should feel that our commitment to one another depended upon knowing certain things about the text we were reading. Like Kip who had a "map of responsibility," as teacher-readers we felt that we had a map of pedagogical responsibility to one another. Because we agreed to come together as a community of readers, we felt a certain obligation, a certain commitment to one another. Because we strongly believed in the importance of this professional community of readers, we felt pressure to prove our commitment. Through our discussions of the relationship between reading commitments and communities of readers, we began to wonder about conventional interpretations of the word "community."

In the field of education, the word "community" has become increasingly popular as a slogan for describing classroom and research structures. Reading and writing instruction, for example, are considered more effective and socially rewarding if accomplished in communities of readers and writers.[55] Concurrent with this interest in the area of language arts instruction has been the promotion of collaborative research structures which are thought to foster this sense of community. Action research, for example, has sought to engage university researchers and classroom teachers in communities of inquirers who collaborate in projects which result in both personal and communal benefit.[56] It is believed that persons who typically serve as "subjects" of research (i.e. teachers, students) are more likely to derive personal and practical benefits from research in which they are meaningfully involved. This involvement is often discussed in terms of "communities" of researchers.

Despite this popularity, the meaning of the word "community" is seldom questioned. What do we mean when we use the term community? As used in educational literature, the word community seems to invoke images of comfortable, familiar, friendly groupings of persons who work together to accomplish collective tasks. From this process individuals are thought to achieve personal knowledge and fulfillment. But is this what communities are like?

The *Oxford English Dictionary*[57] tells us that, like the word "communicate," the word "community" originates in the Latin "communis" meaning "together; bound under obligation." "Communis" eventually became "communa" meaning "to talk together, converse; to hold intimate discourse." The words "community" and "communicate," then, present each other: to be in community requires communication; communication involves some sort of communal structure. Within these communal structures of communication, something is held in common, something is shared. In communication there is implied some form of working together, some sharing of work. This suggests that communication is a kind of collaboration.

The word "collaborate" has its roots in the Latin "collaborare," meaning "to work in conjunction with another or other, to co-operate." Further etymological tracing reveals that "laborare" is derived from "laborem" meaning "exertions of the faculties of the body or mind especially when painful or compulsory." Collaboration, then, must be understood as a form of labour that is often painful and/or difficult. As collaborative structures, communities must not just be seen as places that simply facilitate communication, but rather as places where individuals are somehow bound together in the service of some common goal or good. Therefore, a community seeks to affirm what is held in common and to bind under obligation its members who come together to be of service to the community. As a form of co-laboring, these communal structures must somehow value what is communal over what is personal. At the same time, individuals involved in communal relations must have a sense that these are "personally" rewarding. Somehow the personal and the communal must co-exist.

As suggested in the previous section, communal and public are related, but not always identical. The move from public to communal entails a shift in purpose, for the latter suggests a commitment to some goal, some venture, some idea held in common. The Villa San Girolama in *The English Patient,* for example, was not a public place; it was not a museum. Rather, it was a communal place for the four inhabitants. Because the villa first served as a dwelling place for Hana's committed relationship to the English patient, others who arrived later (Caravaggio and Kip) needed to also commit themselves to this endeavor. Living in the villa and having relationships with each other required that each, in some way, become responsible for the ongoing project of care into which they entered.

In family groupings, communal commitment entails an agreement to create locations for the re-invention of the relations contained within the family structure. In his discussion of the Goodhertz family, for example, Bruner[58] explains that there are "canonical family stories" and particular events that circumscribe family relations. He suggests that gatherings such as traditional family meals (Christmas, Thanksgiving, Seders, etc.) provide places of "joint attention" where members come together to "catch up"—to affirm the narratives that bind them and to re-create relations among themselves. Describing the Goodhertz family Bruner writes:

> They lived within easy reach of one another ... and 'sat around the table together,' to use their phrase, at least once a week. They boasted that nothing was barred around that table. And they had been sitting around it since the children were small. There was also an unwritten rule that you could return home in trouble and reclaim your old room. Nina returned there with her daughter after her divorces; so did Harry after his unhappy breakup.[59]

Although it would be naive to imagine that "everything" is, in fact disclosed in these family communal groupings, it is worth noting that there are several factors that seem to be important to the maintenance of it. First, there is the regularity of meetings. The Goodhertz family seemed to emphasize the importance of the consistency of the rituals that bound them together. Second, there is the ritual of shared meals sponsored a "common-place location" for conversation among them. Without the location sponsored by a ritual, the relations among them would likely not have been maintained. Third, there is, by mutual consent, an agreement that these rituals were places for the sharing of information—even personal (private) information. Although not stated explicitly by Bruner in his report of this family's activities, it could be said that the freedom to "return home" was facilitated by the shared rituals of mealtime, for it was within these shared rituals that family members could announce new events and developments in their "public" lives. The rituals that circumscribed "family life," then, could be said to provide interpretive locations and spaces for reflection and for generativity, for it was within those spaces that family members felt they could re-interpret their current lives in relation to their past lives. Because this family engaged in these "self narrating" activities in the communal space of family rituals, they said they had a deeper knowledge and understanding of one another and their individual and shared histories of interaction in the "public" world.

Although the interaction is communal during ritual meals, the phenomenological experience is one of the personal since it is only "family" that bears witness to the continual transformations being made in the individual's developed sense of self-identity. It is this "bearing witness" that is important, for it points to the fact that these shared relations within specific and regular rituals are, at the same time, comfortable and difficult. The agreement to allow disclosure and locations for interpretation during ritualistic events means that participants must understand that, at times, they will need to witness the unexpected, the unfamiliar, the tragic, the uncomfortable, that someone might announce. It is the commitment to the possibility of a breach in the usual flow of ritualized relations, and the commitment to tolerate the difficulty and ambiguity of these ruptures, that provides the strength to communal groupings. It is this dedication that marks the move to the "co-laboring" necessary for the continued dynamic generation of the fabric of group relations.

Thus far, my comments have been developed around a particular instance of a family grouping. And, following Bruner, I have suggested that it is within the rituals developed in these groupings that family members find a location for the continued interpretation of their evolving senses of self.

What relation is there between the ritualized activities of this mainstream, biologically and phenomenologically interconnected family grouping and a group of teachers who meet regularly to read together?

First, we must remember that moving from a public space to a communal place entails a contract, an agreement, a bargain that is held among those who inhabit that place. It is the bargain, and the ongoing fulfilling of the bargain, that secures viability of communal relations. What we might call a community (a commonplace) functions like Gadamer's formulation of a good conversation. There must be a dedication to what is held among members of that community. It is from being responsible for the maintenance of the commonplace that members develop a map of responsibility. This map of responsibility is not something that pre-determines experiences in the commonplace but, instead, co-emerges with the particular set of interpersonal relations that comprise the commonplace. Like the rituals that occur in family groupings, rituals needed to be established in our reading group. For us this process of ritualizing our relations with one another began with the commitment to read. And it was this reading commitment that announced the possibility for an interpretive location.

It is important to note, however, that *what* we became committed to was not shared discussion of what we *did* as teachers of English or of what we might *do*. Instead, our communal relations developed around the ritual of shared reading and discussion of literary fictions. This is significant for two major reasons. First, it signaled a move from existing in a public space to a more communal commonplace. If we think back to Borgmann's formulation of public spaces as supporting largely instrumental functions, we can see that this is an important shift from formulating our relations through transactions of meaning (reporting on meaning) to enactions of meaning (creating meaning). Second, it meant that we needed to commit ourselves not only to a dedication to the group, but to a dedicated reading of the texts which we held in common. As explained in previous chapters, meanings are not located in readers or in texts but emerge from the evolving relations among readers, texts, and contexts. When these reader-text-context relations become part of an interpretive community of readers, the commitment is twofold: between text and reader and, at the same time, among readers.

Each reader in a community of readers does not merely engage with a text, but always engages with a text as it is implicated in particular ritualized situations with others. When the reading relationships developed in our reading group are discussed, they are not meant to be thought of as something separate from the participants of the group, but understood as inextricable from the complex communal relations formed during acts of shared responses to commonly read literary factions. Like the English patient's annotated copy of *The Histories,* our "personal" relationships with *The English Patient* co-emerged with our commitment to engage in ritualized reading practices with others in our reading group. Because it was through our shared responses that we hoped to gain understanding into our own reading and teaching practices, we each felt that it was necessary to dedicate ourselves, more than we usually might, to the texts we read.

Some of the discomfort that almost all of us expressed about our reading of *The English Patient* can be traced to the desire each of us had to fulfill the contract of our communal life in the reading group. Although it would be convenient to suggest that this discomfort was due to our fore-knowledge of reading for different purposes—or that it was due to the move from the "private" to the "public"—these are likely not very accurate explanations, for neither helps to illuminate the complexity of the reader-text relations as these co-emerged with our relations with one another. Suggesting that being part of the reading group "caused" different reading experiences or that reading particular literary fictions "caused" variations in the relations among group members does not account for the fact that all of these relations (texts-readers-reading group) affect one another. Therefore, rather than attempting to pinpoint and delineate cause and effect relationships between these, it seems more productive to understand how the relations between readers and texts and readers and each other *co-emerged* within the commonplaces of our shared inquiry. Because the commonplaces are founded upon a dedicated, committed co-laboring, the sites at which co-laboring was questioned, difficult, or impossible help to hermeneutically illuminate what is at work at these sites.

Time for Difficulty

I am having difficulty getting through this book. There are so many references to things that I don't know, it makes it hard to understand.

Mena

Read him slowly, dear girl, you must read Kipling slowly. Watch carefully where the commas fall so you can discover the natural pauses.

Michael Ondaatje, *The English Patient* [60]

Much of our group's early discussions of *The English Patient* centered on the difficulty we had forming a relationship with the text. Although we began our reading with great enthusiasm and energy, several of us in the group found this waning as we continued to feel "like a stranger" to this book to which we wanted to become committed. Ruth reported no discomfort with the text, Anna and I reported some discomfort about feeling like an "outsider" to a text that seemed to resist "entry," Ingrid became angry about not being able to "control" the text and almost abandoned her reading of it, and Mena became so overwhelmed with feelings of ambiguity that arose from the difficulty of forming a relationship with it that she was unable to complete her reading.

The difficulty of engaging with this text became an ongoing interest for us in the group, especially as we persevered with our reading since it seemed that it was the ability to live through the ambiguity of not knowing where we were heading with this text (what world this path of reading was bringing forth) that ultimately made this reading experience more evocative and more profound than most others we had had. In the end, all of us who had completed the text believed that we had learned (and were continuing to learn) a great deal about ourselves by having been involved in the experience of shared reading and response. The most important lesson, it seemed, was the value in dedicating ourselves to the difficulty of *not knowing* where our engagement with the text would lead.

But why would not knowing become such a burden for us? Surely, as teachers, we understood the value of not knowing, the value of living within the ambiguity of a tension drawn between a presumed world of knowing and a possible one. Is it not the teacher's task to engage students in events that have the capacity to collect what is known, and through the process of inquiry shake loose the bindings of the familiarity of the known? Is our task not like the artist's—to make the familiar strange in order to provoke new perceptions, responses and interpretations? Or, could it be said that this was not the way our teaching lives were constructed? Perhaps ambiguity and difficulty and not knowing were things that were avoided, smoothed over by the certainty of a daily curriculum which surrounded us and our students with the comfortable, predictable things that were already there. Perhaps our worlds of teaching were circumscribed by three things—what is out there in the world (the objective world), what is inside each human subject (the subjective world), and the artifacts we use to re-attach these (the various texts of curriculum)—instead of one thing: a shared, embodied, co-emerging relationship with the world. If so, could it be that in order for a literary fiction to be a part of that world, it needed to have some immediate, accessible, and well-announced purpose?

In the first part of the year that our group met, there was a strong desire, on the part of most members, to make literary selections that had the potential to be used as classroom texts. "I don't want to become part of this if it's not going to be practical!" was a comment from one teacher who dropped out of the group after a very short time. The need for having something "practical" seemed always to be announced along with the need to be "economical" with one's time. Because reading required some commitment of time, it seemed that the only way in which to justify "extra" reading was to at least not make it "extra-curricular." As a result, the first two meetings were devoted to readings of short stories which were felt by various members of the group to be suitable for classroom instruction. Although this instrumental approach to the meetings was quickly abandoned in favor of the more dedicated reading of lengthier, more complex works, the issues of time and commitment continued to present themselves. What does it mean to "make time" to read, and how does an understanding of this help to illuminate our resistance to the difficulty of our commitment to *The English Patient?*

Margaret Hunsberger provides a phenomenological characterization of time that helps chart a path for this inquiry:

> It is a commonplace for us to speak of time as quantified, segmented, and invariant. We learn in school that a second is a small unit of fixed duration, that sixty of them make a minute, and that every minute is equal in length. This conceptualization is made manageable by, and dominated by, clocks and calendars. In our language, time becomes a sort of commodity; we recognize that we have a limited 'amount' of it and so we 'spend' time and we 'buy' time or we 'waste' a bit of it. But then we also say, do we not, that 'time is money'? And although, according to the clock, each individual has the same twenty-four hours available, some people appear to have more time at their disposal than others. To limit and constrain time in this way is regarded as a convenience to make it manageable.[61]

Being able to use time wisely, then, might be considered a desirable trait within a culture that expects its citizens to be productive. Just as time is founded upon metaphors of money and management, so too is schooling. Students are not to "waste time" in school; teachers, if they are to be considered "effective" must become efficient managers of time so that the learning of students might be maximized. In reading pedagogy, this translates into a fixation on reading quickly and comprehending fully on the first pass through the text. Not surprisingly, then, when the question of what might characterize a "good reader" was raised in one of our group discussions, qualities of speed, fluency, accuracy, and retention were quickly listed. Good readers used time efficiently by reading quickly.

Given these beliefs, it is not surprising that several group members should feel anxious about the time it took to overcome their feeling of strangeness to *The English Patient*. When "good reading" is so closely aligned with speed, efficiency, and effective use of time, the need to "take more time" to read could be seen as a comment on one's abilities as a reader. And, of course, teachers of English are supposed to be good readers! Admitting that the reading of a text required a great deal of time suggests that the reader is less than proficient. Who would want to admit that?

Additionally, because time is understood as a commodity that must be used wisely, teachers who are immersed in the bus(y)ness of schooling feel that it is not their right to take time to engage in what is often considered to be a solipsistic experience. Reading things that are not to become part of the daily curriculum, like books that students read outside the prescribed curriculum, becomes "free" reading. And free reading is something that is done in one's "free" time. Although this is meant to mean the time that is not committed to the many requirements of daily life, "free" can also be understood as something that either "does not cost" or something that is "liberating." But, of course, free reading does cost something: it costs time. And perhaps, in our culture, teachers are not supposed to engage in activities that liberate them, but instead in activities that "confine" them to the prescribed curriculum. In any case, whether understood as something not required, as liberating, or as not having commercial value, free reading is generally thought of as a leisure activity, something that one does when the required work has been accomplished. And so, we could say that free reading is a selfish activity. It is something that one does for oneself;

something that is personal; something that does not contribute to the common good but instead serves some personal purpose. Engaging in free reading, then, is not really proper behaviour for persons designated to act in the service of others. As public servants, teachers are not supposed to demonstrate selfishness; they are supposed to dedicate their energy and time to their students. Taking time to read for oneself, instead of reading in preparation for one's students, could be seen as pedagogically incorrect.

The question of "What has teaching done to teachers?" could be re-configured to read "What has the teaching of literary fictions done to teachers' own readings of them?" Is it possible that the very experiences that inspired many English teachers to enter the profession (i.e., a love of reading) were refused them once they arrived at the schoolroom door? Could it be that treating the literary fiction as a commodity that functions as a vehicle for skills instruction and cultural transmission in the school classroom severely disfigures the teacher's own ability to abandon these instrumental practices during her or his personal reading? Could the way in which the reading of literary fictions is enacted in the secondary school curriculum contribute greatly to not only students' but their teachers' inability to commit themselves to the often-difficult and time-consuming process of engaging personally with a work of literary fiction?

As Deborah Britzman[62] reminds us, teachers in our culture are supposed to "know." Furthermore, teachers must be solely responsible for what they know. Therefore, even though it has been well established that literary fictions are not vehicles for some stable, truthful meaning, the culture of teaching in most schools suggests that, like the math teacher who knows the solution to the riddle of the algebraic equation, the English teacher will know the answer to the riddle of the text. It is not surprising, then, that most teachers in our reading group demonstrated a strong need to *know* all the details of the text:

> *I felt responsible for knowing.... I couldn't read on until I had looked things up that I didn't understand.... I worried when I came to the group and found that others were mentioning details that I hadn't noticed myself.... I guess I'm just not as good at picking out those symbols.... I couldn't find the time to read this book in the way that it asked to be read.... I'm going to have to read this book in the summer when I have more time.... I'm too busy to read something this diffi-cult—I'm too tired to read a book that is this demanding.... I need more time.... There's not enough time.*[63]

In fact, as we continued to reflect upon our reading of *The English Patient,* we realized that the text was not really difficult. The plot was not really complex. Historical knowledge was not really vital to enter into a relationship with the text. Although the events of the plot were not presented chronologically, and although there were few explicit transitions among events, there was indeed a patterned structure to the novel. It was just not one that we expected. The difficulty, the resistance, the ambiguity, it seems, could not really be located in the text, but rather resided in the inability for some readers to "listen" to the text, to wonder what the path of understanding might be, rather than determining the path ahead of time. But of course, as English teachers trained in an era where schema theory insists that "good readers" make predictions about what might happen next, we would, ourselves, both support and engage in this kind of reading behaviour. Although modern readers want to be surprised, they want the surprise to be an unexpected event, not an unorthodox structure.

For us, the difficulty of engaging with *The English Patient* became a demonstration of the other face of resistant reading. Although resistant reading has recently become known as the valued ability to "read across the grain" of the text in order to understand the way in which the text serves to reproduce hegemonic structures,[64] resistance can also be the refusal to engage with the text. Resistance can be recalcitrance, stubbornness, the need to control.[65] As Ingrid, suggested, "With this book I didn't have any control, and I found that frustrating!"

The expressed desire by teachers to control the text should hardly be surprising. In situations of schooling, teachers are required to "control students," students are required to "control themselves," and both teachers and students are to be "in control" of subject matter. Most events of schooling, including events of reading, have as their ultimate goal the "mastery" of the world and of students' actions in it. Success in such a world is not only defined in terms of one's ability to achieve such mastery, but the ease with which one is able to accomplish it. Hence, the emphasis on reading quickly and efficiently, remembering details after one reading, and being able to retell a recently read story accurately. As part of the project of modernity, the reading curriculum, like the pedagogy that announces this curriculum, is founded upon not only expressing the world as it "really is" but being able to do so easily, comfortably, and efficiently.

It is no wonder, then, that modern readers often resist a relationship with a book that requires that they slow down, think, and wonder while they wander through the text. Not only does this take time that cannot be spared, but the reader is in a situation of not knowing what the text will bring. I would argue that this other face of resistance, as made manifest in the difficulty of engaging with the text is, in part, a fear of what this text will announce or what will need to be left behind. Who will this reading ask us to be? New interpretations of ourselves in relation to our world always require the demise of old interpretations. For although every new experience is the end-point of all those which came before it, it is also a point of recursion in which all that was past is understood differently. Although all of life is like that, some things, including committing oneself to a literary fiction can make these re-writings of self more obvious, more dramatic, and more disturbing. For when the literary imagination is invoked through the historically-effected and situated interaction between reader and text, a world is brought forth by a perception that has been altered. And, as Varela et al.[66] suggest, once perception (literally and figuratively) is altered, the world is changed, not just the person.

Breach of Promise

> *This group requires that everyone be here. We're attached to each other. When someone's not here, it's like we've lost a limb.*
>
> Ingrid

> *He slides his open palm along the sweat of her shoulder. This is my shoulder, he thinks, not her husband's, this is my shoulder.*
>
> Michael Ondaatje, *The English Patient* [67]

When Katharine arrived in the desert with her husband Clifton, she did not know that her identity would change. Like any traveler, she assumed that she would simply spend some time in another part of the world, enjoy it, learn about it, and then return enriched with new knowledge and experiences. This is what it is like to be a tourist. As a tourist, one samples, looks, and touches; one collects souvenirs, tokens, and images from the place visited, brings these home and arranges them into an already-there life. And although, of course, these experiences affect one's perception of the world by making it "bigger," touring through a place is not the same as living in a place.   Unlike touring, living in a place requires a commitment, a dedication—but most of all it requires a promise. A promise to do some things and not to do others. These promises become the conditions of living in a particular location.

Touring, of course, does not just happen when one is on vacation. One can "take a tour" through a neighborhood or through a shopping mall. Touring in the latter can be "browsing" without committing oneself to buying. Once the decision is made to buy something, browsing becomes shopping. While browsing has no immediate goal other than the passing of time, shopping has a more distinct goal. One shops *for* something. Like browsing, the goal of touring is ambiguous. And, like free reading, touring is something that is done for pleasure, for oneself, for personal fulfillment. Readers can tour or browse through books. Browsing through a book means "checking it out," determining whether or not one wants to make a commitment to it. Like the browser, little is expected of the tourist. In fact, although we are always aware of tourists, they generally do not meaningfully enter our lives. The mark of touring is faint—almost invisible.

Katharine soon discovered that unlike touring through the desert, living there meant committing herself to a particular set of relations. Although she had no prior history of desert exploration, her recent marriage to Clifton meant that his history now became part of hers. Katharine learned what many of us have experienced: that when we promise ourselves to somebody, we promise ourselves to the world that is brought forth in our relations with them. And so, Katherine's marriage to Clifton meant a marriage to a new world. This was not merely the conflation of her world and his; rather, it was a complete re-configuring of her sense of self in relation to the new situation.

As Katharine lived through the world brought forth through her relationship with her husband and his fellow explorers, she necessarily became re-written. Her identity changed. "Living in" another place, rather than "touring through" that place, meant she needed to become part of the evolving landscape. As she re-drew the boundaries of her self through this process of living, she began to notice things she hadn't noticed before. Her new situation helped her to learn to perceive differently—perceiving not only things around her, but her self and her past self in different ways. Part of this re-configuration included the English patient, Count Ladislav de Almàsy, her husband's colleague. He was a fellow explorer (not a tourist). And as she came to know him by living in a world that situated her with him, she found (to her surprise) that they were sharing a path. It was at this point that Katharine learned the difference between a contract and a promise, and as our reading group read about Katharine, we experienced this difference in our relations with each other.

What is the difference between signing a contract and making a promise? According to the *Oxford English Dictionary*, certain legal texts have recorded precedents that make distinctions between promises and contracts. A contract involves the idea of mutuality while a promise often does not. A contract is something negotiated and agreed upon. A promise is something given, often in the absence of any discussion or negotiation. A contract is explicit while a promise is often not.

Herein lay the greatest conflict for Katharine, for she was involved in a marriage—a contract—with Clifton, and, at the same time, had made a promise to Almàsy (the English patient). Although the promise in their relationship is never announced, it existed in the expectation of what their relationship might bring. Their involvement implied a promise of *more*—more time, more commitment, more of the other one. This illuminates the other difference between the promise and the contract; the contract is cast in the present while a promise is cast in the future. As such, a promise, although tantalizing is, at the same time, often agonizing. Will the promise be fulfilled? Will events allow the fulfillment?

In reading, the difference between the contract and the promise is evident in what we say about our reading. In our reading group, we agreed that we would all complete readings of various texts within particular periods of time. This was like a contract—a mutual agreement. The terms were established. At the same time, there was an implied promise. Although not spoken, it was implied that each person promised to read carefully, to read well. Although not really part of the contract (all we said we'd do is read), our actions unmasked the promise. Each of us, in some way, brought concrete evidence to show that we had read carefully: we had Post-It notes stuck in our books, journal entries to share, jotted scribblings or words and phrases we had looked up in dictionaries and other resource books. Just as Katharine, her husband Clifton, and her lover Almàsy had to live amid a contract and a promise, so too did the members of our reading group: the contract to read; the promise to read carefully.

Like Katharine who needed to decide whether to live with the contract or the promise, so too did each member of our group. For several, the promise was easily subsumed into the contract. For Anna, the primary feeling was one of responsibility:

> *I felt a tremendous responsibility while reading this book. I felt responsible to both the author and the reading group to read well, to do my best.*

Ruth, on the other hand, simply desired to repeat the experience of reading:

> *I don't remember many of the details of the book, but I certainly remember the experience of reading it. That's why I re-read it—to re-claim the experience.*

For Ingrid, however, the contract was chosen over the promise:

> *I couldn't read this book the way I usually do. In order to understand the book I had to read it differently. I skipped ahead and read about the story of one character without interference from the other character's stories.*

For myself, the promise and contract were easily fulfilled:

> *My anxiety about reading carefully ended when I finally became immersed in the lives of the characters. I didn't want this book to end!*

While for Mena, the juxtaposition of contract and promise was impossible:

> *I really want to finish this book, but I can't seem to read it in the same way the others in the group do. I don't see all the images, the symbols. And I think that I should be able to see them.*

As I suggested in chapter four, we do not bring forth a world of understanding by ourselves. Through ongoing interactions with others in particular historically-effected situations we grow to understand *a* world. Although Almàsy had a personal relationship with Katharine, it could never be extricated from their shared world. Therefore, although Clifton was absent during their lovemaking, he was present. Just because things are silenced does not mean they do not exist; it does not mean they do not alter the world of understanding that is brought forth. Was this Clifton's wife's shoulder he was stroking or was it Almàsy's lover's shoulder? Or was it simply Katharine's shoulder? Do we own our own bodies, minds and sense of self? Or do we share them with others during the act of living together? Neither Katharine nor Almàsy were ever able to experience each other without being aware of the way in which each was configured in a situated and distributed identity. Katharine could not be with Almàsy without presenting her husband Clifton's identity as well. Almàsy could not be with Katharine without presenting his historical and cultural self. At the same time, Katharine could not return to the arms of Clifton without bearing the trace of her newly configured identity; one which, of course, was intertwined with Almàsy. What was meant to be a private affair necessarily became part of the public world of perception, interaction and interpretation. Even that which is silenced participates in the world of significance that is brought forth with others.

Is this what it is like to live between a contract and a promise during events of communal reading practices? Although each of us in the reading group had experienced a "personal" reading of *The English Patient,* were we not aware that this book belonged to others as well? Were there not shadows of others in the same room while we read? Did we not feel watched? Did our implicit *promise* to read well not mean that we needed to remain aware of the other, the shadow that existed with us in our reading of the book? Often, we are not really aware of things until they are broken. The English patient is more aware of his skin after it is burned. Hana realizes how much she loved her father only after his death. It is the rupture—the break—that provides the interruption in our usual patterns of living, forcing us to learn to live and perceive differently.[68] Therefore, understanding the importance of the promise to "read well" is better understood in the "breaching" than in the "fulfilling" of that promise. What happens when the promise to dedicate oneself to reading is broken?

During some of the conversations in our reading group the subject came up of what it was like to invite students to read or listen to literary fictions that were personal favorites of the teacher. Whether students were asked to read these texts at home, to themselves in the classroom, or to listen to teachers' oral readings of them, all of us expressed increased anxiety about these shared readings. Because we loved these texts, and had established strong relationships with them, we hoped that our students would love them too. More than with other texts, we expected students to dedicate themselves to them. Although there was seldom a contract (an explicit agreement), there was an implied promise. When we said things to our students like, "This is a favourite of mine that I want to share with you," we were also saying, "Please listen attentively! It's important to me that you read carefully!" When students did not—when they looked bored; when they wrote notes while we were reading to them; when they told us that they couldn't or wouldn't or didn't finish an assigned reading of the text, we felt angry and hurt.[69] Ingrid told us about her experience of this:

> When I look up from my reading and see students looking like they could care less, I feel hurt; then I become angry! Because the story means so much to me.

For Anna, however, anger was not the primary emotion:

> I get hurt very easily. And as a teacher I wish that I could have—over the years developed a thick skin. Because I do go home hurt by kids' comments about stories that I love. And I think that that makes me limit the number of these that I invite them to read.

It is impossible to distinguish our sense of self from the artifacts that co-exist and co-evolve with our relations with others. When students say, "This book is boring," they are not simply commenting on the book; in a very powerful way, they are commenting on our taste in books. They are commenting on us. Boring people read boring books. Although we make comments to our students which suggest that things and people are detachable—"I don't dislike you, it's your behaviour I dislike," or "Don't take it personally, I'm grading the essay, I'm not grading you!"—our own experience of students' comments about our books shows that we don't really believe what we're saying. What we read, what we write, what we produce are all material extensions of ourselves. Our saying, doing, and being are not three things. They cannot be dissected and considered apart from one another. Sometimes we remember this. We would unlikely tell a person whom we care about that we hate their taste in clothes, their haircut, or their new car. Somehow, because these seem more clearly a part of that person we understand that saying "Your haircut is awful!" would hurt them. But because our relationships with books are largely invisible, we forget that they are as much as part of us as our hair. Therefore, we are more inclined to show our feelings about these: "I found that book boring. I couldn't even finish it."

Because the books we care about are part of us, we expect people who are part of our community to care for them in the same way they might care for us. This is likely why most teachers in our reading group reported taking "special" care to introduce books they loved to their students, making sure that the "personal" connection was announced. We seemed to understand that the presentation of the book cannot be separated from the presenter of the book, and since this is the case, the usually-invisible relationship needs to become more visible. When this special care and presentation is ignored or disregarded—when the requested promise to "read well" is breached—a rupture occurs amid *all* of the relations in the classroom, for as discussed earlier, we do not merely form a relationship with a book, we form and maintain relationships with everything that is not-us. In the school classroom, then, the teacher's relationship with the book becomes inextricable from all of the relations in the classroom community. When a student breaks the promise to dedicate him or herself to the text that is held in common, it is not only he or she that feels the rupture, it is the entire community.

The desire that the teacher has for each student to fulfill the promise of reading carefully and reading well is not really a selfish desire. Although it is true that the teacher can become hurt and angry by non-readings or poor readings by students, these feelings do not constitute the greatest consequence of a breach of promise. The most serious consequence arises from the fact that when students do not read, or do not read attentively, they effectively have removed themselves from the interpretive commonplace of curriculum. Not reading means not participating in the process of interpretation. This does not simply mean that the non-reader exists outside of the circle of understanding. Just as Katharine could not banish the shadow of her husband Clifton from her relationship with Almàsy, the community of readers cannot banish the non-participant. Not reading does not merely affect the non-reader, it affects the understanding that is brought forth by the community of readers (in this case the classroom). Non-readers are, at the same time, present and absent. Breaching the promise to read creates a rupture in all relations in the classroom that cannot be ignored.

Similarly, when one of the readers in our group was unable to complete her reading of *The English Patient,* a rupture was created. Although we did not feel personally injured in the same way we did when our students performed this act, we nevertheless clearly experienced the shadow of the absence in our meetings. The breach of promise to read did not merely exclude Mena from the commonplace of reading and interpretation, it effectively excluded her from full participation in all of the shared relations that found their interpretive location in the shared responses to the reading. A sense of loss was felt by all members in the group. The breach created a tension that evolved from Mena's discomfort, our anxiety about her discomfort, and the difficulty of having to continue group relations in the presence of this absence. As Ingrid suggested:

> *This group requires that everyone be here. We're attached to each other. When someone's not here, it's like we've lost a limb.*

Not reading the book and/or not reading carefully is not the opposite of reading. It is not a "non" action. It is part of the ongoing, ever-evolving action in the world. Specifically, "not-reading" becomes part of the "not-us" with which we must maintain ongoing relations in a community of readers. Not doing is as noticeable and significant as doing. It becomes a material part of the commonplace location. And, although participation in these reading commonplaces can bring forth worlds of perception and living which are difficult, it is important to understand that we, the books we read, our relationships to these books, our fulfilled and unfulfilled promises, our commitments, our desires, are inextricable from the not-us with which others maintain relations. Madeleine Grumet suggests that

> because schooling is a complex, ceremonial, and ritual form, it is important to study the status of texts in the exchange systems, totem systems of the classroom. For we have displaced school bodies with school texts. I do not ask my students, 'Do you understand me?' Instead I ask them to understand my reading of the text. We pass texts between us. We touch the text instead of each other and make our marks on it rather than on each other. The text is material, it has texture, it is woven; we pull and tug at it, it winds around us, we are tangled up in it.[70]

Dwelling

> *I was surprised that there were so few pages in this book. It felt like a much bigger experience than the number of pages might suggest.*
>
> Anna

> *And in his commonplace book, his 1890 edition of Herodotus's Histories, are other fragments—maps, diary entries, writings in many languages, paragraphs cut out of other books. All that is missing is his own name.*
>
> Michael Ondaatje, *The English Patient* [71]

Over time, the English patient's copy of *The Histories* became twice its original thickness. It became a collecting place for bits and pieces of a life. Newspaper clippings, notes, cuttings from other books—all became part of a commonplace location. This location was not merely a collecting place. It became inextricable from the complexity of shared relations among he and the others at the villa. As a cultural object it was not merely something he "built"—it was something he "lived." We could say that the commonplace book announced a location for "dwelling."

In his essay *Building Dwelling Thinking,* [72] Heidegger inquires into the words "building" and "dwelling." "Building," he tells us, emerges from the Old High German word "baun," which means to dwell. "Dwelling" is, most essentially, what it is to "be." At the same time, "bauen" means to cherish, protect, preserve and care for. Dwelling, then, is not understood as simply existing; dwelling means living in a place with others with an attitude of caring and attention. Building cannot take place without dwelling, for as Heidegger suggests, "We do not dwell because we have built, but we build and have built because we dwell, that is, because we are dwellers." [73] The construction of things such as buildings and bridges do not result in entities that have meaning in themselves. These constructions become "locations" which, as demarcated by the boundaries of their existence, become spaces for which room has been made. The boundaries that mark these locations are not meant to be understood as demarcations that contain or separate. As originating from the Greek "peras," meaning a place where something "begins its essential unfolding," [74] a boundary marks a place where meaning unfolds. The act of building, then, occurs through a process of dwelling and, at the same time, for the purposes of dwelling. How does this relate to the building and dwelling associated with our relations with literary fictions?

We might say that the literary fiction is something that belongs to dwelling (human existence), but, at the same time, is a deliberate construction (building) in order to create a location (a space) for which room is made. But room for what we might ask? Heidegger's ideas about building and dwelling suggest that the space opened up by the literary fiction becomes a dwelling place for thinking, particularly the kind of thinking that occurs in locations where one dwells "in the middle" with an attitude of listening. The act of listening means being more thoughtfully attuned to the other sense of building, where building is not construction, but cherishing, protecting, preserving and caring for that with which we dwell. This does not refer only to the things or the other persons around us. It means that we must also care for our memories as these collect within the commonplaces of our building and thinking.

The novel The *English Patient* announced such a location for our reading group. It is not surprising that the experience of reading this book should be described as a "large experience"—larger than the book would seem able to support. Like the English patient's commonplace book, our commonplace location was bulging with the experiences that were brought to the readings. But why was this experience so large? Was it large because Ondaatje's novel required us to read in a way that enlarged our experiences? Was this reading a more dedicated dwelling than we usually experienced? Was it that, through our dedication, our contract, our promise to each other, we read more carefully than we might ordinarily, thus making our experience deeper?

Certainly, Ondaatje created a text which asked us to learn to read differently. As already mentioned, we needed to read more slowly, paying closer attention to individual words, phrases, and the idiosyncratic structure of this text. Additionally, our dedication to each other and to our interest in shared reading contributed to a more conscientious reading than might otherwise have occurred for some of us. The "largeness" of the experience of reading, however, does not seem to be adequately accounted for by the structure of the text and our commitment to it and to each other. Rather, the quality of the shared reading experience seems to be most directly related to the interpretive location within which we became situated. Many of us who have read literary fictions and discussed them with others have had this kind of "transformative" experience. We leave our readings and discussions knowing that something has been created—some interpretive location has been announced—that transcends the experience of reading the novel and discussing it with others. Something has been "built" that has altered the way in which we understand our past, present and projected lived experiences. What words can be summoned to describe this experiences?

As derived from "baun," to dwell means to remain in a place. When we read a text in the absence of any group commitment or responsibility, we have a different experience of dwelling, for unless we talk about our reading to others who have also read, the dwelling is limited to our own reflections on our reading. Although our dwelling in the text always lasts longer than the act of reading, and always extends into the after-reading reflections we have of our engagement with the text, "unshared" readings generally have fewer opportunities for "building" (bringing forth) larger response experiences. The act of reading becomes a longer "remaining in a place" when a commitment to share one's response has been made. Aside from the fact that these commitments seem to foster more careful, dedicated readings of the text, the sharing creates a space for dwelling that may not ordinarily occur in the private reading. This "space" is the one that exists *between* the completion of the "private" reading and the planned discussion of these readings with others. When this endpoint (the collective sharing) has been decided in advance, the reader might be encouraged to "dwell" more than he or she would if there were not that known future-point.

This was certainly the case for us. During our readings and discussions of *The English Patient*, our commonplace location was comprised not only of our private readings and public sharing of those readings, but of the space of time between these readings. Each of us explained how usual habits of daily life were altered because of our commitment to read and respond. Several of us explained how we spent lunch hours on the day of the reading group meeting reading and re-reading the chapter(s) that were to be discussed. All of us mentioned the various ways in which we tried to become more attentive to the text by making notes, writing journal entries, looking things up in reference books. As well, we all expressed the need and the desire to re-read the text. In short, there was a general understanding that it was necessary "dwell" for a period of time in the space announced by our reading of the text.

As discussed previously, there is a difference between dwelling and touring. Like Katharine's experience in the desert, we needed to become attuned not only to the geography of the text we were reading, but also to the ongoing evolution of the relations among us that included our reading and response to the novel. Like the English patient's commonplace book which kept on becoming "larger" with each reading, our experience of reading continued to expand. For us, the literary fiction announced a particular location that otherwise would not have existed. However, this location did not function independently; it did not exist apart from the world in which it was contained. Heidegger's description of the function of the bridge has helped me to more deeply understand our shared reading experiences:

> With the banks, the bridge brings to the stream the one and the other expanse of the landscape lying behind them. It brings stream and bank and land into each other's neighborhood. The bridge *gathers* the earth as landscape around the stream. Thus it guides and attends the stream through the meadows.[75]

Heidegger helps us to understand that what we call the banks of a river are always perceived and understood differently when they become the points of attachment for either side of a bridge. The bridge and the banks are not two things which facilitate the crossing of the third thing (the stream). Rather, we perceive the three *in relation* to one another; the significance and experience of each is altered because of and for the others. Similarly, the literary fiction, as the "bridge" which united our disparate historically-effected personal experiences (of reading and of reading as it existed in a life) became one thing—a commonplace. The borders of this commonplace became the site for the unfolding of an active construction—a building that co-emerged with dwelling.

As we continued to incorporate the location announced by shared readings of *The English Patient* into our lives, we became more and more aware of the way in which our co-laboring through the difficulty of this text was "bringing forth" or producing a particular world of significance that was altering our perceptions and actions in the world. This realization challenged us to reconsider what might constitute "good reading." We began to re-assess our understanding of good reading from "speedy tours" to thoughtful engagements with and "dwelling in." We began to realize the need to listen more attentively to the words given in the text, not so much to find their truthful meanings but, instead, to listen for the possible location they announced for us. Most of all, we learned that the commonplaces of our reading together allowed a certain "pointing to the world" which did not exist in our private readings. When Anna mentioned how she had been taken by the image of Hana "unskinning" the plum before giving it to the English patient, we all began to think about the image of "unskinning":

> But here they were shedding skins. They could imitate nothing but what they were. There was no defense but to look for the truth in others.[76]

When this image was shared, Ingrid wondered if that was what we were doing: Were we looking for the truth in each other? Did we expect the other to hold/know the truth in the text? When others pointed to the world they had brought forth through their reading of the text, our own experience became larger. These pointings became like the English patient's clippings in his commonplace book—they re-configured memories of our private reading of the book. Ingrid, for example, pointed to the passage where Hana remembers her father:

> Whenever her father was alone with a dog in a house he would lean over and smell the base of its paw. This, he would say, as if coming away from a brandy snifter, is the greatest smell in the world![77]

She suggested that this was like her experience of paws:

> *That's one thing I loved about my old dog that died. The smell of his paws. When I went to get my new puppy I just had to have a sniff of his paws!*

As Ingrid spoke about dogs' paws, I thought, "Ingrid loves dogs too!" I had not known this. Although I said nothing at the time, this information strengthened my feelings for Ingrid and later became a topic of conversation between us. Loving dogs became part of the commonplace of our shared reading location.

Anna told us that she would not have the courage to smell a dog's paws because she was afraid of dogs, but that this passage had been evocative for her because it reminded her of the importance of hands—especially the way hands become marked by living:

When I look at other people's hands, I am always aware about how hands have a life carved into them.

When Anna said this I began to think of working hands. I thought about hands that become callused, lined, gnarled from hard work. I thought about my mother's hands and shared this memory with the group:

When I think about my mother's hands I see them working. I think of her hands doing things like making bread, ironing—always moving.

The decision to commit ourselves to shared readings and responses to a literary fiction requires a particular kind of thinking which develops with dwelling and building. This thinking is never merely a thinking *about* something, but instead is a thinking *through* something. It is the running of the course. But this running is not a running away, nor is it a running in place. It is an act of building, but not the kind of building that erects monuments of truth. Rather, it is a building that is associated with dwelling—a living location that becomes a meditation.

As our group continued to meet, we began to understand that it was the building and the thinking that existed with "dwelling" that seemed to characterize the way in which we wanted to enact curriculum with our students. For us, important individual and collective transformations emerged from the commonplace location announced by our shared reading. When we first began meeting, I suppose we thought that we might better learn how to more effectively "teach" the literary fiction by investigating shared reading experiences. However, although teaching was often the subject of our conversation, I do not believe that any of us would say that we learned to teach, at least not if learning to teach means learning new techniques and skills for daily instruction. We did learn, however, what it meant to dedicate ourselves to dwelling for a time together with and through the literary fiction. It was through this experience that we learned how to read. Not only how to read the literary fiction, but how to read ourselves.

So, although we came to no conclusions about how we should teach, we each came to consider our own teaching practices. There considerations were usually in the form of questions: "Why were we reading particular texts in our English classes?" This became an important question for Anna:

I'm starting to really question the books that I ask my students to read.

Why did we attempt to read many things rather than dwell for a time in one text with our classes? Mena, too, began questioning her teaching practices:

> *I'm learning the importance of re-reading, and I'm wondering why we don't allow time for our students to re-read?*

Our shared reading experiences provoked us to wonder about whether we had been misguided about the nature of "reading problems" in schools. Perhaps reading problems had very little to do with students' inability to read quickly and efficiently. Perhaps poor reading ability was more closely related to the way in which reading in schools had been subtracted from strong relations around acts of reading. Perhaps there was too much emphasis on "building" in the absence of "dwelling." Was it possible that schooling conditions eliminated the possibility for the kind of reading that we found most valuable in our recent reading experiences? How could dwelling occur in the middle of school life that insists upon touring through many texts? How could dwelling be promoted in schooling locations where the teacher believes he or she must remain "neutral?" Is it really possible to develop commonplace locations in institutions that value predictable productivity rather than the kind of hermeneutic interpretation that occurs with prolonged dwelling?

VI

Laying Down a Path While Walking

I am experience. With each breath. Experience. Regardless of the context, I am running a course.... Currere is to run.

William F. Pinar[1]

In the last chapter I developed six hermeneutic windows to show how reading together is a form of embodied action. As part of the world we bring forth with others, the fictional texts we read become inextricable from other experiences we have had. In this chapter I will provide a brief historical synopsis of conceptions of curriculum followed by a discussion of curriculum as embodied action. Next, I will present another series of six hermeneutic windows that depicts the experience two members of our reading group had reading literary fictions with students in school. These hermeneutic windows will be primarily concerned with the question, "How does the inclusion of a text of literary fiction and a teacher's relationship with such a text contribute to the complexity of curriculum?"

Curriculum as Embodied Action

According to Jackson,[2] the field of curriculum studies has been described by various writers over the past several decades as confusing,[3] in conflict,[4] amorphous and elusive,[5] and moribund.[6] It seems that the study and practice of what we call "curriculum" is difficult to pin down to a neat and tidy definition. However, although there is disagreement among some curriculum theorists, what is shared by most is that curriculum has something to do with what goes on in schools. Whether curriculum is narrowly defined as the subject matter that is taught, more broadly defined in terms of contexts of teaching, or still more broadly as all of the relationships (human or otherwise) that constitute experiences in the school classroom, it is generally agreed that the study of curriculum has something to do with teaching and learning as accomplished by teachers and students within particular courses of study.   Apart from this agreement, the field of curriculum is extremely diverse, complex, and difficult to synthesize. As Pinar, Reynolds, Slattery and Taubman suggest, "Curriculum is an extraordinarily complicated conversation."[7]   It is, however, important to remember that like all of our ideas, those we have about curriculum are historically contextualized and effected.   Therefore, although there is not space in this text for an adequate summary of the historical complexity and disciplinary breadth of the field of curriculum, before describing my understanding of "curriculum as embodied action," I will provide a brief synopsis of several influential curriculum theorists beginning with John Dewey and concluding with William Pinar.

In *The Child and the Curriculum*, Dewey defined curriculum as "The course of study met in school [that] presents material stretching back indefinitely in time and extending outward indefinitely in space."[8] Generally speaking, Dewey believed that subject matter was something to be mastered by students; however, he did not believe that this subject matter should be seen as something fixed. For him, although the child and the curriculum were understood as two things, they could not be understood as operating independently but, instead, as being mutually engaged during the process of learning. Dewey argued that the culturally imposed boundaries between the child and the curriculum must be erased and that the experience of the child must be understood as comprising an integral part of the curriculum.

It is significant that Dewey was born in 1859, the year that Charles Darwin's *Origin of the Species* was published. According to Schubert, there is a clear trace of Darwin's ideas about the connection between experience and biology within all of Dewey's philosophical works in education. This is most evident in Dewey's insistence that knowledge always emerges from human experiences and, as a result, is never fixed. Schubert writes:

> For Dewey, there was no dualistic separation between mind and body, individual
> and society, work and play, nature and culture; rather, these apparent opposites
> had a reciprocal benefit for one another.[9]

In his major work *Democracy and Education*,[10] Dewey clearly explained that schooling must not be understood as a preparation for life, but must be understood as life itself. Dewey believed that schools were societies and, because of this, he believed that schools must be meaningful, purposeful places where students are able to exhibit industry, initiative, social awareness and conscience. This did not mean that schools should be isolated from society, for Dewey clearly saw the role of schools as places for the improvement of society through the preparation of citizens who are able to live effectively within a contingent and ever-evolving social world. However, like Darwin who theorized evolution as a process of natural selection and adaptation, Dewey's philosophy of education typified much of the social Darwinism of the day by suggesting that students needed to become optimally adapted to the current social conditions. For Dewey, curriculum was understood as the complex set of relations among students, teachers, subject matter, and society. The teacher's responsibility was to oversee these relations, creating a set of conditions that would best allow the child to bring her or his experiences and abilities to full potential.

Dewey's attempts to unify school experiences with general life experiences were effectively undermined by Franklin Bobbitt who, in his two influential books, *The Curriculum*[11] and *How to Make a Curriculum*,[12] insisted that the curriculum could be determined by scientifically investigating and delineating the desired qualities of adult life and translating them into behavioral objectives that would frame the school curriculum. Naming this procedure "activity analysis," Bobbitt was influential in directing later work in curriculum towards increased specialization as dictated by the perceived needs of society. Unlike Dewey who saw the curriculum and child as inextricable, Bobbitt viewed these as separate; the child was to be shaped by a curriculum that clearly mirrored the requisites of the social order. For Bobbitt, schooling was a preparation for a future life.

In addition to separating the curriculum from the child, Bobbitt removed the responsibility for curriculum development from teachers and gave it to "scientific workers."[13] These "scientific workers" (whom we now call curriculum developers, planners, and makers) were given the task of analyzing society, determining what knowledge was worth teaching, and translating this knowledge into behavioral objectives and activities. Teachers were given the task of "mak[ing] the educational adjustments"[14] demanded by an ever-changing society and delineated by curriculum scientists. What Bobbitt defined as "the curriculum" was the endpoint of the analysis of a broad range of human experiences within major fields (such as health, citizenship, recreation, the arts) and translating these into smaller "bits" which could be effectively incorporated into existing school subjects. The effective curriculum for Bobbitt was one that guaranteed that students would be given the knowledge necessary to make specific and needed contributions to society.

Bobbitt's ideas had two major impacts on the field of curriculum: First, they removed curriculum development from the day-to-day practice of schooling and transferred it to universities and policy developers' offices. These curriculum developers, of course, participated (and still do) in the policing of knowledge. Curriculum became a way in which to maintain and support the status quo. Second, they provided a recipe for curriculum development which, because of its straightforward, unambiguous and relatively simple-to-follow method, was quickly incorporated into many books and textbooks on the subject.

Beginning as the syllabus for a course which he taught at the University of Chicago, Ralph Tyler's small book *Basic Principles of Curriculum and Instruction* was published in 1949.[15] It quickly became very popular and, according to curriculum writers Pinar et al., [16] Kliebard,[17] and Schubert,[18] remains one of the most influential texts on curriculum ever published. It is considered a bit of an anomaly—not really a textbook, a theoretical treatise, or a philosophical explication of principles—but, instead, a very simply written book of general guidelines which, in his introduction, Tyler summarized as "a rationale by which to examine problems of curriculum and instruction."[19]

Consequently, the general principles outlined in the book have become commonly known as "Tyler's Rationale." This rationale is comprised of four broad questions, which were originally used as the chapter titles of his book: What educational purposes should the school seek to attain? How can learning experiences be selected which are likely to be useful in attaining these objectives? How can learning experiences be organized for effective instruction? and, How can the effectiveness of learning experiences be evaluated? Schubert[20] explains that Tyler did not intend these four chapter titles to be used as a "method" for curriculum development. Rather, Tyler intended these to be conceptual organizers for much of the already-established work in curriculum, including that of Dewey and Bobbitt, but also of Charters,[21] Harap,[22] and Rugg.[23] In any case, the Tyler Rationale came to underpin much of the work in the field of curriculum, particularly within the practice of curriculum development in schools.

It is generally accepted[24] that there was a twofold reason for popularity of the Tyler Rationale: First, Tyler wrote simply and clearly, reducing much of the previously verbose explications of curriculum design and implementation into a form and style more accessible and acceptable to the practitioner. Second, Tyler's rationale appealed to "commonsense" notions about the way things "really were" and, more specifically, about the way human beings were thought to learn. Who could argue that one first identified the purposes of education and then set about trying to find the most likely way to achieve objectives linked to those purposes? Firmly entrenched in an era that valorized the scientific method, rationalism, and empiricism, Tyler's rationale seemed like the voice of clear reason.

Twenty years later, Joseph Schwab wrote the first of four influential essays on the subject of curriculum. Written over a period of fourteen years (1969-1983), these essays remain influential to this day.[25] Primarily concerned with what he termed the "moribund" state of the field of curriculum, Schwab's essays accomplished three tasks. First, they criticized the language of curriculum as being overly theoretical. Schwab felt that too much research and writing in curriculum was done from the sidelines, providing a great deal of commentary about the curriculum but little practical advice to practitioners. Second, the essays clearly defined an approach to curriculum inquiry that was based on what Schwab called the "arts of the eclectic" as these might be applied to the field of curriculum. Third, in the last essay Schwab discussed the role of the university curriculum professor in light of his "practical" method of curriculum inquiry, suggesting that the professor's role must shift from one of developing theories about curriculum to specifically educating individuals who would be able to engage in curriculum development in schools.

Schwab believed that inquiry into curriculum must be accomplished in the midst of the "commonplaces" of schooling: teachers, learners, subject matter, and milieu. Curriculum building and development meant maintaining research into the curriculum of particular schools, classrooms, and situations rather than general applications of over-arching theories applied to these situations. Essentially, Schwab believed that theory and practice specified one another, but he did not believe that effective curriculum building occurred without a conscious deliberation into these processes of co-specification. This ongoing inquiry into educational practice in schools is the essence of what Schwab named the "art of deliberation." These deliberations, suggested Schwab, needed to be concerned with the identification and solving of particular difficulties emerging from the daily practice of schooling.

In his edited collection entitled *Curriculum Theorizing: The Reconceptualists* published in 1975, William F. Pinar announced the need to move away from "conceptual empirical" thinking in curriculum towards what he termed "curriculum theorizing."[26] Using the verb form of theory signaled a radical shift from the instrumental approaches to curriculum inquiry and development to those which were more critically reflective of the existential quality of life in schools. Although Pinar's own writings drew primarily from existential philosophy and literary theory, the group of scholars who supported the shift away from conceptual empirical thinking included critical theorists, feminists, historians, and phenomenologists (to name a few). This loosely knit group was named by Pinar "the Reconceptualists."[27]

Pinar's own reconceptualist work has focused on coming to a deeper understanding of the individual's lived experience of curriculum. In his influential essay, *"Currere:* Towards Reconceptualization," Pinar[28] offered the word "Currere" to describe a method of inquiry appropriate to the study of curriculum experience. Although announced in this book, it was in the collection of essays entitled *Toward a Poor Curriculum*,[29] which he published with Madeleine Grumet, that the method of Currere was offered in a more fully developed form. In it, they describe an approach to curriculum theorizing that moved away from the conceptual empiricism of Bobbitt, Tyler, and Schwab (and their many followers). In addition, they called for a method of curriculum research aimed to

> return to the experience of the individual, respecting all those qualities which disqualify it for consideration in the behavioral sciences: its idiosyncratic history, its preconceptual foundation, its contextual dependency, its innate freedom expressed in choice and self-direction.[30]

Following Pinar's earlier coinage, "Currere" became the word that announced this method. An etymological derivative of the word curriculum, the verb "currere" is the Latin word "to run," as in to run a course. As an approach to curriculum theorizing, Pinar suggested that currere was "not the course to be run, or the artifacts employed in the running of the course" but rather "the running of the course."[31]

Currere signaled an understanding of curriculum as the relationship between the individual and her or his world as it is contained in educational settings. By reconceptualizing curriculum as currere, attention was diverted from the artifacts of curriculum (documents, content, methods, strategies, teachers, students) to the relationships that bound them together and to the way these relationships evolved as they moved through time and space. Understanding curriculum as currere meant a move away from talking about curriculum as the subject or object of experience, to understanding it as the way individuals live a life that includes the experience of schooling.

Similar to Pinar's use of the word "theorizing" to describe the way theory evolves with remembered, lived and projected experiences, currere points to the ever-evolving quality of curriculum. Because currere represents the human subject's existential experience of external structures, Pinar believes that the method of currere must, in some way, help to more clearly disclose this. Beginning always with the experience of the individual, the method of currere seeks a "regressive-progressive-analytic-synthetic" process of inquiry.[32] Any person engaged in curriculum theorizing must involve himself or herself in an ongoing reflection on her or his own past (regressive), ponder about what the future may hold in order to uncover hopes and aspirations (progressive), analyze what is uncovered in the regressive and progressive stages (analysis), and, finally, once the present has been thoroughly and deeply excavated and analyzed, make decisions about one's situation (synthesis):

> More deeply, now, in the present, I choose what of it to honor, what of it to let go. I choose again who it is I aspire to be, how I wish my life history to read. I determine my social commitments; I devise my strategies: whom to work with, for what, how.[33]

In some ways, Pinar's reconceptualization of curriculum through the method of currere is a recollection of Dewey's belief in the importance of attention to the experience of the child and the curriculum. Like Dewey, Pinar believes that curriculum is not to be the pre-determining of the path of life, but rather the "laying of the path while walking." Not only did the method of currere greatly influence the field of curriculum by recognizing the importance of autobiographical, narrative, hermeneutic and phenomeno-logical approaches to curriculum inquiry, but it announced the need for greater attention to detailed analysis and interpretation of the relationships between experiences and expressions of curriculum.[34] Pinar reminds us that like all human engagements with the world, currere is not the course to be run but is the running of the course. Currere explicitly acknowledges that there can be no fixed and clearly defined boundary between schooling and other lived experiences; events of schooling become inextricable from the path of life. Of course, this is not a pre-determined path; the path of life, as Buddhist philosophers have told us, is a path laid down while walking. [35] The path depends upon everything, and everything depends upon the path.

As already discussed, Maturana and Varela have suggested that living organisms and the world are always in a co-specifying relationship. This includes relationships human subjects have with one another and with the world of their experience. Each human subject embodies history and culture. We do not merely inherit a gene pool, we inherit the histories of experiences connected to that gene pool. Both Heidegger and Gadamer knew this; hence their insistence that deep understanding of lived experi-ences must always be understood and interpreted as historical and cultural. Furthermore, human thought, language, and action are autonomous; they exist in a mutually co-determining relationship. Ann Berthoff's description of the experience of writing provides a good analogy for this process of mutual specification:

> When we write, we are simultaneously naming, inferring, referring, recognizing, remembering, marking time, wondering, wandering, envisaging, matching, discarding, checking, inventing: all at once, we are carrying out these acts of mind as we are writing something down—or up—making meaning in the process. The challenge, as I say, is to take advantage of that allatonceness, not to fractionate, reducing composition to skills and subskills. We need to teach ourselves and our students to manage the complexity of allatonceness, to learn to tolerate uncertainty and ambiguity, to recognize the value of *not* knowing what your thesis statement is and thus discovering the uses of chaos.[36]

I have found the word "allatonce" a useful way to conceptualize the complex interaction of lived curricular relations. Her insistence that we "discover the uses of chaos" is particularly pertinent given the recent interest in "chaos theory." Chaos theory, or non-linear dynamic mathematical theory, was first announced by Edward Lorenz in the 1960s. In the process of doing some routine computer runs of a simulated weather system, he discovered that any small interruption in a process could lead to radically different patterns of organization in the final products.[37] Similar to Maturana and Varela's analogy of "natural drift," chaos theory suggests that, in some way, everything matters. The world, our existence in the world, our relations with others, happen all-at-once. Choosing to do "this thing" rather than "that thing" means that our entire pattern of living and the entire set of relationships to which we are connected will be altered for having made that decision. Discovering the uses of chaos, then, does not mean that our lives are to be lived in disarray, disorder, and confusion; rather, it means that we acknowledge that although we have a *sense* of pre-established order in our lives, this order has, in fact, only emerged through our directed involvement in the infinitely contingent nature of our lived experience.

Currere acknowledges the existence and importance of allatonceness. It understands that the path of curriculum is "laid down while walking" and that this path will bend, wind, and turn depending on the particular ways relations among students, texts, teachers, and contexts develop. Dewey, of course, knew this when he insisted that the relationships among the child, the curriculum, and society must be continually acknowledged, particularly by those who have the power to make decisions about the forms in which curriculum is enacted. To a certain degree, even curriculum writers such as Tyler and Schwab who argued for instrumental approaches to curriculum development and inquiry had an understanding of the importance of these relational contingencies, for in the midst of their certainty about the need for pre-determined methods and processes, both insisted that curriculum is fundamentally that which is lived through, not merely something which is the subject or object of discussion or debate.

Much of the literature in the field of curriculum, however, has ignored the allatonce, historically, and culturally situated nature of experience and, instead, has promoted the importance of method. Curriculum has, to a large extent, been understood as the course to be run rather than as the running of the course. Emerging from a tradition of scientific inquiry that has attempted to eliminate the possibility of error by pre-determining a logical and rational method, curriculum has become commonly known as something that is clear, unambiguous, and certain (one could say *truthful*). Work in curriculum has generally been understood as the creation of a clear set of "directions" which guide the interactions between students and teachers so that predictable outcomes might be realized.

It is this approach to curriculum and instruction as "method" that has perpetuated the fundamental severing of curriculum from lived experiences. Hermeneutically speaking, this striving for method is a response to our condition of no longer being at home in the world, which is, according to the writings of David Smith[38] a consequence of being unaware of our historical and cultural presence. Method aims to stand in place of this loss of historical understanding and belonging by substituting reflective knowledge with a form of knowledge that pretends to understand everything in advance. Method seeks to exclude the unexpected, the accidental, the mistake. Just as Descartes believed that disciplined human reason could protect against error, the curriculum that is founded upon pre-determined methods and plans believes that adherence to these will ensure effective teaching and learning.

By focusing on the running of the course, currere acknowledges the importance of the chaotic, the ambiguous, the serendipitous, the unantici- pated, the unexpected, the surprise, the discovery, and the way in which any event, any relationship in some way affects the continual laying of the path of experience. Translator and explicator of *Truth and Method,* Joel Weinsheimer, calls these "haps," suggesting that the hap is something which

> makes its presence felt when one happens onto something, in the haphazard guess, the happenstance situation, in happiness and haplessness.... The Hap eludes the hegemony of method.[39]

The hap, then, is what remains after method; it is what occurs beyond what we predict; it is what exists beyond our willing and doing. The hap may be understood as all the moment-to-moment unpredictable experiences that contribute to our remembered, lived, and projected experiences.

It is important to understand, however, that we should not stand helpless before life believing that errors are unavoidable. Gadamer suggests that "the hermeneutical interest of the philosopher ... arises only where the avoidance of error has already been achieved."[40] The hermeneutical interest, then, is not with the mistake that can be avoided through methods, but rather that which remains—the hap. For it is the hap that usually catches our attention with its unexpected arrival. If interpreted, haplike occasions can bring us to new awareness and understanding of our situation.

We have all experienced the importance of those events that slip between known and predicted categories. We experience "haplike" events on a daily basis. We know that if all life proceeded according to the pre-determined path of methods, nothing new would occur; science, language, relationships, learning would remain fixed, final, complete. The hap, however, is often ignored, marginalized, and devalued in our retrospective discussions of events. Because the hap is seen as "the remainder"—as something which lives outside of planned or valued experience—it, like a daydream or fantasy, is often not accorded status and, as a consequence, not interpreted. Like many of the details of our daily existence that seem too banal or mundane to mention, the hap is often lost in public announcements of past events.

When the idea of the hap is applied to the study of curriculum, the importance of currere becomes evident, for in its emphasis on movement forward, currere embraces the possibility for the hap to not only be noticed, but to be interpreted. Running the course means understanding that there is likely to be some ambiguity, some resistance, and some difficulty to be overcome, as well as unexpected, unanticipated, and surprising events which alter the course. If the course is understood as one which is "laid down while walking," these unexpected details are not ignored, brushed aside, or marginalized, but are always considered part of the course. And, depending upon the value they are ascribed through processes of hermeneutic interpretation, they may fundamentally affect the direction of the path.

This formulation is not meant to suggest that we are determined by the course nor that we determine the course. Instead, it suggests that all components of curriculum cannot be known in themselves, but only in the co-specifying and ever-evolving relations among them. It is not so much the components (i.e. texts, teachers, students, etc.) that we should try to know; it is the relations among these. Curriculum exists in the embodied relations that human subjects have with one another within particular places that we call school.[41] It is the emphasis on the co-emergent qualities of the components of the course of living that signals the most important quality of curriculum as a form of embodied action. By paying attention to what is *happ*ening during the lived curriculum, we can become more attuned to the contingencies that make significant differences in those embodied relations and those that do not. Locating these moments (these haps) amid the planned structures of our lives can help us—as curriculum inquirers, teachers, learners—to initiate the necessary interpretations that help us to more deeply understand the complexities of curricular forms.

This is precisely my task in the second part of this chapter where I present another series of six hermeneutic windows which provide interpretations of events of shared readings of literary fictions among students and teachers. Each of these interpretations takes as its focal point some point of experience that for me, as a teacher and researcher, was "haplike." It is from these that I have attempted to show the fullness of the complex relations that comprise the school curriculum which includes the reading of literary fictions.

Touring

> *The high school English curriculum is very demanding. We have to cover so much material that there is no time for re-reading.*
>
> Anna

> *We've spent a whole month on* The Chrysalids*! All the other grade ten classes are already on Julius Caesar. We're way behind, already.*
>
> Jason, *grade 10 student*

As mentioned in the last chapter, reading *The English Patient* together helped the five members of our reading group re-learn how to read. Our most important discovery was the importance of deliberately taking time to read slowly and to re-read. In order to deepen our relationship with the book, we need to dwell for a time with it. And although we knew that it was this dwelling that allowed the artwork to become most powerfully evoked, we also knew that these experiences seldom occurred in the secondary English classroom. Although there were times in our teaching when we had asked students to read poems more than once, seldom (if ever) did we ask them to do this with novels or short stories. Yet, each of us who finished *The English Patient* realized that the first reading had merely provided us with a rough map of an experience—a mere promise of what might be if we were to re-read. Mapped by desire, we abandoned our touring and began to dwell with the text. And it was this dwelling that permitted a powerful building and thinking.

According to Arthur Applebee's recent study of literature teaching in the United States, engagement with literary fictions contributes to up to eighty percent of activity in the secondary English classroom.[42] James Britton and Merron Chorny have reported similar patterns of instruction in Canada and Great Britain.[43] Now, this might seem encouraging, for it suggests that there is ample opportunity in the English classroom for both students and teachers to develop deep experiences with fictional texts. Clearly, if students and teachers commit themselves to texts which require that the imagination be invoked for meaning-making to occur, the abundance of literary readings would seem to create the kinds of transformative commonplaces that we, as a reading group, experienced in our reading of *The English Patient*. Given the acceptance of various theories of reader-response in day-to-day classroom practice,[44] this possibility would seem to be exponentially greater than previous decades which focused upon "close readings" of texts. But is this really so? Do students in the secondary English classroom dwell with texts or do they merely tour through them? Are there commonplaces for interpretation created in the English classroom, or does the use of the literary fiction amount to a brief stop where students rush off the bus, take a few pictures, grab a bite to eat, relieve themselves, and then rush back on the bus to await the next destination? Are English teachers literary tour guides? Are students' experiences in the English classroom similar to the guided tour?

It is not surprising that many world travelers prefer the comfort of pre-booked guided tours. Given the busyness of modern life, seeing the world is certainly best accomplished according to pre-determined plans which have been drawn up by someone who has been to these places before. Why would anyone want to cope with the difficulty and the ambiguity of traveling through foreign countries on one's own—learning by trial and error—when the alternative is an all-inclusive pre-booked tour to be experienced within the safety and comfort of a friendly group of fellow tourists who speak the same language? In addition to this initial expediency of planning, the guided tour is efficient. Rather than bungling one's way through one or two countries in three weeks, a guided tour allows one to see many countries—and, of course, a vacation is always better if one has seen *more*. But is this really so? Do we see more during the guided tour, or do we merely cover more ground?

Of course, not knowing the precise trajectory of a vacation does not mean that plans are not made. It is clear that travel still needs to be booked and, to some degree, so do accommodations. However, in a more improvised vacation, the plans are not overly determined. Play is left in the system. The differences between touring and dwelling become most apparent when one has arrived at the airport of the foreign country, particularly if it is a country where another language is spoken. Once one has left the safety and familiarity of the airplane, one is thrust into the middle of the unfamiliar. Where is the luggage carousel? Where is the customs office? How do I get to my hotel? What do I do if I am not understood?

As we blunder our way through some of these difficulties—as we lose our way enroute to customs, take the wrong bus, finally get off and find a quaint coffeehouse, abandon our little tourist map and allow ourselves to be led by the ebb and flow of the crowd into the flower market—we learn again what we knew as children. We learn that being thrown into the middle of the world can be exciting if we don't know what is around the next corner. We learn to walk with our eyes and ears wide open; we become more mindful; we notice details we hadn't noticed in our more familiar world. We re-experience the importance of what Merleau-Ponty has called "conducts"[45]— the way our consciousness is shaped by our perceptually guided action in a world which contains others who are similarly involved in such action. When the familiar is rendered strange—as often occurs during travel in foreign countries—we become more aware of the conducts being enacted around us. And, as we simultaneously perceive and act, we learn. We begin to dwell again. At the end of a day filled with new conducts, we usually sleep better—not because our vacation has brought rest and relaxation (for we have probably worked much harder than in our usual world), but because while learning how to locate the toilets, how to order a coffee, and how to find the right bus, we were learning (again) that our bodies and our minds work together in bringing forth a world.

This is precisely what it is like to dwell in a relationship with a literary fiction. Engaging with the literary fiction means becoming immersed in situations which are not completely given—ones which require that the reader invoke the imagination, as conditioned by the text, to learn to see again. As Madeleine Grumet reminds us, "It is the function of art to reorganize experience so it is perceived freshly."[46] And, like the feeling of finding oneself lost in the middle of some foreign city, it has, as Susan Sontag suggests, the ability to "make us nervous."[47] But as products of the modern age of reason, we, in the Western world at least, do not value feeling lost or nervous.[48] We don't like dwelling; we like touring. However, as shown in the last chapter, the literary fiction asks for dwelling, for it is only by dedicating oneself to the difficulty and ambiguity of dwelling with the text that a commonplace for interpretation and understanding can be evoked.

We who choose to commit ourselves to literary fictions know this. We know that dwelling with texts requires a dedication and commitment. Although we do not do it with all of the literary fictions we read, there are some with which we choose to deepen our relationship. Over the course of our lifetime we re-read them, not to recapture the original experience of reading but to re-engage our most recent experiences within the location announced by the text. Like the English patient's commonplace book, the location gathered together through our engagements with these texts becomes increasingly larger for, like memory itself, the commonplaces of reading are collective phenomena.

Because the shared readings of *The English Patient* existed alongside the day-to-day teaching of the high school teachers in the group, our recently articulated desire to promote dwelling with texts rather than touring through them began to have an affect on the curriculum decisions that were being made. Mena, for example, decided that she would try not to cover as many poems and short stories in her upcoming thematic unit on "War" as she had in the past and would, instead, select several to read and re-read with her students. However, reducing the number of items taught was a difficult decision for Mena and for the other teachers since, like any tour, the tour through literature seems better if more is covered. Like many schools that are large enough to have an English department, teaching success and efficiency was marked by where one "was" in the mandated curriculum. This had nothing to do with dwelling, but instead with locating. In the staffroom it was common to hear comments such as: "I'm just finishing my short story unit and moving on to poetry." It also had to do with the efficient movement and distribution of materials: "I'm starting my novel unit next week. Will you be through with the class sets of *To Kill a Mockingbird?*"[49]

Even though the teachers in our group had recently understood the importance of dwelling with a text, they remained caught up in a school culture which defined effectiveness by the amount of material covered and the efficiency with which one was able to work within pre-designated time schedules. Not only would dwelling longer in a text be understood as a sign of ineffectiveness, it would create a hitch in the materials distribution system. It would be like missing a bus. And in schools one is not supposed to miss buses. One is supposed to be on time, on schedule. Times and places are things to be mastered—ironically, making both teachers and students slaves to them.

The desire to be on time and in the right place has led to the phenomenon known as "covering the curriculum." In the English classroom, this has generally meant that the reading of literary fictions has become buried under the covering of the efficient use of materials, time and space. Although students and teachers still sometimes find themselves dwelling with texts, this dwelling is often buried alive by the thick patchwork quilt of syncretism. For although many teachers have taken up reader-response in the classroom, they have largely not abandoned the close reading of texts.[50] It is a somewhat uneasy alliance, with the former being generally used as a mechanism for efficient entries into and exits from the text (with pre-reading questions like: "What sorts of things do people do to get more power?" before reading *Hamlet*; or post-reading questions like: "Did this play remind you of anything in your own life?") while the latter serves to satisfy the ranking and sorting functions of schools by asking questions that have predetermined answers (What is the theme of *Hamlet*? What symbols are used?).

Although these largely opposing critical practices have been adopted in the school curriculum, this has not occurred without creating some tension. Both Anna and Ingrid, for example, who were about to begin units which included readings of novels, questioned the way they might approach these readings with their students. Although Ingrid had, in the past, assigned chapters to be read followed by a series of questions for each chapter, she was not convinced that this was the best way to help her students develop a strong reading relation with *The Chrysalids*,[51] a book she had chosen for her academic stream grade ten class. Because this book formed the focal point for her planned anti-racism unit, she wanted students to have as deep a relationship with this book as possible and was not convinced that this would happen if she intervened too forcefully while that relationship was being established. At the same time, Anna was wondering how her non-academic grade eleven class might successfully read the novel *Forbidden City*[52] that she had chosen for them. Although she found herself very much caught up in the book and felt that students would identify with the characters and their situations, she was not convinced that they would have the reading skills or the patience to form a meaningful relationship with it.

Important questions began to present themselves. How should teachers read with students? Did dwelling with a text in the English classroom mean reading the entire text to oneself? Did it mean keeping a response journal while reading? Did it mean reading chapters aloud in class together and talking about these readings? Did it mean stopping at the end of each chapter to critically reflect upon one's understanding of the text and the relationship one was forming with it? What was the teacher's responsibility in all of this? Was the teacher to become a "tour guide," taking students through the text, pointing to sites along the way? Or was the teacher simply to allow students to wander through the location announced by the inclusion of the literary fiction in the classroom?

If one understands reading as embodied action, where the text becomes part of the world with which we strive to maintain a relationship, it would seem that neither "touring" nor "wandering" are appropriate. Touring suggests that the world of the text is "out there" waiting to be experienced, appropriated, collected in a series of snapshots that then becomes part of having "been there and done that." Touring suggests that some sort of orienting "map" is required and some decisions about the purposes for touring be made in advance. It also implies that outside help might be required. These might be book reviews or recommendations from friends, teachers, or other sources. Wandering is more like aimless browsing without any particular purpose or any pre-determined assistance or advice. Wandering (what we might call "allowing students their own experience with a text") can lead to discovery and dwelling, but it can also lead to becoming lost and never found.

Recent literature that addresses the experience of reading suggests that experienced, skilled readers choose literary fictions for a variety of purposes and approach their reading differently depending on these purposes.[53] Sometimes browsing and wandering through texts is appropriate and necessary; sometimes guided tours are essential; often dwelling, in the form of re-reading, is valued.[54] Most of this literature, however, discusses the kind of reading that occurs between one reader and one text, which, although providing important insight into the experience of reading, falls short of considering shared readings in the classroom setting. Generally speaking, literary fictions that are used in the classroom are meant to fulfill functions other than might be expected of one-on-one reading encounters. It is common practice for literary fictions to function as vehicles for skills instruction and for transmission of cultural heritage.[55] Although there has been a movement in the last two decades toward promoting personal response to reading,[56] because this movement has been accompanied by a desire to teach students to read critically and with some resistance,[57] there has been considerable anxiety among English teachers as to how all of these approaches to reading might be incorporated into day-to-day classroom practice.[58]

It is not surprising, then, that all of the teachers in the reading group proved to be syncretists, using various approaches for reading and teaching the literary fiction. However, even though they all demonstrated a general understanding of these various teaching approaches, it seemed that the literary fiction was used largely as a site for touring. From our discussions, it was apparent that most of the teachers guided students through assigned readings of one text, followed by some personal response, some critical response, general class discussions, all ending with a writing assign-ment—usually an expository essay. Response journals were largely not used, because, according to the teachers, they were overused in junior high school. "The kids were journaled to death in junior high school. They don't even want to hear the word 'journal' in high school!" was Anna's comment.

Therefore, as in many high school classrooms, students' and teachers' engagements with literary fictions were largely events where the text served as a site for touring. Teachers were tour guides, students were tourists. The tours included some pre-touring information (a bit about the book), sometimes some research into the pending tour site (background informa-tion), some pointing out of the most important sites (notice the character development here, the symbols there, the use of language here), and some general discussion and response, usually led by the tour guide (Any questions? How did you feel about that?).[59]

In our discussions of our own reading, we agreed that although guided tours through literary fictions were sometimes necessary, especially for students who were unfamiliar with the geography of the literary texts, our recent experiences led us to believe that there needed to be more dwelling and less touring. Therefore, although Ingrid was accustomed to leading students through tours of texts, she decided that the class reading of *The Chrysalids* would not be a tour. Because she wished her students to develop a strong personal relationship with the text, she asked students to read on their own.

> *I want them to form their own relationship with the book, without my influence, or anyone else's influence in the class. It's really important that they experience this on their own. I don't think that some of my students know what it means to be marginalized and hated. I think that they need to understand what that feels like. This book will give them that experience.*

Although Anna, too, had selected a novel with which she wanted her students to form a personal relationship, she was unconvinced that her grade eleven, non-academic stream students would be able to do this by themselves. Not only had most of them never read an entire novel on their own, she knew that nothing she could say or do could entice them to read *Forbidden City* by themselves.

> *Many of my students will not read this on their own. Some can't read very well, some just don't and won't read. Many of them have very difficult lives; several live on their own without the support of parents or family. I think that they might learn something by reading this book, and so I think that I need to read it aloud with them in class.*

Both Ingrid and Anna believed that if their students could enter into a relationship with these novels, the students would learn something about themselves and their relationship with their world. Although they both acknowledged the importance of developing literacy skills, it was made abundantly clear in our conversations that for them the reading of a novel had the potential to announce a particular location—an interpretive commonplace—for their students. However, each, in her own way, wanted to ensure that her students' experience would be neither a guided tour, nor an inattentive wandering through the text. Anna had some concerns about the appropriateness of the novel she had selected:

> *Some of the other teachers think that this book is too difficult for these students, but I want to use it because I think that, like the Chinese students in the book who have very few choices, some of my students believe that they have few choices. I think that if we can really get into this book, they might understand their own situation more deeply.*

Although Ingrid did not question her choice of material, she was concerned how her students might engage with it:

> *I am hesitant to just let them read this book on their own, for although I think they are all able to read it, I am concerned that they may not read it carefully enough. If they're going to have a strong relationship with the book they have to listen to what it is saying!*

Does reading the literary fiction aloud to one's students imply touring? Does asking them to negotiate the readings on their own risk aimless, inattentive wandering? Can either of these approaches lead to the kind of dwelling that we valued in our reading of *The English Patient?*

Tucking

> *When I was a kid ... I believed I could fill myself up with what older people taught me. I believed I could carry that knowledge, slowly altering it, but in any case passing it beyond me to another.*
>
> Michael Ondaatje, *The English Patient*[60]

> *I was surprised that there were so few pages in this book. It felt like a much bigger experience than the pages might suggest.*
>
> Anna

Many of the students in Anna's non-academic stream grade eleven class had experiences that were unusual for their age. Several were parents; some lived on their own without the support of family; a few were recent immigrants from non-English speaking countries and were in the process of learning the English language; several were prone to emotional outbursts in

class. According to Anna, many felt that school had little to offer them.
Like the characters in *The English Patient*, many were wanderers—
nomads—unaccustomed to dwelling. And so, it was not surprising that
although most of them could read, they generally chose not to. Anna
worried about this resistance to reading, not only because she felt that they
needed reading skills, but because she believed that they might benefit from
a more meditative, reading life:

> *I would like these students to be able to understand what life is like for young
> people their age in countries like China. Because I think that they think that most
> of the world is like theirs. Even though they watch TV, they don't seem to really
> understand the differences between life in this country and life elsewhere. They
> have such small lives right now, and they think that they must choose from within
> that life. I would like their world to be bigger!*

And so Anna was disappointed when, as she passed out new copies of
Forbidden City to this class, students responded negatively. "This book is
too thick!" "Look how small the print is!" "This looks really boring!"
Anna couldn't help but think that maybe her colleagues were right. Maybe
she should have found a simpler book, one that would offer them a more
accessible, comfortable reading experience. But Anna didn't want them to
feel comfortable. She didn't want to remain in the confining boundaries of
the world they knew and understood. She wanted to re-map their experience
and help them to understand that boundaries were meant to unfold into new
paths, not confine old ones. Although she was hesitant about making the
decision to use the novel *Forbidden City*, she felt certain that if students
could tolerate the difficulty of the experience of reading it, they would
somehow bring forth a different world of understanding.

Forbidden City is an historical fiction founded upon the events leading
up to and including the massacre of Chinese university students in Tian An
Men Square in 1989. The main character is a Canadian teenager named
Alex who has come to Beijing with his father, a news cameraman posted to
China for one year. Shortly after their arrival, the pro-democracy demonstrations in Tian An Men Square begin, and later, when the demonstrations are
at their peak, Alex is wounded, separated from his father, and ends up taking
refuge in a traditional Chinese home. Here he is cared for by two university
students, their parents, and their grandparents. Because Alex has videotape

footage of the massacre which will likely be some of the only evidence of the event, he hopes to try to smuggle these out of the country. One of the students, a teenage girl Alex's age named Xin-hua, decides to help Alex get to the safety of the airport where foreigners were being evacuated. Because it would seem odd for a Chinese girl to be associating with a Caucasian boy, she dyes his hair black, gives him Chinese clothes and, on her bicycle, attempts to get him to safety. Enroute, they are stopped by the military and questioned, and when it is apparent that Alex is not Chinese, Xin-hua is interrogated on the spot, taken behind some trees and shot. Alex eventually finds his way to the airport, locates his father and, although he returns home safely, finds his own perception of Canada to have become remarkably altered by his experiences in China.

In our reading group discussion of this novel, and in private conversations between Anna and myself,[61] it became apparent that this novel had particular significance for her. Although it seemed at first that this was because Anna and her husband had spent some time in China several years prior, I learned that, in fact, it was the bravery of the Chinese students that prompted a strong response from Anna:

> *As I read and re-read this novel I came to realize how much we take our freedoms for granted, and how we sometimes fail to understand that we need to become personally responsible for maintaining them.*

It was particularly significant that during the time that Anna was reading and teaching *Forbidden City,* there was a movement within her school system to eliminate the marking time for English teachers. Although Anna had previously described herself as "not political," her reading of this novel, juxtaposed with this event, prompted unusual action:

> *I kept having all these powerful personal responses to the book as I re-read it, because of all the stuff that is happening in our school district right now. I was at a meeting the other night where a teacher stood up and spoke about the need for us to join voices in order to offer some resistance to the controlling politics. It reminded me that we are not as free as we think we are, and that even in Canada we need to continually resist this kind of oppression. After that meeting, several English teachers and I from this school decided that we would prepare a presentation to our faculty, defending our need for marking time. We are also going to try to organize meetings with teachers from other schools. This is not*

something that I would usually do. My reading of Forbidden City *has really affected me.*

It is not surprising that Anna's actions should be affected by her reading of the book and, more particularly, through her reading of the book *with* her students. Thinking about their own need for "bigger worlds" seemed to illuminate this important idea for her. It is crucial to understand, however, that it was not her reading that sponsored her political actions, nor was it the political action that somehow altered the reading. Rather, these co-emerged as Anna continued to maintain a viable relationship with her world—a world that included students, literary fictions, and politicized action. As Maturana and Varela have suggested:

> We do not see what we do not see, and what we do not see does not exist. Only when some interaction dislodges us—such as being suddenly located to a different cultural environment—and we reflect upon it, do we bring forth new constellations of relation that we explain by saying that we were not aware of them, or that we took them for granted.[62]

Although we may consider the interaction with a literary fiction imaginary, it is the conditioned imagination, as it co-exists with our other lived experiences, that can serve as the interruption, the breach, the rupture in the familiar world. And it is this interruption, this newly configured set of relations, that can help us to perceive what had previously not been perceived. As the present world is viewed freshly, so too is the past world, for as hermeneutics reminds us, not only are we historically-effected, but we effect history. Seeing freshly—differently—means understanding our past relations differently. It is an ever moving circle of understanding. A circle, one might argue, that becomes "bigger" when the literary imagination is invoked.

And so it is not really surprising that as Anna became more involved in the "marking time issue," she became even more deeply involved in the re-reading of *Forbidden City* with her class. Although she had originally planned to alternate between reading chapters aloud to her students and having them read chapters on their own, she eventually chose, instead, to orally read the entire novel to them over a two week period. What can we say about this? We could say that Anna was denying her students their own experience of the novel. We could say that by reading aloud they were not being offered the opportunity to develop their own path of reading. We could say that reading to them effectively altered the reader-text power relations, placing the greatest authority for the map of reading in the teacher's hands.

Or, we could say that by reading the novel orally with her students, Anna presented the possibility for an encounter with a text that many of them would never have by themselves. Not only would many not have read the book on their own, several simply could not read. We could also say that by reading the author's words out loud, Anna was standing with the author and her students in the evocation of the kind of meaning that occurs when persons gather together in the bringing forth of a world. And perhaps it was the publicly performed enunciation of the author's text that helped students to understand that literary fictions are always embodied by a reader. Although the activity between reader and text is invisible, the "calling out" of the text by the teacher is a reminder that words require the resonating chamber of the body. Madeleine Grumet suggests that teachers must remember the intimate connection between bodies and words:

> Touch and voice are the sensual passages between parent and child. Because these modes of contact are associated with the intimacy of familial or erotic relations, they are barred from the classroom where sensuality in any form is anathema.[63]

And so, like the infant who, while lying against her mother's breast, feels the resonance of the voice through the body, like the thrill of turning up music full-volume on the stereo so that the music pierces the body, perhaps the teacher needs to use her own body as a chamber for the text. Perhaps by speaking the words in the presence of her students, the reading of the text becomes not just another task to be accomplished but an event of living—a performance—something that Albert Borgmann would call a communal celebration:

> People who have been captivated by music make their children take lessons; they invite their neighbors and urge their friends to go to concerts. They will make music themselves.... In a community of celebration, the terms are defined by the reality being celebrated. When people join for Saturday morning softball games on Chicago's lakefront, they do not pretend to share their possessions or beliefs; they have gathered just to play.[64]

But the event of teachers reading to and with their students is not just any communal event. Although it may be compared to a softball game, the character of gathering together to participate in readings of literary fictions is not just any playing. As Iser reminds us:

> [I]t is an integral feature of literature that ... it is not *created* for any one specific use.... In fact, literature seems constantly to provoke translations of itself into terms of prevailing social situations, which in turn makes it into a sort of divining rod for those impulses that have given rise to whatever use has been attributed to it.[65]

If the literary fiction is a type of divining rod, then teachers who call out the text become part of this divining process. Although the students may be situated in a public place, they can only perceive of the text what they are structurally able to perceive and, as a result, the meanings they make can only emerge from the way in which the public event of reading exists in the us/not-us.

Madeleine Grumet has described this divining function as a form of "pointing to the world," suggesting that teachers who choose to read with their students "point" to some aspects of the world and not others. Like the parent who teaches the child by pointing, announcing and naming (There's a kitty!), teachers who live and read with children identify that which may go unnoticed:

> When we select a story to read to a group of children, when we choose texts for a curriculum, we are extending this process of identifying what parts of the world, what relationships, creatures and events are worthy of their notice.[66]

But, of course, as Grumet reminds us later, "The task of pointing out the world is dangerous. If we point to everything, we relinquish order."[67] What does it mean for a teacher to live with students during shared readings of texts? And how is the idea of "pointing to the world" particularly significant for this sort of dwelling together?

Towards the end of the school year, Anna and Ingrid invited me into their classrooms to observe some of the lessons that centered around shared readings with their students of *Forbidden City* and *The Chrysalids*. Unlike other research that I had done in classrooms, these observations had no specific pre-determined purposes. The three of us were simply interested in the question of what it was like to share readings of literary fictions with our students as these readings became part of the high school English curriculum. And so, although I did ask Anna and Ingrid to wear a portable tape recorder, and although I did bring along a notepad, and although I was introduced as a "researcher from the university" to the students, I was not really entirely sure what I was looking for or what I would find. One could say that we agreed to allow the "path" of inquiry to be "laid down while walking."

Significantly, however, unlike previous research that I had done with teachers whom I barely knew, this classroom intervention was accomplished with persons with whom I had read—with persons whom I had engaged in mutual "world pointing"—and so, more than that at any other time, I felt that Ingrid, Anna and I—collectively—were bringing forth a very particular world of significance that had been made possible through our discussions of literary fictions. Like the collective at the villa, we agreed that our history of interactions with each other through reading together had enabled us to notice a world of significance that we had not noticed before.

And so, as I sat in Anna's classroom one unseasonably warm Spring day, with the breeze from the window flipping the pages of my notepad, I was again reminded that my function in this classroom was not to "report" on Anna's or her students' activities, nor was it to attempt to distinguish between effective and ineffective routines, processes, or practices. Rather, it was to situate myself, as another reader who was also a teacher and researcher, in this group of persons who were reading together in order to come to some understanding of what it means for teachers and students to engage in this activity in schools. More specifically, it was to try to understand both the deep relationships among the teacher's life, the way her own reading of literary fictions becomes part of this life, and how that life commingles with students' lives and their readings. Although this important insight eventually led to the sort of thinking and reading that led to a great deal of the writing in preceding chapters, it is not the insight—nor was it the pleasant warmness of the spring day—which has etched this particular classroom visit in my memory. Rather, it was a small incident—a hap, we could say—that most clearly announced for me the importance of pointing.

As she had done for several days prior, Anna was engaged in reading aloud *Forbidden City* to this class of twenty-six grade eleven students. I had been quite enjoying these classes, for Anna did not simply read aloud an entire chapter from beginning to end and then question her students or engage them in discussion. Instead, she would stop her reading every now and again and engage in what I called "pointing to herself." She would ask questions like, "I wonder why Alex did that? Could it be that he really cares about Xin-hua?" And sometimes she would answer them. "I get the feeling that he is really changing, and I like these changes; it makes him seem more human to me!" Sometimes she talked about her experience of visiting China, her feelings about the difficult political situation, her wondering about the kinds of freedom that she most valued in Canada. On this day, in the middle of her reading, she stopped to tell students that she had thought about *Forbidden City* during the teacher meeting she was at the previous night, and had been reminded of the importance of standing up for what one believes is right and just. And she asked students if they were thinking about their own lives differently by being immersed in this book.

As I spent days in Anna's class being immersed in this event of shared reading, I realized that although one could easily list the "techniques" that were contributing to the attention students were giving this text, these could not somehow account for the difference between this particular event and others I had witnessed. Students who had originally shown distaste for this novel were engaged. Attendance was almost one hundred percent (even on this warm spring day). As I continued to think about this, Anna continued her reading, slowly moving around the classroom, stopping periodically to think out loud. And during this choreography of movement and recitation, she steered over to the back corner of the room where Kathy and Jamal had begun a whispering session. Without comment, she slipped herself between them, all the while continuing her reading. Jamal immediately tried to find his place in the text; Anna (still reading) placed her finger on his book at the right spot. Kathy did not attend to her text, but looked at Anna, and asked, "Mrs. Powell, why do you always tuck yourself in like that?" Somewhat startled, Anna stopped reading, smiled, shrugged her shoulders, and said, "I guess I do that quite a lot, don't I?"

Yes she did. Anna did tuck herself into the classes she taught. Completely. Anna did not "tour" through her classes. She did not tour through her reading. Reading, for Anna, was a commitment which she took very seriously and, as evidenced by her attentiveness to *The English Patient,* it was a commitment that emerged from her desire to dwell in life, not tour through it. And so, it is not surprising that, when Anna brought forward *Forbidden City* for her students, she brought forward, as fully and deeply as she was able, her own relationship with that novel. Not just a relationship which had been established prior to the school day, but a relationship that unfolded and developed *with* Anna and her students during the event of curriculum. As Anna read each word of the text, as her body became the chamber through which the words resonated, she *showed* her students the way that literary fictions course through a body. As she stopped and pointed to the text, to her reading of the text, to her past and present living in and through a life that contained this literary fiction, she created a location—a commonplace for interpretation.

And so, when she read the words that announced Xin-hua's murder by the Chinese soldiers, her students understood why there was a small tremor in her voice, a hesitation in her reading. For they knew that this was not just any reading of any text; they understood that this was an event of dwelling with Anna in a transformative moment of curriculum. A moment in which, because Anna was fully invested in her shared reading, so too were they. This is not simply because of the power of the literary fiction, nor is it the power of the teacher. Rather, it is what happens when the teacher is able to show her students what it is like to commit oneself to a relationship with a world which is made somewhat larger, somewhat more "strange," because of the conditioned imagination.

Tucking-in is what Heidegger has called "building dwelling thinking." It is like the location announced by the bridge that does not merely join, but "gathers the earth as landscape around the stream ... guid[ing] and attend[ing] the stream through the meadows."[68] When the literary fiction is brought into the school classroom and the literary imagination is invoked, it is not the text that does the gathering; it is the teacher who dwells with her students in the commonplace location of shared reading.

Occasioning

It is not so much our judgments as it is our prejudices that constitute our being.
Hans-Georg Gadamer [69]

Some of my students don't know what it means to be hated. I think that they need to know.

Ingrid

The school curriculum does not and cannot exist apart from the world. For Ingrid, choosing to read the novel *The Chrysalids* with students was largely a response to the increasing racial tension in the inner-city high school where she taught. Ingrid was concerned that these escalating tensions were not being addressed as effectively as they could be across the school curriculum. At the same time, she was becoming increasingly frightened by the way in which this climate at school was being supported by public displays of the racist, sexist and homophobic attitudes of the provincial Premier and other prominent elected officials. For Ingrid, who had experienced a great deal of persecution in her life, the kind of intolerance and hatred being expressed in the community and the school was simply unbearable:

> *It seems that there are still some forms of discrimination that are publicly sanctioned. Usually I can ignore displays of it ... but when I read about and hear the comments made by elected officials about gays and lesbians—comments that they would not dare publicly make about other groups—I become very concerned.*

And so, because her own reading of *The Chrysalids* had evoked a particularly powerful personal response, Ingrid decided that she would use it as the focal point for what she came to call her "anti-hatred" unit. Since she wanted students to have their "own experience" of the novel, at the beginning of the unit she asked that they spend one week reading on their own. This decision was largely from Ingrid's experience of reading *The English Patient* in our reading group:

> *Although I found The English Patient difficult and frustrating, it was important for me to have my own relationship with the book. I don't usually let my students have that kind of experience. Usually, because I want them to learn particular things from their reading, I carefully guide them through the reading with questions and discussion.*

Written in 1955, *The Chrysalids* is a science fiction novel set within a community called Waknuk where any kind of deviation from the norm is rooted out and destroyed. The narrator and main character is David who can communicate telepathically with a small group of other young people in the community. Because this deviation is invisible, it goes unnoticed for many years until one of their group, Anne, withdraws herself and, in a desperate attempt to be "normal," marries a non-telepathic man from the community. Soon after, David and his friends' secret is disclosed by Anne to her husband and eventually to others in the community. At the same time, Petra, David's sister whose telepathic powers are much stronger than the others', has been sending and receiving messages from the "Sealand" people who, it turns out, are an entire civilization able to communicate telepathically. In the end, drawn by Petra's great power, the Sealand people arrive, kill a number of the oppressors who aim to dispose of David and his friends, and return to Sealand with Petra and several others.

In our reading group discussion of this novel, we all agreed that the themes of oppression were anything but subtle. Although the story was engaging, it was obvious that the reader was being placed within a textual structure that was meant to evoke feelings of what it would be like to be despised for non-conformity. Barthes would likely call this a "readerly" text[70] while Iser likely would suggest that although it required some suspension of disbelief, it had fewer "gaps and spaces" than most contemporary novels. Unlike *The English Patient* which requires that the reader work diligently to make connections between elements of the text, *The Chrysalids* presents a tightly bound set of circumstances. Therefore, we believed that Ingrid was correct in believing that her students would gain a deeper understanding of issues of racism and hatred in their own world by reading the novel.

We were wrong. Although most of the students completed their reading of the novel in the required week, it became clear to both Ingrid and myself that the intended experience had not evolved for most students. Unlike ourselves, most of them did not articulate the kind of emotional response to the text that we had expected. In fact, most students suggested that the book was rather dull and slow-moving. Although their written personal responses indicated that they understood the issues presented, it seemed that they were unable to make the connection between the text and their lives. Marla's response was typical:

I found the book quite boring and hard to get into. Nothing happened for a long time. It got interesting when we found out about Sophie's six toes, and then a bit at the end when the Sealand people came, but that's about all.

When asked if she thought that the kind of oppression depicted in the book happened in the school or in the city she suggested:

Not really. I mean, yeah, there's kids that get bugged in the school for different things—like if they're overweight or something—but nothing really bad. I think we all get along really well here in this school.

Ingrid became quite depressed. How could a novel that had provoked so powerful a response in her, seemingly do so little for her students?

I don't understand what's going on here. Most of these students just don't seem to feel the way that I feel about this book. Or the way that most of us in the reading group felt about it. There isn't the same kind of emotional reaction. They don't seem to be having the experience that I thought they would have.

There were several students who did have this experience. Alvina, a Chinese Canadian student, told me:

I became really involved in the book. I couldn't put it down. I was quite upset when Sophie was killed.

For Alvina, the book mirrored her and some of her friends' experience of attending this large, predominantly Caucasian inner-city high school:

In this school you have to be white and good looking to be popular. If you're a girl you need to have a boyfriend who is on the basketball or football team. I don't have many friends here.

We do not see what we do not see. While the experience of reading *The Chrysalids* had illuminated Alvina's situation for her, it had not helped Marla or many of her classmates "see" any more in their world than they had seen before. Although the literary imagination had been invoked to a certain degree, it had not significantly changed their perception of their world. What could account for the difference between Ingrid's experience of reading and the experience of many of her students?

Like most skilled readers, during the course of her reading life, Ingrid
had experienced the transformative effects of her engagement with literary
fictions. For her, books like *The English Patient* announced a location—a
commonplace for interpretation—within which she was able to engage in a
period of reflective meditation on her circumstances in the world. Hermeneutics and reader-response theories, however, have taught us that these
experiences, although different from those that do not include the literary
fiction, always emerge from historically-effected structures. Not only is this
governed by our history of personal experiences in the world but, as
suggested in chapter four, these very experiences are inextricable from our
biological history as a species on this planet. Any interactions that we have
in the world, then, are, as Maturana suggests, always structure-determined:

> Living systems, if they are to be explainable, must be treated as structure-
> determined systems, defined by certain organizations. Hence they must be
> systems in which whatever happens to them is determined in them by their
> structure. The interactions they undergo will only trigger changes in them; they
> will not specify what happens to them.[71]

Now, this is not a popular view of reading or learning, for it flies in the
face of the sort of freedom, self-control, and self-determination that we, as
modern subjects, would like to believe that we have. It is important to
understand, however, that Maturana is not suggesting that the living system
we call a human being does not have choices, or that varieties of paths of
interaction are not possible. He is merely suggesting the obvious: that our
very historically-effected structures (phenomenological and biological)
determine what sorts of interactions in the world are possible. This does not
mean that our paths in life are *pre*-determined, for while we are structure-
determined, so too is the medium with which we must maintain a viable
relationship—which, as explained in chapter four, I call *us/not-us*.
Therefore, just as we are structure-determined, so too is our medium
(environment) and thus only capable of admitting changes that are structurally possible. Because these interactions are constant, it is impossible to
trace their beginnings and endings, and so questions of cause and effect are
uninteresting and unproductive. When discussing any sort of us/not-us
interaction, the idea of *correspondence* gives way to the importance of
coherence, for it is only by maintaining coherence among us/not-us that

continued action (structural coupling) is possible. Hermeneutically speaking, we would call this the circle of understanding where our prejudices are always the backdrop for our ongoing action in the world, but, at the same time, become altered—re-written—as new information is added to the system.

Events of living—including the experience of reading the literary fiction—are not syncretic, but recursive. Although a literary fiction can offer an opportunity for a particular experience, it cannot *cause* the experience to happen in the reader. The reader can only admit a response that is structurally possible. Therefore, given their prior histories of experience, it is not surprising that Ingrid and Alvina were emotionally moved by *The Chrysalids* while Marla, Donna and Jason were not. Simply being able to read the words in the text did not guarantee the same experience.

What implications does this have for the school curriculum, particularly situations where the aesthetic rather than efferent experience with the literary fiction is meant to contribute to the path of curriculum? This is an important question, for although we understand that the literary fiction is meant to invoke the literary imagination, conventional school practices suggest that it is the efferent rather than the aesthetic reading that is valued in the secondary English classroom. That is why it is not really necessary that Ingrid's students leave their reading experience with anything other than an ability to know what happened, be able to name particular literary conventions in the text, and be able to discuss these in relation to their own opinions. None of these require that they have "felt" or "experienced" what it was like to be hated through their reading of the book. Essentially, none of what is typically asked a secondary English student (including journal responses) really requires that they have any deep and enduring relationships with the text—relationships such as the ones Ingrid and the rest of us experienced in our reading of *The English Patient*.

Through the various written and oral responses given by students in class, as well as from interviews that I had with students who volunteered to talk to me about their experience with this reading,[72] it became clear that those students who admitted to having experienced discrimination (particularly racial) in their lives had a powerful emotional response to the novel while those who told me that they had not experienced discrimination did not have the same sort of response. Therefore, the very persons whom Ingrid hoped to affect with this novel were not affected. Their historically-effected structures, it seems, simply could not admit this new experience.

However, like any literary fiction, this one did not stand alone in its relationship to its readers. Like all things in the world, it existed as part of the world with which students needed to remain viable. And because this reading was only a part of Ingrid's "anti-hatred" unit, it existed alongside other experiences she presented to them, including the viewing of films, the reading of expository material on the subject of racism and hatred, and presentations from two guest speakers—Dayna, from the local Jewish Federation and Tony, from the city's gay and lesbian association. Therefore, as I interviewed students about their experience of reading *The Chrysalids,* I was also interested in the larger text of curriculum in which this reading existed. This meant that my questions about their experience of reading the novel were always positioned next to questions about their impressions of other aspects of the unit, particularly their impressions of what the guest speakers had to say about what it was like being a member of a marginalized group.

It was this approach which, within the context of a discussion with fifteen year old Kelsey, helped me to understand the importance of *occasioning.* Occasioning was a word that I had heard mathematics education researcher, Thomas Kieren, use when discussing the idea of cognition as embodied action in relation to teaching experiments he had done with public school and university mathematics students. I had often heard Tom say things like: "The teacher must occasion learning with the students."[73] Although I had always sensed the importance of what he was saying, I could never quite make sense of this unusual use of occasion. What is the significance between this shift from the noun form of occasion to the verb? I had always thought of an "occasion" as some sort of special event or celebration, such as a birthday, a wedding anniversary, Christmas, Hanukkah, or a graduation. When the word "occasion" is used to describe classroom events, it is often thought of in such terms. It is not uncommon, for example, to hear of classroom occasions as "celebrating students' learning."

According to the Oxford English Dictionary, however, the original Latin meaning of occasion (occasion-em) has more to do with an opportunity arising from a "falling of things towards each other"—something that presents itself in the middle of a set of circumstances. Occasion, understood in this way, is more like a hap—more like the kind of situation that is not predictable but which, if taken up, can lead to a new and previously unknown path of understanding. The move from noun to verb, from occasion to occasioning, when applied to a discussion of curriculum, is similar to the move from curriculum to currere. The teacher occasions when she is able to notice a moment that occurs when aspects of curriculum have "fallen together" in unexpected, but interesting ways. With her students, she is able to lay a path of understanding that was previously unknown. From such events of curriculum, some students come to understand what they had previously been unable to understanding. Such was the case with Kelsey.

Like most others in Ingrid's class, Kelsey had shown little interest in *The Chrysalids*. Although his written responses indicated that he had read it and could discuss elements of the novel (character, theme, etc.), his response to Ingrid's announcement that a member of the gay and lesbian community would be coming to speak to the class indicated that, if he had experienced what it was like to be hated by reading the novel, he was not generalizing this to his life, for as he left class that day I heard him mutter to himself, "I'm not coming to class if there's gonna be a fag in here!" However, Kelsey did come to class on that day. And although he, like many of the other students in the class, entered the classroom hesitantly and sat back in his seat, arms folded—rigid, resistant, recalcitrant—he became visibly more alert as Tony spoke. And, towards the end of the period when Tony asked if there were questions, Kelsey was among the first to raise his hand: "Did you ever play hockey or football when you were a kid? Do gay people do that?"

During our interview I asked Kelsey about his experience of reading *The Chrysalids*:

> *I just couldn't get into this book. And it took me forever to write about anything about it—mainly because nothing stuck in my head. I had to read things over and over again—but nothing seemed to stick.*

Nothing seemed to stick. Even re-reading sections did not seem to help. Clearly, re-reading is no guarantee that dwelling has occurred. Nor is the desire to know, for it was apparent from my discussions with Kelsey that he wanted to understand the issues which seemed to be so important to Ingrid:

I knew that there was something about the book that was really important to Mrs.
Matisz—something that we were supposed to get. But I just couldn't get it from
reading the book.

A relationship with a text is always part of a relationship with everything
that is not the reader (but which, of course includes the reader—us/not-us)
and so I was not surprised when Kelsey told me that what he had previously
not "seen" in the novel, he could after listening to Tony speak:

I didn't really catch on to the book until after Tony had spoken to us. It was
weird—like, I was able to understand what the book was saying after listening to
him talk to us about what it was like to be gay. When I think of the book now, I
think of some of the things that Tony said and how, all of a sudden, I understood
what life was like for him—how difficult it was.

Ingrid knew that the presentations from Dayna and Tony had had an
effect on her students. She could tell by the way in which they had become
engaged in class—by their attention; by their questions, by the way in which
they came into class on the days following the presentations. Occasioning
had begun. However, in order for occasioning to fully develop, there needed
to be time for re-collection, re-vision, re-reading. And so, following the
occasions of curriculum that featured readings of a literary fiction and the
extra-textual occasions featuring the guest speakers, there were class
discussions of issues that emerged from these events. What was life like for
the characters who were banished to the fringes? What would it be like to
grow up as a visible minority? An invisible minority? Why is it so difficult
for us to understand the way in which we are implicated in the architecture
of hatred in our society? Could it be that as structure-determined creatures
we simply "cannot see what we cannot see?"

Varela uses the analogy of wind chimes to illustrate what it means to be
structure-determined:

Imagine in your mind's eye and ear a mobile, with thin pieces of glass dangling
like leaves off branches, and so on. Any gust of wind will cause the mobile to
tinkle, the whole structure changing its speed, torsion of branches, etc. Clearly,
how the mobile sounds is not determined or instructed by the wind or the gentle
push we may give it. The way it sounds has more to do with the kinds of
structural configurations it has when it receives a perturbation or imbalance.
Every mobile will have a typical melody and tone proper to its constitution. In

other words, it is obvious from this example that in order to understand the sound patterns we hear, we turn to the nature of the chimes and not to the wind that hits them.[74]

But, of course, although the chimes have only a "possible" range of sounds, the intensity of the perturbation—the wind—will determine the intensity of the sound, and, if we take the metaphor a little further, will determine whether or not the glass will be able to sustain the force or whether the force will shatter them. In any case, although the structure is in place, it requires some disturbance, some occasion of wind to effect a sound. A limitation of this metaphor is that, although true to the notion of structure-determined behaviors (i.e., the possible range of movements and sounds of the mobile is determined by its structure, as occasioned by the wind), the comparison fails to illustrate the way in which a structure-determined entity's history of interactions with an occasioning agent leads to change in not only the entity's path of movement, but in its very structure. Suzanne Langer's use of the relationship between form and motion in the waterfall is perhaps a better depiction of the ideas of structure-determination, coupling and occasioning:

> The waterfall has a shape, moving somewhat, its long streamers seeming to shift like ribbons in a wind, but its mobile shape is a permanent datum in the landscape, among rocks and trees and other things. Yet the water does not really ever stand before us. Scarcely a drop stays there for the length of one glance. The material composition of the waterfall changes all the time; only the form is permanent; and what gives any shape at all to the water is the motion. The waterfall exhibits a *form of motion,* or a *dynamic form.*[75]

Suggesting that "the material composition of the waterfall changes all the time" depicts the way in which two structurally-determined unities (water and environment) can only function within the range of their mutual possibilities, but from this each evolves somewhat differently from their history of occasioning with one another.

But what occasions the waterfall and what does the waterfall occasion? Melting snow from distant mountains, run off from August thunderstorms, the very structure of the land, the very *history of previous occasionings* that have cut a path (not *the* path, but *one* path from a possible many that may have been cut). The interesting question becomes one of what constitutes the waterfall. Is it the water? The riverbed through which the water passes? The conditions of water collection that lead to the forming of a river that eventually flows over a cliff? All of these, it seems. The various occasionings that lead to the maintenance of the dynamic form which we call the waterfall happen *allatonce*. And even if the water supply ends, there remains evidence of motion, for cut into the rock of the riverbed is the history of the water's effect. Something like scars from childhood cuts, stretch marks from childbearing, notes in the margins of a book.

What is the significance of the idea of occasioning, of the structure-determined action of wind chimes, and the dynamic form of the waterfall to curriculum? Madeleine Grumet suggests that

> Curriculum is a moving form. That is why we have trouble capturing it, fixing it in language, lodging it in our matrix. Whether we talk about it as history, as syllabi, as classroom discourse, as intended learning outcomes, or as experience, we are trying to grasp a moving form, to catch it at the moment that it slides from being the figure, the object and goal of action, and collapses into the ground of action.[76]

It is difficult to describe a moving form since it is the nature of language to freeze, to fix, to isolate, and to present one-word-after-the-other a stream of some interpretation of a world. Activities in the classroom are often like that. First we prepare to read by talking about the author and the historical circumstances of the text; then we read; we respond; we answer questions about our reading; we discuss our reading; we write about it. One-thing-after-the-other. This in itself is not problematic, for it is really the way life is. What *is* problematic is pretending that learning experiences are linear, incremental, and cumulative. And it is here that even the waterfall metaphor breaks down, for unlike the waterfall that cannot help but flow downstream collecting into rivers, lakes and the ocean in an ever-forward-flowing stream, humans have the ability to back-up, and, through the process of reflection, to re-configure their structures—change their mind and change their direction. Curriculum is a moving form, but unlike the waterfall, it moves forward and backward—sometimes allatonce.

What does this suggest about Kelsey's experience in the curriculum announced by the various experiences surrounding his reading of *The Chrysalids?* First of all, the readings of literary fictions will not, as Ingrid expected, "give" students like Kelsey an experience that falls outside the realm of their structure-determined possibilities. Some paths simply are not possible, even with the assistance of the literary imagination. However, reading does not necessarily end upon the completion of the physical act of reading. Reading can re-occur as new events unfold within the dynamic form of curriculum, particularly if the teacher understands that students' engagements with literary fictions are structure-dependent. As a consequence, the teacher does not insist upon *optimal* readings of these texts, but instead merely expects *sufficient* readings. Kelsey's reading was sufficient. He knew enough about the text to be able to talk and write about it. It is from the point of the sufficient reading that the teacher who understands the importance of occasioning begins to present events that allow many paths of learning to unfold. The text and the extra-textual activities are not boundaries that confine, but rather are processes of occasioning which unfold into new understanding.

Specifically, this means understanding that events such as the guest speakers' presentations, when subject to a deliberate period of reflection, have the capacity to affect the way in which the literary imagination is invoked and conditioned. Although Kelsey did not re-read *The Chrysalids* after hearing from Tony, the opportunity to re-collect the details of reading in relation to a reading self that had been involved in this curriculum occasioning allowed Kelsey a deeper, richer interpretation of the text. This is an important point for those of us who believe that new worlds can be opened up for students when the literary imagination is invoked by in-class readings of the literary fiction, for it shows how we must neither ignore nor feel powerless by the fact that relationships with literary fictions are always structure-determined. For although the initial reading of the text is always conditioned by the reader's existing structure, the history of interactions between that reading and critical reflections on it can offer clearings for new paths of understanding. This is the power of sharing readings and interpretations of literary fictions with our students.

Hijacking

Mr. Sweeney was a completely lazy man. I don't remember him reading at his desk, grading papers, or even looking at us. He just sat there for the entire semester, like a middle aged mannequin. Though the authors we read were good

*choices, our sixteen-year-old minds had trouble understanding those short stories
without the help of a teacher. But it was nice for an hour in the school day just
to be left alone and I remember that.*

Natalie Goldberg[77]

*But here they were shedding skins. They could imitate nothing but what they
were. There was no defense but to look for the truth in others.*

Michael Ondaatje, *The English Patient*[78]

In his book *Becoming a Reader,* J. A. Appleyard suggests there are important differences between the adolescent's and the adult's experiences of reading literary fictions.[79] Most adults, he explains, read literary fictions in order to escape from the pressures of daily life, to search for wisdom or truth, and/or to find usable images that help them negotiate their lives in a more productive and satisfying manner. Generally speaking, the adult reader can be described as pragmatic, for although the text is experienced aesthetically, most adult readers expect some real-world, non-imaginary benefit. The adolescent reader, according to Appleyard, generally expects to be able to identify with the main characters and, even if they are contained in science fiction or fantasy settings, expects them to be realistic. Most important, however, is that they expect their engagement with the literary fiction to make them think about various competing truths in their own lives. Unlike adults who generally use their experience with literary fictions to reflect on the already-walked path of their lives, adolescents are more concerned with using their relationship with the text to make immediate decisions and to project a path of possibility.

The experiences shared by members of our teacher reading group, along with my interviews with twenty-five students from Anna's and Ingrid's classes, largely confirm Appleyard's general conclusions about these different reading experiences. As I spoke to adolescent readers about their experience of reading *The Chrysalids* and *Forbidden City,* it became clear that, for a number of them, their relationship with the text had become an important referential experience—a reference text. Kevin, for example, confided that he had not really expected to "get into" *The Chrysalids,* but was unexpectedly swept in when the character Sophie's six toes are announced to the reader:

I couldn't believe it when I read that. I've never told anyone at school this, but I had six toes on each foot when I was born, and had to have them cut off. It didn't really bother me all that much until reading this book—because look what happened to Sophie! I guess I never thought that something like that would be thought of as a deviation. I sort of felt like a freak when I read that.

Because it caused Kevin to wonder about his status as a "normal" person, his relationship with the novel was not a comfortable one. In high school where conformity is highly desired, feelings of abnormality can be distressing. Malcolm, who had emigrated with his family from Northern Ireland five years prior, also felt considerable discomfort:

When I read about the way the deviations were handled in the book I remembered how people always noticed my accent.

I had not noticed an accent, and told him so. His response was:

I've worked hard to suppress it. I don't want to sound different. I hated having attention drawn to myself all the time.

There are two issues that emerge from these readers' comments. First is the fact that many of the "responses" that are reported in the English classroom are, in themselves, fictives. Students like Kevin and Malcolm, whose entire relationship with a book seemed to hinge on a particular life experience that they wished to remain private, felt tremendous dissonance between their actual experience of reading and that which was reported (in written or oral form) in class. Excluding these relational pivot points, for them, meant needing to "construct" responses in order to fulfill curricular expectations. Second is the ethical issue of the appropriateness of using students' relationships with texts as material for the curriculum. Although is it significant, and likely important, that students are able to better understand the relationship between their personal experiences and those of others as a result of his reading a novel, it does not follow that these experiences should be used as classroom texts. John Elliott has used the term "hijacking" to describe the way in which university-based researchers have appropriated the experience of practicing teachers and used them for their own benefit:

We take an idea which underpins teachers' practices, distort it through translation
into academic jargon, and thereby 'hijack' it from its practical context and the web
of interlocking ideas which operate within that context.[80]

Are teachers hijacking student response by making response to literary
fictions a requirement in the English classroom? What really functions as
the text of curriculum in the secondary English classroom? Is it the literary
fiction? Or is the students' responses to these fictions?

Before these questions can be addressed, it is important to understand
that English as a school subject is a fairly recent phenomenon. For most of
the eighteenth and nineteenth centuries, the English language arts found their
way into the curriculum through subjects like spelling, grammar, rhetoric,
literary history, reading, oratory, and elocution.[81] Literary fictions were
generally used as materials through which skills and cultural heritage were
taught. The push towards universal public education and the importance
ascribed to the reading of religious materials and classical texts eventually
led to greater use of particular literary fictions in schools. However, again
these had specific purposes: to engender in students moral virtues and an
appreciation of literary works of art. It is not surprising that even to this day,
the literary fiction functions as a vehicle for transmission of cultural heritage,
for moral education, social reproduction, and skills instruction.

The popularity of "personal response" to literature in the English
classroom, although sporadically practiced for the last sixty years or so,[82] has
only gained general popularity in the past two decades. The importance of
personal response has coincided with considerable research on reading
which has convincingly shown the importance of the reader's response to
meaning making, the push towards student-centered instruction in schools,
and the general Western cultural belief in the importance of individualism.
Not only has personal response been seen as vital to the enactment of the
literary fiction, but it has been understood as a personal right to be supported
and maintained in the school curriculum. These beliefs, however, when
asked to co-exist with the sorting and ranking functions of schools (where
right answers are important), require that the reader-text relation (another
way of talking about response) become an artifact of curriculum that must
become subject to the gaze of the teacher. When the evaluative gaze of the
English teacher is considered in light of the previous chapters, which have
shown the way in which the reader's (student's) relationship is *always* part

of the world with which he or she is coupled, it becomes clear that evaluation has become a dangerous form of "panopticism."

Panopticism, as discussed by Michel Foucault in his book *Discipline and Punish*,[83]—is derived from the word "panopticon"—a plan for an efficient prison designed by Jeremy Bentham and described in his book *Panopticon*, published in 1791. The panopticon's most innovative feature was a design that allowed the warden constant surveillance of the prisoners from a vantage point in a tower surrounded by cells for individuals. These cells, because they were fully open in the front (bars only), and lit from behind, exposed prisoners at all times. Foucault writes:

> They are like so many cages, so many small theatres, in which each actor is alone, perfectly individualized and constantly visible. The panoptic mechanism arranges spatial unities that make it possible to see constantly and to recognize immediately.[84]

The idea of the panopticon, Foucault suggests, has polyvalent applications:

> It is a type of location of bodies in space, of distribution of individuals in relation to one another, of hierarchical organization, of disposition of centres and channels of power, of definition of instruments and modes of intervention of power, which can be implemented in hospitals, workshops, schools, prisons.[85]

The English patient, of course, experiences panopticism in various ways. As a patient unable to care for his own needs, he is continually exposed to the ministrations of others. At the same time, his very elusiveness about his identity coupled with the intriguing bits of it which are revealed through his commonplace book prove irresistible to Caravaggio who is determined to excavate the truth of his past. There are times, however, when the constant surveillance is simply too much to bear:

> You must talk to me, Caravaggio. Or am I just a book? Something to be read, some creature to be tempted out of a loch and shot full of morphine, full of corridors, lies, loose vegetation, pockets of stones.[86]

There were times when members of our reading group felt the panoptic gaze. Ingrid commented on this:

I remember coming to the reading group after having missed one session. All of a sudden everybody had these little notes. And I thought, "Ah, everybody's keeping notes! I should keep notes too."

As discussed in chapter five, the need to publicly demonstrate dedication to reading, along with the knowledge that private reading relationships were to become the subject of conversation, was stressful for most group members. And although it was also productive, it is important to remember that each of us ultimately *chose* to be involved in that shared reading situation and could also choose to opt out. Like prisoners in the cells of the Panopticon, however, the students in the English classroom often do not have an opportunity to freely move out of the panoptic gaze. And, of course, in schools, panopticism is heightened, for unlike the prisoners in the panoptic prison who are not able to see one another, the students are continually subject to the gaze of their peers. As sixteen year old Taylor remarked:

High school is hell. Most adults forget how awful it really is. There is no place to hide. If it's not the teachers watching you, it's all the other kids.

For many of Ingrid's and Anna's students, prior experiences in English language arts classes had taught them to grow leery of anything related to "journals" or "personal response," for they had learned that "personal response" was simply another way of checking to see whether or not they had read the book and, if they had, how well they had understood it. For some students this seemed like an inefficient way to check on them. Tim suggested:

It would have been a lot easier if my grade nine teacher had just given us questions at the end of each chapter like all the other teachers I had. Cause that's all he was really interested in anyway—whether we had read the book.

For many others, however, whether it was in the form of a response journal or occasional response assignments, the need to respond personally was often distasteful—sometimes impossible. Not only did students feel unable and unwilling to share with their teacher the direction their literary imagination had taken them, they often found it quite impossible to do so when surrounded by their peers in the school classroom. This should not be surprising. For as Iser has suggested, "the act of fictionalizing is a crossing of boundaries. It amounts to nothing short of an act of transgression."[87] Students who are unaccustomed to being visible at all times in the school classroom cannot and should not be expected to participate in this coerced disclosure. Darby was most articulate on this subject:

> *I just couldn't write very much about* The Chrysalids. *And it wasn't because I didn't have anything to write about. It's just that even before Tony came in to talk to us, I had thought about how gays and lesbians are discriminated against, because I have friends who are gay and lesbian. But I couldn't write about that. Mrs. Matisz doesn't know I have these friends, and no-one in the class does either. So I just pretended that I didn't like the book.*

When one is constantly exposed, there is a desperate desire to cover up—to become hidden, invisible, not there. It's easy to be not-there when working on a grammar unit, a spelling list, a set of questions about who said and did what in act three, scene five of *Hamlet*. It's hard to become not-there when asked to uncover a relationship that has been formed with a literary fiction. Now, there are those who might say, "Well, students don't have to respond. It is their choice." I wonder if it is? Do students really believe that saying nothing will not affect their grades? Others might suggest that personal response can be kept personal since what is often graded is the "expository" material that is written anyway. But if we understand reading as embodied action, we must also understand that there are no real boundaries between what we call "personal" and what we call "public."

When the reader establishes a relationship with a literary fiction, when the literary imagination is invoked, the response is not fragmented. Although readers may choose what to disclose and what not to disclose, it is important to remember that what is *not* chosen—what is absent—is always present. And so, when Kevin did not mention the fact that he also at one time had had six toes, when Malcolm felt uneasy because the book reminded him that he too was "different," when Darby pretended she had not liked the book because she was not able to "construct" a fitting fictive response to the classroom text, an event of curriculum was unfolding that served to reinforce the authority of the teacher as the primary arbiter of what is said and not said in the English classroom. For although there are some students who are able to integrate their relationship with a literary fiction into the school curriculum, there seem to be many who are not. This means that the literary imagination is not really able to do its job in the school classroom. The panoptic stare has glued some readers in place. As Greg told me:

> *I've read all four volumes of* The Lord of the Rings *twice. I hate reading novels for school though. I can't enjoy a book when I know that I have to answer questions or say something about it in class.*

As teachers we know this. In a comment during one of our reading group discussions Ingrid suggested:

> *Reading in school is not the same as reading at home. At home you can control your relationship with the book. At school you can't.*

These feelings, of course, are not only conditioned by our current experience as teachers in school, but are conditioned by our prior experiences as students. Announcements of changes to reading pedagogy, such as an emphasis on "personal response" does not guarantee different reading experiences. As Mena explained:

> *When I was growing up and going to school, reading really was a private thing. We wrote about our reading—in the form of essays—but we never did any personal response. I guess I'm still not used to it.*

For some students and teachers the question of what the literary imagination has done for the school curriculum is not nearly as important or as interesting as what the process of schooling has done to the literary imagination.

Counterfeiting

> *And in his commonplace book, his 1890 edition of Herodotus' Histories, are other fragments—maps, diary entries, writings in many languages, paragraphs cut out of other books. All that is missing is his own name.*
>
> Michael Ondaatje, *The English Patient*[88]

As a teacher I always try to determine what the most appropriate response to students would be in any given situation while I, myself, remain detached from that response.

Ingrid

In his book *Narrative and the Self,* Anthony Kerby explains that what we call the "self" is the product of ongoing acts of self-narration. Our sense of personal identity is not something that develops through a process of accretion where new experiences are simply piled up on top of old ones. Instead, identity is constantly in the process of being written through the narrative interpretations we give to our remembered past, our lived present, and our projected future. He writes:

> [I]dentity ... is not the persistence of an entity, a thing (substance, subject, ego), but is a meaning constituted by a relation of figure to ground or part to whole. It is an identity in difference constituted by framing the flux of particular experiences by a broader story.[89]

This "broader story" is what I have described as everything that we perceive as not ourselves (not-us)—the world to which we endeavor to maintain a viable and meaningful relationship. Maintaining this relationship requires that interpretations of who we think we are and what we think the world is like must remain coherent. Confronting something or someone unfamiliar requires a re-interpretation of who we are (us) and a re-interpretation of the world that contains the unfamiliar (not-us). Our feelings of discomfort in a new situation (like traveling in a foreign country or beginning a new job) demonstrate what it is like to have this coherence disrupted. In these situations we are less sure about our established and familiar identity, for we have not yet learned what we need to know in order for a comfortable coherence to be formed. We could say that our own personal history has not yet been re-written in terms of the unfamiliar circumstances being presented to us. And so, we tend to be more alert and more inquiring in such situations, striving to close the gap between our presently understood sense of self and an evolving self.

This phenomenon was evident in the discomfort that members of our teacher reading group felt while reading *The English Patient.* It was also announced in the novel itself through the descriptions of the dis-ease felt by the characters when they were unable to learn very much about the burned

pilot whom Hana has been tending. For much of the novel he is presumed
to be of English descent, and so he is called the English patient. Eventually,
it is learned that he is not English but is the famous Hungarian spy, Count
Ladislav de Almàsy. And, of course, once the others learn about this
previously concealed history and identity—once his counterfeit identity has
been disclosed—the relations among the four of them were immediately and
unalterably re-configured. Not only did present and future relations change,
but memories of past relations were necessarily re-written.

What can we say about the idea of the counterfeit identity in relation to
shared readings of literary fictions and events of schooling? We must begin
by understanding that the act of counterfeiting is not the same as the act of
fictionalizing—at least not when fictionalizing refers to a literary work of art.
As discussed in chapters two and three, the fiction which we call literary is
a set of invented details and circumstances which, in order to function as a
literary fiction, must be unmasked as such. Unless the presented circumstances are unmasked as fictional, the imagination of the reader will not be
invoked and conditioned which means that the literary fiction will not be
allowed to do its work. This is what distinguishes the literary fiction (as an
example of fictionalizing) from something counterfeit, for in order for a
counterfeit to do its work, it *must not* be unmasked. It must not be identified
as a fake. Disclosures of this sort mean that the counterfeit is seen for what
it is *not*. It is understood as a deceit, a sham, a forgery. The unmasking of
counterfeit money or a forged signature renders each valueless—although
they retain material structure in the world, they lose material value. This
distinction between "real" and "counterfeit" points to two things that are
significant to a discussion of our relations with literary fictions: First, it
shows that a known "fake" is valueless and becomes disconnected from the
world of exchange. Second, it illuminates how the objects of human
production become locations for a sense of self.

This is particularly evident in the case of the signature that is meant to
represent an individual's identity. Like the fingerprint, the signature is
thought to be unique to the individual and how, when produced on a
document, it becomes a material extension of the self. When we discover
that our signature has been forged we feel violated, for by producing a
counterfeit signature, the forger is appropriating an aspect of our identity.
This is why the unmasking of the forged signature renders it valueless, for

although it has been produced by someone, it is not relationally attached to its rightful owner. This is also why the signature is so crucial on visual works of art; there is a sense that there needs to be evidence of the producer on the work. Even though the artwork is a material extension of the producer, the signature is still considered a more powerful one. This is proven by the fact that in this age of reproduction of visual and literary works, we are content with the copy if there is an original signature of the artist or author on it. The signature changes a poster into a valued work of art, a book into a more valued artifact.

Understanding the signature as a material extension of the self helps us to understand the way our responses to literary fictions function. Although these relations are not generally visible like the signature, they share its most important characteristic: the response that one has to a literary fiction is inextricable from the person. Like the signature, it is a material extension of the self. And, like the signature, the response to a literary fiction can be subject to the act of counterfeiting. This counterfeiting can become manifest in two ways: through an act of unmasked fictionalizing where a response is deliberately invented for presentation, or through an act of withholding where no response is disclosed. The presentation of the counterfeit response is something that is seldom raised in the reader-response literature, yet it seems that if the counterfeit response functions in the same way as the counterfeit signature, it too will profoundly affect the us/not-us relations of which it becomes a part.

The importance of the actual and the counterfeit response to the literary fiction became most apparent to me as I attempted to unravel a knot of confusion which I had concerning student interactions with the two novels being taught by two different teachers. Why was it that most of Anna's students reported highly developed personal relationships with the novel *Forbidden City,* while most of Ingrid's did not report such relationships with *The Chrysalids?* Was it because *Forbidden City* contained situations that students found more interesting and characters whom they thought were more realistic? Or did it have more to do with the way in which the readings were enacted in the classroom? Did the different experiences reported by the two groups of students have more to do with the fact that one novel was read orally (performed) while the other was read silently by each student? Or was it that one class was an academic stream class while the other was not? Or was it that Anna presented her response to the novel as she read with her students while the Ingrid did not? Although I suspected that all of these factors contributed to the different reading experiences, I came to believe that it was the last one—the way the teacher's relationship with the novel did or did not become part of the text—that was most influential. Important questions began to present themselves: How significant is the teacher's relationship with the literary fiction and, furthermore, how important is it that this relation becomes disclosed? What happens when a counterfeit response is used in place of an actual response?

Earlier in this chapter, I discussed the way in which Anna "tucked" her emerging relations with the literary fiction into the in-class oral readings of this novel. As she read, she reported to her students her developing response and relationship to the book as it existed in the ongoing relationship she was maintaining with her world. Embedded in these disclosures of her responses were continual "pointings" to connections from her past and present world. Frequent references to her trip to China, her involvement in "the marking time" issue, her husband and daughter, other books she had read, other books that she had read with this class, other discussions that she had had with this class, things that she knew about the life of the students in her class—all these became a material part of the actual text that was being read. Through this pointing Anna was demonstrating that the meaning was not to be found in the text, in herself, in some critic's remarks, or in the students. Neither was "meaning" some independent entity floating around in the room. By pointing to the text, her own experiences, her past experiences with her students, her students' experiences, Anna was helping them to understand that meaning is arrived at through continued reflections on the ongoing relationship that each reader/interpreter tries to maintain with a world that is shared with others. Through specific processes of reflection, synthesis, and re-symbolization, Anna and her students were performing the method of *currere*. That is why it was not surprising that several of her students were unable to separate information in the novel from information that they received from Anna. Kathy, for example, when telling me about an incident from the book, gave details about Tian An Men Square that had not been in the book at all, but instead were details mentioned by Anna about her own trip to China. When I pointed this out to Kathy, she became rather flustered and replied, "Well, I can't separate what's in the book from what Mrs. Powell tells us! It's all one thing to me!"

Indeed it is. This is what it is like when teachers bring forward their actual response to a literary fiction as it unfolds during events of schooling. Like the signature, Anna's continued disclosures of her response became a material part of an identity that functioned, along with the text, as part of the not-us world with which each student needed to maintain a coherent relationship. The teacher is not someone who mediates between text and curriculum. Nor is her response to a literary fiction the mediating object. When the teacher brings forth her emerging response to the text during the event of curriculum, in relation to her students and their responses, *occasioning* is in process. And when occasioning is in process, the usually confining boundaries of the curriculum become transformed into boundaries that gather up the students, the texts, and the teacher into a set of relations that unfold into new understandings and new possibilities. When this occurs students notice the difference.

> Kyle: *I never liked English until this year. And I never read a whole book until we read this one [Forbidden City] with Mrs. Powell ... It helped when she read to us, especially when she stopped and talked about what she thought about.*
>
> Jessica: *This is the only class where I feel like I can say what I want to say. There's always lots of time for us to talk about what we think about. Especially while we're reading stories.*
>
> Paul: *I've never heard a teacher talk about a book like Mrs. Powell does. It's interesting hearing her think out loud.*

Although the student comments about Anna's way of teaching were sometimes rather vague, I knew what they were trying to express, for as I spent time in Anna's class, I also noticed how she became invested in the curriculum. As discussed in chapter five, Anna was the kind of person who dedicated herself to the literary fiction and who attempted to continually interpret the evolving relationship between herself and the text. Her teaching mirrored this practice. Not only did she frequently interrupt her oral reading to explain to her students the personal connections she was making to particular passages, she encouraged students to do this as well, and she provided significant periods of time for these exchanges. It was this move from relating her response, to listening to, and responding to student response that created an important interpretive location in the classroom. It was Anna's ability to listen that most students seemed to notice and distinguish from other teachers' practices. Ray's comment was typical of what students told me:

> *I usually don't say anything in my other classes—teachers don't really care what we think anyway. But I do in this one. Mrs. Powell really listens to me. Like, yesterday when we were reading about AK 47's she remembered that I knew a lot about military weapons and asked me to explain what an AK 47 was.*

For the students, these in-class discussions created locations for interpretation that helped them to re-connect the usually disconnected relations among texts and student and teacher responses to the text. I believe that this was largely because Anna was able and willing to insert her own evolving responses alongside shared readings of the text and student response to the text. By making public her own responses, Anna enlarged the usually-constricting space of the school curriculum. Because the function of the literary imagination is to render the familiar strange—to broaden the range of perception and understanding—Anna was successful in making the commonplace for interpretation, as announced by the inclusion of the literary fiction, a larger than usual experience.

But this was not the case in Ingrid's classroom, for although Ingrid felt a deep commitment to the novel she was teaching and an equally deep one to her students, she did not feel able, in the same way as Anna did, to include as part of the curriculum her actual response to *The Chrysalids*. In large part, this was because Ingrid felt very strongly that students should develop their own opinions without the influence of the teacher. Therefore, even though she wished them to have a particular experience with the novel that she hoped would influence their actions in the world, she did not wish to impose her opinions upon them:

> *I have very strong opinions. I know that. And I have worked very hard to try to remain neutral in the classroom, because I think that my students need to form their own opinions from the information presented. Now, I know that I control that information, and in a way, in doing so, control what they might decide about certain things. And I accept that. But I am always very careful about keeping my personal life and my personal opinions to myself.*

Of course, this could be interpreted as a pedagogically appropriate and correct response. However, as I came to know Ingrid, it became clear that her need to remain silent had little to do with any belief about the need for English teachers to suppress their response and, instead, privilege students' responses. Rather, the silencing of response emerged from fear of disclosure. Like most teachers who are gay or lesbian, Ingrid kept her sexual identity, and the entire life that she had developed with it, a secret. She had already suffered the consequences of an "outing" in a previous teaching position, and was terrified of another. Keeping her strong emotional response to *The Chrysalids* secret, therefore, was an act of personal protection. As a former secondary school English teacher and a gay man, I could easily identify with Ingrid. For most gay and lesbian teachers the role "teacher" needs to be carefully constructed and, for the most part, needs to remain distinct from any "non-teacher" identity. In both my experience and Ingrid's, every word uttered in the classroom was carefully censored, for it was important for us to never cross the line into the "personal." For both of us, pedagogical relationships were always developed around the "professional"—around discussions of the text, of student responses to the text, around themes announced by the text. For Ingrid, discussions of *The Chrysalids* occurred in the absence of the very close, intimate, and powerful relation that she had developed with the novel:

> *It's so easy to identify with the characters in the book as they grow into adulthood. Like me, they're people who have to keep secrets, to be on guard all the time, to lead a double life with two completely distinct and separate identities. I'm so emotionally caught up in this story!*

And so, although I knew that Ingrid had had a strong personal response to *The Chrysalids,* there was little evidence of this in her discussions of the novel with her students. Given the importance of the general themes emerging from this novel and the unit that it announced, I expected a great deal of class discussion. However, even when there was opportunity for this, students remained strangely reticent and withdrawn. Ingrid had commented on this in one of our early conversations:

> *This class doesn't discuss. They just won't talk to me or to each other about anything. Nothing I do to encourage them seems to work. I've just about given up trying to have a discussion about anything with this class.*

When I asked students why they were so reluctant to speak in class there was general agreement among them that their silence emerged, in large part, from an inability to know what to say—to know what was expected and what was appropriate. This was relatively unproblematic with lessons that emerged from the reading of texts of non-fiction or with lessons that dealt with topics about literary fictions (figurative devices, writing style, etc.), for in each Ingrid could be consulted for a "correct" response. However, when the literary fiction was used as the primary text for response and the kind of thinking that announced a location for reflective thought in the classroom, students felt some confusion about what was expected of them. Over time, I began to suspect that much of their silence in class had to do with Ingrid's silence. Although she was adept at framing discussions about the novel, at no point did she make any disclosures of her response to that novel. Michelle explained to me how she felt about this absence:

> *Why should I say how I felt about the book? Ms. Matisz doesn't say anything about how she felt! Maybe if I knew what she thought about it I might want to say more.*

Withholding is a form of counterfeiting. By withholding personal response to a literary fiction, the teacher is withholding all of her relations in the world connected to that response. She is withholding herself. This means that the identity that is brought forth in the school classroom is a wholly invented one. It is an identity that has been fictionalized through acts of suppression. As Deborah Britzman suggests:

> For those who leave this world to enter teacher education their first culture shock may well occur with the realization of the overwhelming complexity of the teacher's work and the myriad ways this complexity is masked and misunderstood. But what occurs as well is the startling idea that the taking up of an identity means suppressing aspects of the self. So at first glance, becoming a teacher may mean becoming someone you are not.[90]

When curricular relations are developed around discursive practices that situate teachers as persons who know and students as persons who must learn to know from teachers, the texts that mediate these relations simply become understood as fuel for the curriculum learning machine. In such instances the masking of the teacher's out-of-class identity is seldom problematic, for when learning is constructed as an object that exists between students and teachers, it is relatively easy for the teacher to stand outside of the engagement between learner and what is to be learned and to serve as a pedagogical tour guide. However, because the literary fiction depends upon the personal engagement of the reader in order for the literary imagination to become invoked, the school curriculum can less easily discount the teacher's relationship with the text. As discussed in earlier chapters, the meaning evoked by the literary imagination is not to be found in the reader or in the text, but in the *relations* between the reader and a world that contains that text and the reader.

This is an important point, for it helps to move us beyond the transactional model of reading, where the meaning is understood as a "third thing" between readers and texts, to an enactive understanding of reading where reading is understood as inextricable from the us/not-us relationship. The shift from transaction to enaction means that when theorizing the experience of reading we must understand that like all other components of our experience, literary meaning is always evoked amid the complex, ever-evolving relation readers have with a perceived world of significance. As I suggested in chapter four, we do not interact with things or persons one-by-one as they occur in our environment—our environment is comprised of everything that is not-us. When we read we do not form a relationship with some sort of free-floating thing called a novel, a poem, a short story. We form a relationship with a literary fiction that is part of a constantly evolving world of complexity. The text can never emerge independent from a context, nor can a context emerge apart from the text. The reader and the world of which the literary fiction is a part are re-invented through the act of reading.

Thinking about reading as inextricable from the unity of us/not-us helps us to understand the consequences of the counterfeit response in the school curriculum. It is not that students are unable to have a strong and deep relation with a work of literary fiction in the absence of knowledge about the teacher's response, it is simply that when the teacher's response is withheld, the relations among teacher and students become developed around the presence of an absence. Even if a response is invented for presentation in the classroom, because it is not connected to the teacher's actual reading of the text and her or his remembered world, it becomes a thin facsimile—a simulacrum—that begins to function as a third thing. Usually, however, as in Ingrid's case, the forgery exits in the withholding of the response. Whether this is done for purposes of professional neutrality or personal protection, it becomes a form of counterfeiting, for excluding the response means excluding anything but some fictionalized version of the person that is the teacher. It means that the teacher is not able to "point" to herself in discussion of the literary fiction. And when the teacher does not (or feels unable to) point to herself or himself, but only to her or his students and the literary fiction, students begin to believe that meaning occurs in the text, in knowledge about the text the teacher has, or in themselves. This formulation shows how closely the phenomenon of the counterfeit response to the literary fiction is connected to the fictionalizing (counterfeiting) of personal identity for presentation in the school classroom. One cannot present an invented response without constructing an invented identity.

These acts of counterfeiting lead to a type of curriculum touring. By excluding her or his personal response to the text, the teacher is not able to deeply explore with students the interpretive possibilities of the common-place location announced by the reading of a literary fiction. Because Ingrid did not feel able to reveal her personal response to this novel as it evolved with the ongoing classroom activities, a breach developed between Ingrid and her students, and between the students and a world that included her and the literary fiction. Because the literary fiction is only a component of the not-us world with which each student must maintain coherence in the classroom, it is impossible for students to ignore the teacher during class readings of the text. When the teacher discloses nothing of herself, she is unable to disclose much of her actual relation to the text, for the two are inextricable. It was a dilemma that caused Ingrid a great deal of stress:

Teaching this novel has affected me more than I ever thought that it would. I am finding it so hard to not tell students how I am feeling—not just about what happens in the book, but also what is happening with their response to it. I'm just so distressed that there are so many of them that don't seem to understand how they are implicated in the very same kind of oppressive social structures that are described in the novel. How can they begin to understand what it is like to be hated for just being who you are?

Despite this increasing anxiety, Ingrid felt compelled to continue to keep her non-teaching identity separate from her teaching identity. Because she was afraid of where any personal disclosures might lead, she chose to say nothing about her out-of-school life. Like my own experiences teaching in public schools, Ingrid neatly severed subject matter from the teacher and teaching identity from non-teaching identity. It was an act of subtraction which, like any act of "taking away," left a discernible breach in the relational fabric of the school classroom. Like many who bring the subtracted self into the classroom, Ingrid justified her decision by suggesting that it was the teacher's job to guide and direct, not to disclose and personally influence. However, subtraction has its consequences. In this situation, although Ingrid had hoped that the reading of this novel might help her students to see what they had previously not been able to see, it seemed to me that it was the counterfeit, subtracted self of the teacher that, at least in part, created an insurmountable perceptual barrier for some students. As Kyla explained:

> *I think that Mrs. Matisz is really good at teaching English. She knows more about the subject than any other teacher that I have ever had. And I don't mind coming to her class because I know that what I learn here will help me next year.... She really seems to care about this subject. But I don't think that she cares about me.*

I knew that Ingrid, like Anna, did not just care about the subject matter, but cared deeply for her students—the kind of pedagogical caring that Max van Manen has called "thoughtful and tactful" caring.[91] Van Manen has made an important distinction between the conventional uses of the word pedagogy.[92] He suggests that pedagogy must not be isolated from the idea of the "pedagogical relation" which, as he describes it, might help us to better understand how teaching is always a cultural activity steeped in various competing discursive practices. The pedagogical relation, under-stood in this way, does not merely depend on what the teacher knows or what the teacher does, but depends upon who the teacher *is*. The teacher's beliefs, her own virtues, her character, her relationship with a world that includes her students, must always be considered in any discussion of pedagogy. The teacher must not only guide learners through effective learning programs; the teacher must invest herself or himself into the complex set of relations that comprise the school curriculum.

It would seem difficult to establish and maintain the pedagogical relation that van Manen describes with the counterfeit identity—whether this is an identity of absence or whether it is a deliberate fictive construction. If we believe that our relations with each other and our world are embodied, historically-effected, and recursive, then we must believe that identity is inextricable from any relations we have in the world. In fact identity always co-emerges with the world of significance that we bring forward with others. If we believe this, then it becomes clear that the commonplaces for interpretation announced by shared readings of literary fictions will be considerably reduced if the teacher's relationship with the literary fiction is excluded. Furthermore, the literary imagination will not be able to function as it might in the school classroom that is ruptured by the exclusion of the teacher's relationship with it, for the absence of the relationship with the text requires the absence of the teacher's identity.

Even though the counterfeit identity is only meant to stand in place of the teacher's out-of-school identity, it cannot help but become a part of the teacher's life and the teacher's world. And so, the question of what teaching has done to teachers presents itself. And the question of what teaching has done to teacher's reading of literary fictions is again presented. For although the inclusion of the literary fiction in the school curriculum is meant to encourage out-of-school relationships with literary fictions, it seems that perhaps the opposite is being accomplished. Perhaps the kinds of relationships developed around counterfeit identities (for it is not just teachers who bring these to their school readings; students do too) have ruined us for out-of-school readings. Perhaps this is why some high school students who love to read at home, hate to read at school. And perhaps this is why many high school English teachers whom I know *only* read for school. Perhaps the counterfeit identity has, from years of teaching, finally gained dominance.

Unmasking

> *In Ortona she had held cigarettes to the mouth of the boy with no arms. Nothing stopped her. She had continued her duties while she secretly pulled her personal self back.*

Michael Ondaatje, *The English Patient*[93]

When I first started teaching this unit, and all these emotions came up, I thought that I would just do like always—subtract myself from them. But that hasn't been very easy. I'm not sure you can do that without causing a great deal of harm to yourself.

                                                                                        Ingrid

It is not surprising that beginning teachers experience a great deal of anxiety in the classroom, for the act of assuming the identity of "the teacher" has not yet become a habit. I have come to believe that beginning teachers construct a "fictive" teacher identity that functions as a bridge between conceptions of self that they bring to teaching and conceptions of themselves as "teacher" that eventually are developed with teaching experience. These "fictive" identities are, in large part, drawn from their experiences in university teacher education programs, memories of teachers they have had when they were in school, and various cultural beliefs about what teachers should be like. As Deborah Britzman suggests:

> In the case of learning to teach, cultural myths partly structure the individual's taken-for-granted views of power, authority, knowledge, and identity. They work to cloak the more vulnerable condition of learning to teach and the myriad negotiations it requires.[94]

The fictive identity becomes a mask worn by the beginning teacher—a mask that conceals and discloses at the same time. The non-teaching life of the teacher is concealed; the "teaching" identity is revealed. Beginning teachers who, in appearance, manner and lifestyle, closely conform to cultural expectations about teaching and teachers generally have little difficulty constructing a "fictive" identity that mediates between pre-teaching and experienced teaching identities. However, teachers who do not lead such lives—gay and lesbian teachers, for example—must construct a much more intricate and elaborate fictive identity, for the dissonance between pre-teaching experience and cultural expectations of "teacher" are great.

For most teachers, what was once the "fictive" identity eventually becomes transformed into a more internalized and coherent "lived" identity.[95] It is not surprising for teachers to take on "teacherly" qualities in their out-of-school lives and, as they gain confidence and experience, to bring their non-teaching identities into the classroom. The identity "teacher" eventually becomes integrated into all aspects of the individual's senses of self identity. Again, this is more true for some teachers than for others. For some, the mask "teacher" is always in evidence, both for the teacher and for the students. In discussions of our experiences as teachers, for example, Ingrid and I agreed that we were always aware of the fictive identities that we donned in order to negotiate our teaching lives. For both of us, the identity "teacher" was a carefully constructed one that, for the most part, remained separate from our non-teaching lives.[96] We both felt that even though we had assumed this identity for many years, it did not, for us, seem like our "real" selves. For us, assuming the identity "teacher" was a counterfeiting activity which we knew had consequences both for ourselves and for our students.

One of these consequences was that the development of a strong and well-developed fictionalized version of ourselves meant we became adept at maintaining classroom relations around attention to subject matter and not necessarily to the way in which subject matter was attached to us and to our students. When teaching literary fictions, however, we found this more difficult to do since, as discussed in the previous section, the literary fiction depends upon the personal response of the reader in order for meaning to become evoked. Even though we each were always able to "construct" some invented response to the text, or were successful in withholding responses to the text, we still felt that our out-of-school identities were more at risk of becoming unmasked during the process of reading literary fictions with our students. Generally speaking, we believed it was possible for us to simultaneously maintain "actual" and "counterfeit" responses to the literary text.

We also believed that many of our students, including those from Ingrid's class who read *The Chrysalids*, were able to accomplish this feat. It is possible for teachers and students to have a "personal" response to a literary fiction that remains private, and a schooled response that becomes used in the school curriculum. In fact, it is probably *desirable* for students to invent responses to literary fictions when these are read for school purposes. For although reader-response theories have been integrated into the philosophical underpinnings of most English language arts curricula, most classroom practices are still developed around excavating meaning from texts or from the teacher who apparently knows about the text. Most students in secondary schools quickly learn that it is the schooled response that is required in readings of literary fictions rather than a response that might emerge from their own imagination as conditioned by the literary fiction. Because most teachers have had similar reading experiences in both high school and university English courses, they too often gravitate toward the "schooled" response.

This phenomenon is apparent when listening to teachers talk about their reading of literary fictions which they might be considering for use in the classroom. My experience has been that teachers (and I include myself in this group) seem unable to talk about these books in the same way as they do about books that they read for their own pleasure. This became especially apparent in our reading group as we moved from discussion of *The English Patient* to discussions of young adult fiction. Although there was some discussion of how each of us felt personally about these books, the discussions were more oriented toward what we might *do* with these books rather than how we *were* with them. It seemed to me that once these books were announced as ones that might be used in the school curriculum, the literary imagination was suppressed by the need to read with the "teacher" identity. The schooled response gained dominance.

As Ingrid and I continued to discuss the connection between our relations with literary fictions and our relations with our students, it became clear to us that the construction of the fictionalized "teacher" identity and the "schooled" response to the literary fiction were inextricable. This insight raised some questions for us: What happens when one or the other of these is unmasked? What happens when it is discovered that identities and/or responses have been deliberately invented for school purposes? Is it important for teachers to be able to disclose to their students their actual response to a literary fiction that is read in the school classroom?

My experiences have led me to believe that teachers who construct pedagogical relations around a counterfeit identity seldom learn very much about their students, nor do students learn very much about them. This is likely why students are often surprised to see teachers shopping for groceries, swimming at the local pool, or going to a movie with a spouse, partner, or friend. The construction of teacher identity has effectively been removed from communal life and re-situated in some closed social construction we call the public school. As Madeleine Grumet has suggested, the classroom often becomes a "bunker" where teachers hide the work they care about behind the classroom door.[97] The trouble is, often only the self who is the teacher is allowed into the bunker, leaving the non-teacher self waiting outside that closed door. And although this other self—the one that is not the teacher—waits patiently, the day eventually comes when, after the final bell has rung and the classroom door is flung open, there is no other self waiting. Counterfeiting has its consequences.

Some teachers, however, are able to invite the other one into the classroom before closing the door. These are the ones who tell their students that they feel tired today because it was a rough night with a colicky baby. These are the ones who, like Anna, feel that it is okay to let their students know that when they read books they sometimes are emotionally moved by them, that they sometimes become politically motivated by reading them. They are the ones who let their students know that the reading of literary fictions, for them, is part of a life. And that is why teachers like Anna, who bring forth their actual identity into the school curriculum, are known to their students and know about their students.

When asked, Anna's students were all able to tell me many things about her out-of-school life. They knew about her husband, her daughter, where she lived, where she had vacationed, what her hobbies were, how she felt about political and social issues and so on. And Anna knew about her students. She knew about their living situations, their interests, their out-of-school lives. The pedagogical relation was not simply founded upon what one "did "; it was founded upon who one "was." Ingrid's students, however, were not able to tell me anything about her. Nor did Ingrid seem to know much about her students. The pedagogical relations between Ingrid and her students were largely founded upon knowing and doing. Although this point may seem trivial, it is, I believe, a difference that makes a difference during events of schooled reading of the literary fiction. When the lives of students and teachers are invited into the day-to-day activities of the classroom, the literary imagination is able to do its work.

My reading of *The English Patient* with other teachers helped me to understand this, for it was through this experience that I was reminded of the importance of fully dedicating oneself to a relationship with a text and to those with whom I was reading. Because our relationships with this text were meant to be shared in a communal situation, we needed to also dedicate ourselves to each other—and this meant that we needed to drop any fictionalized identities and responses that we might usually bring to schooled readings. However, this did not happen with all of us. It did not happen with me. Although there were members of the group who were certainly aware that my relationships with books were inextricable from my identity as a gay male, it is not something that I announced. And, like Ingrid, I deliberately either withheld responses I had to works of fiction we were discussing or invented responses that would allow me to continue to defer references to my gay identity. A type of counterfeiting.

However, it was not the reading group experiences that caused me great discomfort. Instead, it was the experience of sitting in Ingrid's class the day Tony came to class to talk about what it was like to live as a gay man that became almost unbearable. For although I had felt fairly comfortable in Ingrid's classroom on previous days, I felt exposed on that day. Even though I had dressed more conservatively than usual and sat at the back of the room rather than in the front corner where I generally sat, I still felt more visible than usual. I felt like I had on that first day of teaching at W. R. Myers School in Taber, Alberta , thirteen years prior when I overheard a student in one of my classes wonder out loud whether—like last year's music teacher whom they had tormented out of the school—I was gay too. That same wave of fear washed over me. And as I watched the students coming in the room making jokes about the fact that a "fag" would be in class that day, I could not help but wonder if they would notice that there were at least two of us. What would Tony tell them? Would students become more "tuned in" after his visit? Would I (and others) no longer be able to "pass" as straight?

But as I listened to Tony speak to the students about his life as an openly gay man occupying a very prominent public position in our community, I began to understand the importance of unmasking. And as Tony shared with the students how reading *The Chrysalids* had affected him, it became clear that this disclosure also affected Ingrid's students. They became more relaxed. Some who had demonstrated a well-developed homophobia began to participate in the class discussion in a way which indicated to me that they were seeing things that they had not been previously able to see. However, it was Karleen's question to Tony that seemed to finally open up the world that Ingrid had so desperately wanted her students to see:

Do people at work treat you normally?

It was a question that Tony did not answer. Instead, he paused for a moment, looked at all of the students and said:

> *The question is: "Do people at work treat me normally?" Do people treat me normally? Let me ask you that question: Are you treating me normally?*

There was silence. Uncomfortable silence. I know that I was uncomfortable even though I knew that this was the right question. And then a burst of response from the students and Tony:

> *What is normal? ... Well, that's the question! ... Am I being treated like other people? ... We're being just as polite as we were for other guest speakers.... But I'm not the same as other people.... Well, yeah—we are asking you different kinds of questions! ... So is that normal? ... But, we're not treating you badly or anything! ... No, not to my face, you're not! ... I know that I didn't know what to expect before you came, but now that you're here, I see things differently.*

Yes, I think that most of us "saw" things differently on that day, including Ingrid:

> *After Tony was here I realized how much of a difference it made that he was able to tell students about his own experiences and his own feelings. I have never heard them discuss like that before. They were like different people. And they seem to finally understand the book better. Having Tony talk about how he felt reading it really made a difference for some of my students.*

It made a difference for me too. It helped me to understand that although none of our relations in the school curriculum are really able to be neatly separated out, the relationship with the literary fiction, if it is to perform its culturally announced function, must be allowed its *gathering* function. Like the bridge which gathers up the banks, the river, and the world beyond any visible horizon, the literary fiction must be allowed to gather up the students, the teacher, their historically-effected experiences, their in-and-out-of-school-identities that co-emerge with these experiences—in an event of curriculum that *occasions*. And when occasioning is allowed during shared readings of literary fictions the literary imagination becomes what Iser has called a type of "literary anthropology" where our contemplated relationships with literary fictions reveal as much (or more) about us as about the text. This is the special function of the commonplace location announced by the act of reading a literary work of art.

Although one could argue that it was Tony's interaction with the students and not the literary fiction which was the difference that made the difference for these grade ten students, for Ingrid, and for myself, I would suggest that it was the space opened up by the invoked literary imagination that was the important difference. For although many of the students had not felt the experience of oppression by reading *The Chrysalids,* they had a map of a possible experience that was not there before their interaction with the text. And as Tony narrated his own experiences, the students were able to re-situate themselves (and their reading map) within the world of under-standing which they brought forth with Tony on that day. Jason explains:

> *When Tony talked about the phone calls he got—where people said that people like him should be shot, I thought about Sophie [from The Chrysalids] and how she was shot. And I thought about the Jews in World War II and the slides that Dayna showed us.*

Some students explained that the history of their interactions in their English classroom had not only changed their understanding, it affected their action in the world. Michelle spoke to me at length about how she had been affected:

> *At first I didn't get much out of the book. But after Tony came and told us how he had been beat up for being gay—how he got phone calls saying he should be shot, and how that made him feel, I began to think about this girl that my friends and I used to bug when we were in Junior High. We were really awful to her. Sometimes she would cry.... She goes to this school. I see her sometimes. I tried to say "Hi" to her the other day. But I don't think she likes me too much.*

This is what it is like to be able to see what one had previously been unable to see. The various activities occasioned by Ingrid in the location announced by shared readings of a literary fiction in the school curriculum led to a new path of understanding for many of the students. As an event of *currere,* this path did not, like the waterfall simply move forward, but moved backward and forward—allatonce. And through the history of interactions in the school curriculum, which included the literary imagination, structures were altered, perceptions were changed. The hermeneutic imagination was invoked. David Smith reminds us that:

> [T]he hermeneutic imagination works to rescue the specificities of our lives from the burden of their everydayness to show how they reverberate within grander schemes of things. Hermeneutics is about finding ourselves, which also, curiously enough, is also about losing ourselves.[98]

Like the game of hide and seek, losing and finding depend on one another and on the dedicated playing of its players. When the literary imagination is invoked as part of the school curriculum, and students and teachers are prepared to become lost for a time in the relations inspired by the text, the thrill of being found is announced. Experienced readers know that this is so. Hana knew it:

> She entered the story knowing she would emerge from it feeling she had been immersed in the lives of others, in plots that stretched back twenty years, her body full of sentences and moments, as if awaking from sleep with a heaviness caused by unremembered dreams.[99]

But we must wake up! We must shed the heaviness caused by unremembered dreams. We must learn how to see what we had previously been unable to see. And if this is to be accomplished through shared readings of literary fictions in schools, we, as teachers, must stop hiding behind talk *about* texts and start living through them with our students. That means re-discovering the self that stands behind the teacher.

It is an unmasking. But it is important. The importance of unmasking.

VII

Unskinning Curriculum

The past is not a language lost to the present, not a language sealed off in the unconscious, forever buried. It is here, and now, in the son I try to father, the friends I cherish, the students with whom I work, the books I read, the papers I write.

William F. Pinar[1]

In the essay from which this passage is taken, William Pinar[2] uses the interpretive location announced by his reading of David Leavitt's[3] book *The Lost Language of Cranes* to perform an autobiographical reading. For Pinar, autobiographical reflection is "not about wandering around in one's own house of mirrors, Narcissus-like, but remembering that the language we speak now derives from what and whom we saw through our windows as infants and children and young adults."[4] As hermeneutics teaches us, we are always already at the intersection of remembered, lived, and projected experiences. We are historically present beings. However, as Pinar reminds us, not all history is necessarily apparent to us—suppressions exist alongside expressions. What seems absent is always present.

Unfortunately, the school curriculum usually seeks to express what is readily available to everyday perception. Curriculum is a normalizing experience. Too often, curriculum is an exercise of sounding out other people's words. These words are generally ones that point to what is present—if not to the teachers, then to those who make decisions about what shall and shall not be taught. Teachers become tour guides, showing students which sites must be noticed. These sites, of course, become the images that become etched into the individual and collective identities of students and teachers. As a daily performance, teaching becomes a pointing ritual that seldom pierces underneath the skin of the everyday. I have suggested that there needs to be more poking, prodding and piercing of the familiar during events of schooling—more curriculum unskinning. Schools must become places to know the unknown and to say the unsayable.

In this book I have suggested that shared reading of literary fictions in schools has the potential to permit the unskinning of curriculum. I have also tried to show that schooling structures often militate against this possibility. Literary fictions that are meant to provide a space for autobiographical and cultural interpretation are usually stripped of these possibilities in schools and used, instead, as fuel for the curriculum learning machine. Although students may be able to explain the difference between a metaphor and a simile, they are often unable to interpret their involvement in the complex, continually evolving historical-present that I have called the ecology of us/not-us. The obsession with what is considered "the real" has created schooling events that suffocate the fantastical, the imaginative, the erotic, the not-present.

Because of this, schooling events have become repetitions of the familiar, which, in my view, are not the same as repetitions of the everyday. In schools, the everyday exists in the school corridor, but not usually in the classroom. It exists in the often unacknowledged relations among students, their families, their neighborhoods, their cultures—relations that are typically rendered invisible in the classroom. These are not always relations that are necessarily what might be considered "positive." All of us who have lived through events of public schooling know about the underbelly of school life. However, in schools the "visible," the "familiar," and the "possible" have become dominant discourses. Suzanne de Castell reminds us, however, that as educators it is our responsibility to find words to articulate the impossible. In her view teachers must

> speak not just about things that are difficult, or challenging, but about things that are impossible—voices that may not be heard; about dangers lived out daily; about what is not permitted to be seen or, if seen may not be acknowledged—or, if acknowledged, about the cost of that speaking.... [5]

As I have explained, however, before speaking out can occur, locations that re-arrange the familiar must be announced. Perception does not guarantee understanding. As biological and phenomenological creatures, we can only see what we can see. And so, I believe it is important for each teacher to create locations that occasion opportunities for re-viewing, re-interpreting, and re-conceptualizing. For me, locations such as these have been developed around shared readings of literary fictions and the critically interpretive practices associated with these. In this book I have attempted to show how I and other teachers have lived lives that have included some of these practices. Although I, following Patti Lather,[6] acknowledge that all re-presented experiences are partial tellings and, like her, do not believe them to be reproducible or generalizable, it is my hope that through the telling of these narratives of experience, windows into the imaginative (which is, for me, often synonymous with the impossible) have been created. Producing these interpretive opportunities in schools is important. As those of us who have worked in public schools know, immersion in the normalizing practices of schooling events has buried many of the openings that existed when we began our careers. Institutional rituals, particularly panoptic rituals, have anaesthetized life in schools. Even when the skin of the daily curriculum is pierced, many have become too numbed to notice. I have tried to show that interpreted engagements with works of literary fiction can transform the anaesthetic to the aesthetic. It is the move from not-art to art. And, because I concur with Susan Sontag who suggests that "art has the capacity to make nervous,"[7] I expect that these are not always spaces that are seen by many as "positive," nor are they necessarily places that are "safe." It is much easier and safer to point to what we find in the text than it is to point to what the text finds in us.

What about the space taken up by this book? For me, this collection of printed pages has become very much like the English patient's commonplace book. Beginning with my own and other's experiences, I have produced a text that offers some of my interpretations. In order to accomplish this task, I have needed to learn to not only include the practices of reading, teaching and researching in my life, I have had to learn to include the practice of writing. This has made a difference for me, since, as Natalie Goldberg suggests, "A writer's life is about self-examination."[8] And so, I have learned that in order to accomplish these hermeneutic interpretations and writings, I have had to live a life that is more meditative than the one to which I had become accustomed. As David Smith has suggested in his work,[9] and as he has demonstrated through the meditative life the he has developed with this work,[10] hermeneutic inquiry requires a contemplative attitude. Like Smith, for me this has meant confronting myself in relation to the ongoing experiences of reading, teaching, and researching. The work that has led to and included this writing has helped me to understand what Smith means when he suggests that hermeneutic inquiry must always be a form of personal inquiry:

> The conversational quality of hermeneutic truth points to the requirement that any study carried on in the name of hermeneutics should provide a report of the researcher's own transformations undergone in the process of inquiry; a showing of the dialogical journey, we might call it.[11]

Because this book was announced as a hermeneutic inquiry into reading and teaching, it is important for me to reconnect my personal journey to the interpretations that have been presented. The reader will likely have noticed, for example, that woven into my interpretations of reading and teaching literary fictions are the voices of those who are not me. It is important for me to say that although there are a number of these voices are of persons that I do not know personally, there are several whose lives have become woven into mine. These voices include those of the teachers with whom I have read and worked—Anna, Ingrid, Ruth, and Mena. Although many of the details of their lives have been fictionalized for purposes of confidentiality, for me, our many meetings and discussions continue to live in the collection of memories I call my life. Other influential voices are those of persons whose scholarship and friendship have been influential—Madeleine Grumet, William Pinar, Deborah Britzman, Rebecca Luce-Kapler, Terry Carson, Margaret Hunsberger, David Smith, Paula Salvio, Tom Kieren, Max van Manen (and many others). They include those voices who exist for me as books—Gadamer, Rosenblatt, Iser, Ondaatje, Derrida, Heidegger, Bruner (and many others). And, of course, they exist for me as fictional characters who now inhabit my world of remembered experience—Hana, Caravaggio, Kip, the English patient. All of these voices live alongside memories I have of other experiences—dinners I have eaten, movies I have seen, conversations I have had, teaching I have done. All of these voices, these readings, these experiences, are, in some way, collected in this book, for as Gadamer has suggested, our past is always caught up in our present and projected experiences.

As a reader, I am always curious about the specific conditions that surrounded the production of a written text—of the life that co-existed with the writing. And so, although I cannot know if the reader shares this interest, I will forge ahead and describe some of the conditions that co-existed with the writing of this book. Throughout all of the inquiries and the writing that have led to this book, I have lived and worked with my partner, Brent Davis, who teaches in the Department of Curriculum Studies at the University of British Columbia. During the months that included the writing of this book, Brent was in the process of writing his book on mathematics teaching.[12] We live in a ground-floor apartment condominium on the corner of Robson and Denman streets in the west-end of Vancouver, British Columbia, several blocks away from a large park called "Stanley Park" which sits on the edge of the mainland facing the Pacific Ocean. During intense periods of writing, we would rise, eat a cereal and toast breakfast while flipping through the *Vancouver Sun*, and then retreat to our respective offices (mine in the back of the apartment, his in the front) and sit in front of our computers until we could no longer bear to do so (usually about mid-day). On most days, I would head out for a run or walk through the park and on the seawall, returning to a lunch that we would prepare and eat together. In the latter part of our writing projects this seems to have consisted mainly of Campbell's tomato soup and tuna fish sandwiches. Over lunch, we would sometimes discuss what we had been writing that morning but, more often than not, we spoke very little. For us, writing seems to require rituals of silence. Afternoons usually included reading of materials relevant to whatever we happened to be writing, more writing, some re-writing, and usually a nap. Evenings included more of the same. We believe that Mary Catherine Bateson[13] is correct when she suggests in her book *Peripheral Visions,* that deep learning often means becoming obsessed with the topic of inquiry. We have often wondered why these obsessive rituals are not permitted in school. Of course, we have also learned that an element of obsession is distraction. Sometimes we would walk down Robson Street to the Blockbuster Video and rent a movie. And, on rare occasions, we would walk to Dede's or Delilah's for a martini (with two olives). Although our pets Sophie (a sealpoint Siamese), Finnegan (a lilac-point Balinese) and Scooter (a whippet) do not figure prominently in our writing, they are completely woven into our writing routines, always wandering in and out of our respective work locations, reminding us with a few insistent miaows or the nudge of a hound-nose that there actually is a life to be lived away from the computer screen.

Just as Anna's students found it impossible to separate what the teacher had told them from what was contained in *Forbidden City*, I find it finally impossible to extricate the words appearing in this book from the complex set of relations I have with others in the world. As Pinar suggests, "Engagement with the world ... keeps one eye looking out the window, where the worlds of past, present, and future collide in the chaos and order of the historical present."[14] Experience is always larger than expression. It spills over and slips between the words selected to account for it. However, not all words function in the same way. Not all sayings and not all readings do the same work. As I have attempted to show throughout this book, the locations announced by readings of literary fictions become the common-places through which we have an opportunity to grasp and interpret the complexity of our lived experiences. Therefore, although descriptions of writing rituals are not usually included in the pages of a text such as this, they are necessary if readers are to remember that all writing emerges from *particular* experiences, relations, and selections from the world.

Of course, there have been other events, other reading and writing rituals, that have influenced the formulations about reading and teaching that I have presented. While scanning my bookshelves for something to read on a rainy Sunday afternoon a few months ago, for example, (it rains a lot in Vancouver) I came across a yet-unread copy of Michael Ondaatje's poetry collection *The Cinnamon Peeler.*[15] I had bought this book some months prior while browsing the University of Calgary bookstore with my friend and colleague Rebecca Luce-Kapler. Now, Rebecca is a poet, and so when I go to bookstores with her I find myself standing in front of books of poetry. On that day, she surveyed the shelves and reached for Michael Ondaatje's The *Cinnamon Peeler.* Because I know that Rebecca likes Ondaatje's work, it was not surprising to me that she would immediately notice this book. And so, because I have learned to trust Rebecca's intuitions about books, I too reached for a copy of this book, already anticipating my engagement with it.

Upon returning home, however, the book somehow found its way from my backpack, to my desk, to the shelf with a number of other unread books. Like other times in my life, there seemed to be no time for reading amid the flurry of teaching, marking papers, painting the bathroom, and going to meetings. Until, of course, that rainy Sunday when I made myself comfort-able on the couch and began to read the first poem entitled "Light." Within a minute I was immersed in the world of the narrator/poet who tells of sitting on the front verandah in the middle of an electrical storm on a sultry summer night looking at old photographs of family. Vancouver rain-spatter on the window behind me became a steamy Ontario cloud-burst, Ondaatje's poetry appearing between flashes of lightning and claps of thunder:

> Midnight storm. Trees walking off across the fields in fury
> naked in the spark of lightning.
> I sit on the white porch on the brown hanging cane chair
> coffee in my hand midnight storm midsummer night.
> The past, friends and family, drift into the rain shower.
> Those relatives in my favourite slides
> re-shot from old minute photographs so they now stand
> complex ambiguous grainy on my wall.[16]

As I read and re-read this beautiful poem describing the way inter-generational memories become announced by family photographs, I had a memory flash of a photograph that I do not own, but which I vividly recall. It is a Polaroid snapshot of my mother Celia and her two friends Sophie (no, not the cat, another Sophie—and no, the cat was not named after this Sophie) and Isobel standing in the alley behind Park's Dry Cleaners after a long-day's work there. It was an image that stayed in my mind most of that day until I was finally provoked to open a file on my computer and write about it:

> I can't get the image of that photograph out of my mind. And, like Ondaatje
> suggests in the poem, the representation of the picture becomes a placeholder for
> a complex fabric of memories—memories that we continue to re-interpret each
> time we think about them in relation to new experiences.

"This is why we read fiction," I thought. We don't just read to add new knowledge or experiences to our lives, we read in order to find a location to re-interpret past experiences in relation to present and projected experiences. This is precisely what Ondaatje's poem had done for me. A commonplace location for interpretation was announced. Inhabiting this location was a memory of a picture. I did not even have the picture itself but, instead, a simulacrum—a copy with no original—floating around in my memories. Although I have not written much poetry in my life, it was this thought that provided the impetus for a poem that I eventually wrote. In fact, the title of it, "Three Women Pictured," came to me first; the lines seemed to write themselves. In interesting ways it is a poem about my mother's experiences, and yet, like all poems, all literary fictions, it transcends the specificity of the described event. I have reproduced it here:

THREE WOMEN PICTURED

    Three women pictured
linked arm in arm
purses tucked in elbow crooks
wrapped in nubbed cotton and smudged white duty shoes
wearing newly lipsticked camera-smiles
for Celia's husband Mike
              who captures them
    with the Polaroid camera
         in the alley
    near the back door of Park's Dry Cleaners
a five-o'clock city wind cooling the hot dampness of hair
pushing past skirts to the place where
the bones of girdles and brassieres cut deeply into soft flesh.

Like the pictures taken at Auschwitz they stand
smears of red around white teeth
bodies pressed together
looking through the dark cheek stubble of the photographer
    past the alley
        past the post office
            to the park of shadowed trees and clipped grasses
thinking that they should drop their arms and
        run
out of the alley
to the fountain-pool in the park,
           peel dresses, brassieres, girdles,
           Woolworth's nylons,
wade into the water and wash the sweat
        of other people's laundry,
        the grooves of tight clothing,
        the red lipstick from each other,
until they are once again plump and fresh and whole.

Three women pictured
in a wood-frame house with a purple garden
where they plant seeds of
> butter lettuce,
African marigolds,
> > ice beans,
> blood beets.
On scorched prairie nights
they sit together
in the cooling kitchen by the open aluminum door with the pheasant grill
a puff of breeze nudging soft linen dresses.

Now, this is not likely what my mother and her friends were thinking while standing in the alley having their picture taken (although it may be). I do know, however, that there were many times over those difficult years when she wished for an easier life—one removed from the daily work in the dry cleaners. And so, I suppose that like most immigrant women who arrived in Canada after World War II, my mother and her friends likely thought of fleeing the difficulty of their lives. And, as the poem sponsored by my memory of this photograph unfolded, I began to wonder about the connection among my sense of self, my parents, my historical situation, the pictures that depict events from these, and the "fragments" that announce the interrelation among them. All of these fragments were becoming collected in the commonplace location announced by my reading of Ondaatje's poem "Light." Of course, that event of reading, of memory, of response, of writing, of interpretation, is situated alongside the circumstances of my life which have led to the writing of this book.

Paulo Freire has suggested that when we read the word we read the world.[17] Reading is not merely an act that facilitates the accumulation of knowledge; reading becomes an act of interpreting the complex world of intertextual relations. Reading announces a specific location in which the reader is able to discern the usually invisible and uninterpreted relations among herself or himself in the world. In his book *Occupied Reading*, Alan Block[18] has shown that reading is more than a process of naming and pointing to the world: for Block, reading the text means inventing the self. He writes:

> [R]eading is a creative process ... [W]hat is created in reading is the reader and the text s/he reads. A pedagogy of reading can do nothing less than permit the reader to come to being not by teaching reading but by permitting its being learned.[19]

Each new reading is a new invention. Following Freire and Block, I have suggested that reading the word is a reading of the world and of the self. I have also suggested that the experience of reading literary fictions is a particular kind of world/self reading. Literary fictions have a very specific cultural function. Like other art forms, the literary fiction is meant to condition our imagination and our experience so that remembered, lived, and projected experiences in the world are understood differently. Like our reading group's reading of *The English Patient,* Ingrid's class's reading of *The Chrysalids,* and Anna's class's reading of *Forbidden City*, my reading of Ondaatje's poem "Light" created a set of conditions that facilitated personal and cultural interpretation. A commonplace location was announced that became more complex and elaborate as I continued to integrate various experiences and interpretations of those experiences into that location. This literary experience, then, was not a vicarious experience but, because it contributed to continued interpretations of my involvement in the us/not-us relation, was inextricable from other experiences I have had. When the commonplace location came to include intergenerational memories of my family's histories, and the composing and interpreting of "Three Women Pictured," a focal practice began to take form. The material evidence of the poem on paper became a way for me to better understand my involvement in history and the present ecology of communal life.

As a newly formed cultural object, this poem is not merely a personal re-symbolization of my own readings. Because it now exists in the world, it, like other literary fictions, becomes part of the complexity of any reader's us/not-us relation. As a teacher, it is important for me to continue to remind myself that curriculum must be understood as an intertwining of mutually specifying relations among students, texts, teachers, and contexts. It is not so much the study of any of the components of curriculum that is illuminating, it is the study of the relations between and among these components. Applied to the study of reading of literary fictions in schools, this suggests that it is not the text or the reader or the teaching that should be interpreted, but the relations among these.

For me, it has become clear that the study of these reader-text-teacher-context relations function as what Iser has called a "literary anthropology"[20] where, through the process of interpreting the text, the reader interprets her or himself. And, because the literary fiction is *always* read in relation to the world, it is impossible for readers to read texts and to interpret themselves without interpreting the world of significance that readers bring forth with others. As Block[21] has explained, these mutually specifying actions occur within a complex ecology of intertextual and interpersonal relations. This is, of course, not only true for student readers, it is true for teachers who read with students. Even if the teacher has read a literary fiction many times prior, each reading with a new class is always a new reading. As I suggested in chapter one, even though I had read *Bridge to Teribithia* with many other classes over a number of years, it was one particular reading with one particular class during one particular period in my life that provoked a wholly new and unanticipated personal response.

It is time, however to stop writing and to end this book. Like the ending of the life of anything, however, there needs to be ritual. I would like to offer the ritual of reinterpretation, of reclaiming that which was announced at the beginning of this book and offer a re-reading of it in relation to what has been presented in the intervening chapters. I would like to return to my initial wondering about my unanticipated emotional response to *Bridge to Teribithia* while reading it aloud to my grade seven class. In my initial reporting of that response, I indicated that, although the response became apparent to my students, I felt unable to discuss it with them. Although the response was announced, it remained uninterpreted. An uninterpreted *hap* we might say. But, in the end, although it occurred years later, it was this hap that inspired me to investigate the experience of sharing readings of literary texts with students in places we call school. And so, although I initially expressed some concern about the fact that this hap remained uninterpreted, I have come to understand that, hermeneutically speaking, interpretation need not be immediate. In fact, hermeneutic interpretation is likely *not* to occur in action. Hermeneutic reflection and interpretation requires time. It requires meditation. It requires a hermeneutic location.

What, then, might I say about this event within the interpretive location announced by this text? What has this research and this writing taught me about that moment? Hermeneutics teaches us that experiences must be understood in terms of their historically-effected circumstances and so, before this question is explored, an excavation of that moment in time is necessary.

As already mentioned, this public oral reading occurred during a time when our school staff and I were still mourning the loss of our school Principal. And, certainly, this must have contributed to my feelings of empathy for Jesse and Mrs. Myers. But I knew then, and I know now, that there were other events that contributed to that response. That reading occurred during the 1986-87 school year in a mid-sized rural school in southwestern Alberta. Now, this part of Alberta is farming country. The people are hardy, steadfast, resolute. They live in a geographical location that is hot, dry and windy in the summer, cold and unforgiving in the winter. It is a stark land, with little ornamentation. The geography is flat, definite, obvious, straightforward. It is the prairie, and on the prairie little is hidden. There is no-where to hide. As my mother told me forty years after emigrating to this land from the south of Germany: "It is a place where I feel exposed and confined. I have never felt comfortable here."

Tourist brochures call it "Big Sky Country." The sky *is* big. It looms. It watches over a definite land. And so, it is not surprising that over the last hundred years this land has attracted persons who were also definite. Christian fundamentalism and right wing politics seem to go well with the land. Being right is important. Being definite. Knowing the way things should be. Including the way the land should be. This once-arid desert-like environment was forced to grow things that it was not meant to grow. New crops became possible because the rivers were dammed, the water collected and allowed to trickle through the prairie grasses. It is important to be definite. It is important to know the way things should be. The land submits; it yields: corn, onions, potatoes, sugar beets.

The rhythm of the school year was marked by the sugar beet season. In late spring it was easy to identify students who lived on farms where sugar beets were grown. They arrived at school sleepy and tired, for sugar beets need to be watered frequently in the spring and many farmers still had to move the irrigation pipes manually. Every four hours—10 p.m., 2 a.m., 6 a.m. The pipes needed to be moved on time, because, of course, it is important for things to occur on time. The land is recalcitrant; it resists submission. And later in the spring—in late May and early June—the sugar beets needed to be thinned. "Hoeing beets," it was called. This was back-breaking, low-paying labour which was largely done by seasonal workers. Some were Mexican Mennonites who traveled north after working the winter in the California vegetable fields. Sometimes their younger children came to school for a month. They spoke a strange combination of German, Spanish and English. We were never really sure what to do with them. Some of them lived in the "beet shacks" that dotted the fields.

My Polish father and German mother emigrated to southern Alberta in the early 1950s. After two years of working as farm laborers in southern Saskatchewan, they took their few possessions and three hundred dollars they had saved, drove to the city of Lethbridge in southwestern Alberta and purchased a tiny two-room house. It was a beet shack that had been moved to the edge of town. Because they had no more money and because banks were unwilling to lend to immigrants (displaced persons or DPs they were called), they built a new house around this shack using discarded materials from the old Municipal hospital that was being torn down. Each night after work they would drive their old Vauxhall to the construction site and fill the trunk and backseat with whatever they could salvage. It was my mother's task to chip the old mortar off the bricks and old tiles and to pull the nails from the boards. Tiles from the operating room that once collected blood-spatter were used to cover the walls of the downstairs shower stall.

In October the sugar beets were harvested and deposited in piles the size of small mountains alongside the highway that took me to school each morning. After a week or two they began fermenting. On cold mornings alcoholic steam rose from those gray-brown beet mountains. The sugar factory was one kilometer from the junior high school where I taught. I could see it and smell it from my classroom window. In the mid-eighties it was discovered that it cost more than twice as much to grow and process sugar beets than the sugar was worth. Only government subsidies allowed beet farming to remain profitable and these subsidies were in danger of being lost. A large delegation of farmers went to Ottawa to protest the loss of a livelihood. Sugar beets are still grown in southern Alberta. It is important to be definite. It is important to be right. It takes a ton of sugar beets to produce a small bag of sugar. It is important that the land yield.

Many of my students belonged to the Church of Jesus Christ of Latter Day Saints, more commonly known as the Mormons. Most Mormon teenagers attended seminary every morning for one hour before school began. One day before class, I overheard two grade nine girls discussing their lesson from that morning. For homework they had been asked to think about what they would do if they found themselves in love with "Norman the non-Mormon." I asked them if they thought they would marry Norman. "Definitely not," they said. It is important to be definite. It is important to be right. It is important to yield. The same girls told me that once they finished high school they would go to Brigham Young University in Provo, Utah. They were going to pursue a degree in Home Economics. In the staffroom I had heard some of the teachers (Mormon and non-Mormon) say that young women went to BYU to pursue their MRS. Every now and then over the years I would find a copy of *The Book of Mormon* on my desk with pages marked for me to read. I had a collection of them in the bottom drawer of my filing cabinet. Unread. It is important to be definite.

Our deceased principal had not identified himself as Mormon and, as far as I knew, did not attend any church. However, he had gone to BYU many years prior on a basketball scholarship. Upon his sudden passing, the local Mormon community kindly took care of all the funeral arrangements. Before Don's funeral on that unseasonably hot day in May, I had not set foot in a Mormon church. It seemed strange seeing him in that place. I had purchased a new tie for the funeral and felt choked by it.

In his novel about life in a small prairie town, W. O. Mitchell writes about the way in which the people of the town were depicted in the local newspaper:

> In the pages of the *Shelby Chinook* the people of the town and district lived blameless lives. They neither raped nor were raped. They were heterosexual. They held rodeos and church suppers, ran curling bonspiels, turkey shoots, community bingo games, bridge and whist parties; they paraded and observed three minutes of silence on Remembrance Day, and danced at Thanksgiving, Hallowe'en, New Year's, and Valentine's Day. They became engaged, married, went into hospital, and were born always in wedlock, died of old age, accident, or sickness, but never of suicide or murder. From railways, chartered banks, implement firms, the civil service, and grain elevator and lumber companies they were transferred or retired; they did not embezzle, nor were they ever debauched, disrobed, or defrocked.[22]

It is important to be right. It is important to be definite.

During that same year in southern Alberta a dozen or so men died of complications from AIDS. This was not a well-known statistic, for one did not often hear people speak of such things. Unless it was related to some tasteless joke told by one of the junior high kids or, on occasion, by one of the teachers. Those jokes, along with ones about "fags" and "lezzies" was the one form of hatred that was generally approved in our school. And so, it was not surprising that when David, a young man who had graduated from the local high school ten years prior, died at his parents home after a long battle with AIDS, no-one seemed to know about it. At least I heard no-one speak of it. Although human sexuality was taught as part of the health curriculum, the section about homosexuality was deleted. It is important to be definite.

In this writing I have tried to show the way in which literary fictions are always read in relation to the world which announces them. They always exist in a location. And, like Heidegger's image of the bridge, the literary fiction has the potential to gather up the experiential landscape around it. It has this ability, not because of what it *is,* but because of the way it is allowed to stand in the world. It is, at the same time, familiar and strange, and it is this very juxtaposition of known and unknown that allows experience to become re-organized. And so, it is not surprising that when readers become part of a location gathered up by a literary fiction, unexpected responses occur.

I have also tried to show how what is silenced, what is deferred, what is marginalized, and what is invisible is an absence that is always present. This includes the invisible landscape that exists with our readings of literary fictions. It includes the histories that we bring into places like classrooms, and it includes the history of interactions that comprise our lived experience in those classrooms. Therefore, although the curriculum is something deliberately designed to provoke, to point out, to illuminate, at the same time, it is something that silences, hides, covers. There is much that is covered during events of curriculum. Unskinning seldom occurs.

Although we often pretend that literary fictions are read vertically, I have tried to show that they are not. Any literary fiction has a life that exists in the horizontal and vertical landscape of our experience in the world. And so, it is important to understand that reading *Bridge to Teribithia* to a group of grade seven students from Taber, Alberta, under the shadow of the sugar factory, in the presence of the memory of the dead, in the middle of a school day which included a censored health curriculum, after the fact that my parents lived in a beet shack, alongside readings of *The Book of Mormon*, was a re-reading of a world and a re-reading of a self.

Most of all, I have tried to show that when private readings of literary fictions become public, the usual configuration of remembered, lived, and projected experiences in the school classroom become reorganized. The literary fiction, because it asks the reader to perceive differently in order for meaning to be evoked, sometimes alters the world of significance that is brought forth with others. And so, there are times during the reading of a literary fiction when we suddenly notice (but often only briefly) that a new vista of perception and understanding has been illuminated. And we respond. Sometimes these responses uncover previously unnoticed components of the world. Sometimes unskinning occurs. When this happens the reader notices. It is a difference that makes a difference.

Notes

I.   A Life that Includes Reading

1.   Sylvia Ashton-Warner, *Teacher* (New York: Simon and Schuster, 1963), 33.
2.   Ibid.
3.   For example: J. A. Appleyard, *Becoming a reader: The experience of fiction from childhood to adulthood* (New York: Cambridge University Press, 1990); Madeleine Grumet, "Lost places, potential spaces and possible worlds: Why we read books with other people," *Margins* 1, no. 1 (Spring 1991): 35-53; Margaret Hunsberger, "The experience of re-reading," *Phenomenology + Pedagogy* 3, no. 3 (1985): 161–166; Margaret Hunsberger, "The time of texts," in *Understanding curriculum as phenomenological and deconstructed text*, edited by William F. Pinar and William M. Reynolds (New York: Teachers College Press, 1992); Max van Manen, "Phenomenology of the novel, or how do novels teach?" *Phenomenology + Pedagogy* 3, no. 3 (1985): 167–181.
4.   Katherine Paterson, *Bridge to Teribithia* (New York: Harper and Row, 1977).
5.   Ibid., 124–125.
6.   Cynthia Chambers explains how shared readings of literary texts reintegrate public and private experiences in teacher education classes. In her article, "Student journals: Private lessons in public" (in *WestCAST Proceedings*, edited by Louisa M. Kozey and Caroline D. Krentz [Regina, SK: Saskatchewan Instructional and Development Research Unit]), she writes: "I invite reflection through children's literature and its exploration of the phenomenology of the lived experience of being a child and of being human. One of my intentions in reading a children's novel aloud to the class is to demonstrate good language arts practices.... On the other hand, these novels themselves and my oral interpretation of the text 'bear witness' to things that matter most in our lives—the experience of friendship, of death, of being a student" (163). (The article has been revised and reprinted as "Private lessons in public," *Analytic Teaching* 42, no. 4 [1992]: 37–42.)
7.   Hunsberger, "The time of texts."

8.   Natalie Goldberg, *Long quiet highway: Waking up in America* (New York: Bantam Books, 1993), 92.

9.   I offer a fuller explanation of this in chapter four.

10.   Maurice Merleau-Ponty, *Phenomenology of perception*, translated by Colin Smith (London: Routledge), xx.

11.   Martin Heidegger, *Being and time*, translated by John Macquarrie and Edward Robinson (New York: Harper and Row, 1966). I offer a fuller explanation of some of Heidegger's ideas in later chapters.

12.   Alan Lightman, *Einstein's dreams* (Toronto: Alfred A. Knopf, 1993).

13.   Gordon Mills, *Hamlet's castle: The study of literature as a social experience* (Austin: University of Texas Press, 1976), in Jerome Bruner, *Actual minds possible worlds* (Cambridge, MA: Harvard University Press, 1986), 45.

14.   Wendell Berry, "The futility of global thinking," *Harpers* (June, 1990): 22.

15.   Albert Borgmann, *Crossing the postmodern divide* (Chicago: The University of Chicago Press, 1992).

16.   Ibid., 119.

17.   Ursula Franklin, *The real world of technology* (Concord, ON: Anansi, 1990).

18.   Madeleine Grumet, *Bitter milk: Women and teaching* (Amherst: University of Massachusetts Press, 1988), 136.

19.   Richard Bach, *Jonathan Livingston Seagull* (New York: Macmillan, 1970).

20.   Antoine de Saint-Exupéry, *Le petit prince* (Bourges, France: Editions Gallimard, 1946).

21.   Madeleine Grumet, "Lost places, potential spaces and possible worlds."

22.   All names of persons and places used in this book are pseudonyms. As well, in order to ensure anonymity, some details about persons and places have been changed.

23.   My interest in action research was initially sparked by a course I took on the subject from my doctoral supervisor, Terrance Carson. In that course we read John Elliott's *Action research for educational change* (Milton Keynes: The Open University Press, 1991); William Carr and Stephen Kemmis' *Becoming critical: Education, knowledge and action research* (Philadelphia: The Falmer Press, 1986); Stephen Kemmis and Robin McTaggart, editors, *The action research planner* (Victoria, Australia: Deakin University Press, 1988); Terrance Carson and Jean-Claude Couture, editors, *Collaborative action research: Experience and reflections* (Improvement of instruction series, monograph no. 18,

Edmonton, AB: Alberta Teachers' Association, 1988); as well as a number of articles written by researchers in Canada, Great Britain, and Australia on the subject of action research. I found, however, that I was most influenced by a one hour talk given by Ted Aoki, Professor Emeritus from the University of Alberta, who helped me to understand how we always "enter into the middle of things." Good research, he suggested, is like a good life. It requires commitment, dedication, thoughtfulness—all of which require a dedication to that for whom and among which we live.

24. Early in my research process Margaret Hunsberger warned me about getting involved in hermeneutic/phenomenological work: "Be prepared to live with a lot of ambiguity!" I have thought of those words many times during the past couple of years!

25. Madeleine Grumet, "Bodyreading," in *Bitter milk*, 145.

26. Roland Barthes. *S/Z* (New York: Hill and Wang, 1974).

II. Schooling the Literary Imagination

1. Wolfgang Iser, *The fictive and the imaginary: Charting literary anthropology* (Baltimore: The Johns Hopkins University Press, 1993), 21.

2. William Bell, *Forbidden city* (Toronto: Doubleday, 1990), 52.

3. Peter Rabinowitz, in *Before reading: Narrative conventions and the politics of interpretation* (Ithaca: Cornell, 1987), outlines the culturally determined "rules" which enable the author-text-reader transaction. Although these rules are in a constant flux and evolution, his careful explication of these as used by contemporary authors and readers helps to de-mystify and de-romanticize the process of text-reader interaction. Rabinowitz discusses four major "rules": 1. Rules of notice (to help readers determine what is important and what is not); 2. Rules of signification (to help readers decide the source, the ethical value, the kind of attention to give the rules of notice); 3. Rules of configuration (textual conventions that help readers to make transitions between disparate bits of the story in relation to their own experience); 4. Rules of coherence (the reflective activities that readers impose on the text, helping them to see the work as a whole).

4. Susanna Moodie, *Roughing it in the bush* (Toronto: McClelland and Stewart, 1962). It is noteworthy that Margaret Atwood, in *The journals of Susanna Moodie* (Toronto: Oxford University Press, 1970)—a book of poems based on Susanna Moodie's writings—had this to say about the reading which inspired her to write her collection:

> Although I had heard of Susanna Moodie I had never read her two books about Canada, *Roughing it in the Bush* and *Life in the Clearings*. When I did read them I was disappointed. The prose was discursive and ornamental and the books had little shape: they were collections of disconnected anecdotes. The only thing that held them together was the personality of Mrs. Moodie, and what struck me most about this personality was the way in which it reflects many of the obsessions still with us." (62)

Which, then, more clearly re-presents the truth of Susanna Moodie's life in the Ontario wilderness: her own written work, or the poetic interpretations of Margaret Atwood? Or is "truth" to be found in the dialogue which (implicitly) exists between the two?

5.   Anne Frank, *Anne Frank: Diary of a young girl* (New York: Pocket Books, 1958).

6.   Margaret Hunsberger told me of her experience of visiting China after having read *Forbidden City*. She said that in her drive from the airport to Beijing, she was surprised to notice that the actual arrangement of bushes and trees by the side of the road did not correspond to the mental image that she had constructed from reading the novel. In our conversation about these dissonant images, we wondered which was more real for her, concluding that fictional imaginings and constructions became as much a part of our memories and experiences as those which are actually lived.

7.   As part of the process of researching this chapter, I browsed through a dozen or so English language arts "methods" textbooks (those produced for use in teacher education) and, to my surprise, found that most took for granted that "literature" meant "fiction," several made a distinction between "fictional and non-fictional" literature, and only one rendered problematic the idea of "literature" as "literary."

8.   Terry Eagleton, *Literary theory* (Minneapolis: University of Minnesota Press, 1983).

9.   For a selection of provocative essays on the intersection of poetics, aesthetics, politics, philosophy and ethnography see *Writing culture: The poetics and politics of ethnography*, edited by James Clifford and George E. Marcus (Los Angeles: University of California Press, 1986).

10. See, for example, Clifford Geertz, *Works and lives: The anthropologist as author* (Stanford, CA: Stanford University Press, 1988); Deborah Britzman, "The Question of Belief: Writing Post-Structural Ethnography," *Educational Theory* 8, no. 3 (1995); and Norman K. Denzin and Yvonna S. Lincoln's introduction to their edited book, *Handbook of qualitative*

research (Thousand Oaks, CA: Sage, 1994).

11.   Described in I. A. Richards, *Practical criticism* (New York: Harcourt Brace, 1929).

12.   See J. A. Appleyard's *Becoming a reader* for an insightful description of this and other phenomena related to the experience of reading.

13.   Susanne Langer, in *Problems of art* (New York: Charles Scribner's Sons, 1957), equates the virtual in creative objects as a space created by the artist (or in this case the author) which is "new in the sense that it never existed before" (29). Wolfgang Iser, in *The act of reading* (Baltimore: The Johns Hopkins University Press, 1978)—his phenomenological account of reading—implies this use of virtuality within the fictional text itself when he says that "the meaning of a literary text is not a definable entity, but, if anything, a dynamic happening" (22) and when he explains that "literary texts initiate 'performances of meaning' rather than actually formulating meaning themselves" (22).

14.   Langer, *Problems of art*, 149.

15.   Ibid., 148.

16.   I am grateful to Susan Pirie for this phrase. I use it here to describe the location announced by the conditioning, but not overly determining, quality associated with engagement with a literary fiction.

17.   Jerome Bruner, Actual minds, possible worlds.

18.   Ibid., 13.

19.   Ibid.

20.   Ibid., 26.

21.   Tzvetan Todorov, *The poetics of prose* (Ithaca: Cornell University Press, 1977).

22.   As first described in *The act of reading*. For Iser, the literary text exists "primarily as a means of communication, while the process of reading is basically a kind of dyadic interaction" (66). In reading, the reader is required to reduce the indeterminacies that exist between the text and the reader, and the text and reality, and to build a situational frame which will encompass her/himself and the text. Through the structuring and ordering of signifiers, the author creates a text in which the potential reader is to interact. The fulfillment of this interaction occurs when the reader applies his/her reading skills to the already constructed language of the text. The situation is not found in the text, but rather in the interaction between reader and text. If the author has been skillful, the reader will be able to use his or her reading skills to engage in the text in a manner which facilitates that sort of construction. The reader, then, must carefully follow the textual clues in order to form the sort of horizontal reality that is

derived from the interaction of his or her understanding of the text combined with her or his own experiences. The text, then, establishes a guiding framework for this interaction, one in which "author and reader are to share the game of imagination" in which the text becomes "a set of governing rules" (108).

23. Barthes, in *S/Z*, argues that the literary text, if it is to summon up the reader's imagination in a way which becomes productive rather than merely re-productive, must be "writerly" rather than "readerly." For Barthes the writerly text is one which requires that readers engage in indeterminacy filling constructions, while the readerly are those which are over-determined, didactic, allowing little space for the reader.

24. Bruner, *Actual minds, possible worlds*, 25.

25. Although she does not explicitly align herself with the hermeneutic phenomenology of Heidegger or Gadamer, it is clear that her theory of meaning-making is compatible with Heidegger's Dasein and Gadamer's insistence that coming to an understanding of this being can only occur through a dialectical hermeneutic where understanding of Self and Other occurs through questions that present themselves in conversation, for it was through Rosenblatt that the "conversation" between text and reader gained priority and prominence.

26. Louise Rosenblatt's *Literature as exploration* (New York: Appleton-Century, 1938), written in the heyday of the new critical movement, was revolutionary in its alliance with the philosophy of John Dewey and the progressive education movement of the time. See John Willinsky's *The new literacy* (New York: Routledge, 1990), esp. 99–104, for an excellent summary.

27. Louise Rosenblatt, *The reader, the text, the poem* (Carbondale, IL: Southern Illinois University Press, 1978).

28. Rosenblatt, *Literature as exploration*, 212.

29. John Dixon, *Growth through English* (Oxford: Oxford University Press, 1967).

30. Interestingly, in her own discussions and responses to her first reading of the novel, Anna, his teacher, also seemed pre-occupied with the efferent. In her case, however, her efferent reading seemed to be conditioned by the fact that she wished to use this novel as the basis for a teaching unit. Although in later conversations emerging from a group reading of the novel, she demonstrated a more personal involvement with the book, emerging largely from some parallels between the characters' political struggles and her own wranglings with political oppression in her school, the "efferent" always remained foregrounded in her comments.

31. See the chapter entitled "Adolescence: The reader as thinker," in J. A. Appleyard's *Becoming a reader*, 94–120.
32. Hans-Georg Gadamer, *Truth and method* (2nd revised edition), translated by Joel Weinsheimer and Donald Marshall (New York: Crossroad, 1990).
33. In *Truth and method*, Gadamer states that "understanding is, essentially, an historically effected event" (300). For him, this meant that all of the traditions of the past (as carried in the language we learn) pre-conditions and effects our present consciousness. Gadamer suggests that historical effect means "that we cannot extricate ourselves from it in such a way that the past becomes completely objective for us.... We are always situated in history.... I mean that our consciousness is determined by a real historical process, in such a way that we are not free to simply juxtapose ourselves to the past." Cited by Shaun Gallagher, *Hermeneutics and education* (Albany, NY: SUNY Press, 1992), 90.
34. Gadamer, *Truth and method*, 88.
35. Joel Weinsheimer, in his book *A reading of "Truth and method"* (New Haven, CT: Yale University Press, 1985), explains that Gadamer began with a discussion of aesthetics because he realized that "An aesthetics that would be more adequate to the full scope of art must surpass the pure aesthetic judgment—in Gadamer's view and Kant's ... Gadamer does not transcend aesthetics by viewing it from above; rather, in his interpretation of Kant, aesthetics transcends itself. There can be no free play of imagination if understanding are thus reaffirmed as the surplus by which art exceeds pure aesthetic judgment" (83).
36. Gadamer, *Truth and method*, 163.
37. Because this concept deals more with the experience of reading, than the condition of the literary work of art itself, I will elaborate on these ideas in chapter three in my discussion of the experience of reading.
38. Gadamer, *Truth and method*, 97–98.
39. Jacques Derrida, *Acts of literature* (New York: Routledge, 1992).
40. Ibid., 73.
41. Ibid., 37.
42. Ibid., 44.
43. Jacques Derrida, *Positions*, translated by Alan Bass (London: Athlone, 1981), 70.
44. Derek Attridge, in his introduction to Derrida's *Acts of literature*, 16.
45. Such as in the judicial system where the meaning of the law is always considered in relation to the specific application of the law and at the same time the general meaning of the law.

46. Especially in E. D. Hirsch's book, *The aims of interpretation* (Chicago: The University of Chicago Press, 1976).

47. Derrida, *Acts of literature*, 64.

48. Ibid., 74.

49. As Martin Heidegger explicated in his seminal work *Being and time*.

50. The students' teacher told me that the students seemed unable to understand the experience of living in a non-democratic country. Although they could recite clichés of democracy (equal opportunity, freedom of speech, etc.) they did not really seem to understand that embedded within democratic ideals were necessary constraints for individuals. At the same time, they found it virtually impossible to understand how one could not "choose" a career in Communist China. These ideas seemed to become much clearer for students after they had "lived through" the experience of reading the novel, which, one could suggest, points to the importance of the virtual in understanding the "real."

51. Wolfgang Iser's writings include *The implied reader* (1975), *The act of reading* (1978), *Prospecting: From reader response to literary anthropology* (1989), and *The fictive and the imaginary* (1993), all published by the Johns Hopkins University Press, Baltimore.

52. Iser, *Prospecting*, 10 (emphasis added).

53. Ibid., 28–29.

54. Such as the conceptual literary art of Jenny Holzer who rents electronic signs in places such as Times Square in New York City, and flashes across the screen reflections such as "Fathers often use too much force," "Money creates taste," or "Go where people sleep and see if they're safe." The matter is discussed by John Willinsky in *The new literacy*.

55. Iser, *The fictive and the imaginary*, 11–12.

56. Hans-Georg Gadamer, *Philosophical hermeneutics*, translated and edited by David E. Linge (Los Angeles: University of California Press, 1976), 8.

57. Gadamer's use of the word "spiritual" here seems to refer to the importance of being tuned into the invisible connections between human subjects and their world.

58. David Smith, "Hermeneutic inquiry: The hermeneutic imagination and the pedagogic text," in *Forms of curriculum inquiry*, edited by Edmund C. Short (New York: State University of New York Press, 1991), 196.

59. Ibid., 195–196.

60. Hans-Georg Gadamer, *Philosophical hermeneutics*, 13.

61. Plato, in *The republic* (Oxford: Clarendon Press, 1945), attacked art and the artist on two fundamental issues. In the first place, Plato not only viewed the artist as an imitator, he believed that the product of the artist's

technique is an imitation of an imitation. The artist borrows his or her subject matter from another art, and moreover, is ignorant of the function of the art he or she copies. Secondly, Plato believed that the poet invoked the emotions in a dangerous way, making persons who should be controlled by reason mastered by passion.

62.   Smith, "Hermeneutic inquiry," 188–189.

III. Tracing Intertextual Desire

1.   Ondaatje, *The English patient*, 12.
2.   *The English patient* won the prestigious Booker Award (1992) as well as the prized Canadian award, The Governor General's Gold Medal for Literature (1992).
3.   There are numerous editions of Herodotus' *The histories* in circulation. The one that I eventually used as a reference was the translation by Aubrey de Sélincourt (Middlesex, UK: Penguin, 1954).
4.   Ibid., 13.
5.   Walter Ong, *Orality and literacy: The technologizing of the word* (New York: Methuen, 1982).
6.   Forms of this "oral tradition" still exist (although less and less) in unwritten "family stories" that are passed from one generation to the other. Oftentimes artifacts such as family heirlooms and photographs serve as "collecting places" for these stories.
7.   Aristotle, *On poetry and music*, translated by S. H. Butcher (New York: Bobs-Merrill Co., 1948).
8.   No one is sure of the dates. I have chosen these from a span suggested by John Gould in his explication of *The histories* (Herodotus [London: Weidenfeld and Nicolson, 1989]) and Aubrey de Sélincourt's introduction to his translation of *The histories*.
9.   This is discussed by Norman K. Denzin and Yvonna S. Lincoln in the introduction to their edited collection *Handbook of qualitative research*, 2–3.
10.   Ibid.
11.   Following his teacher Franz Brentano's work, Edmund Husserl formed the idea that consciousness is intentional or possesses intentionality. For Brentano and Husserl, intentionality indicated the way in which the human subject is inextricably connected to the world. Consciousness, then, is always about something, even if it is something which is imagined or remembered (i.e., something not immediately given in the world). All

human consciousness, all human thinking and action, therefore is intentional; it is about something. All human activity and thinking is oriented to something and, at the same time, directed by that which orients it. For clear explications of Husserl's complex philosophy of the transcendent ego and intentionality, see Max van Manen's *Researching lived experience* (New York: State University of New York Press, 1990) and Michael Hammond, Jane Howarth and Russell Keat's *Understanding phenomenology* (Oxford: Blackwell, 1991), particularly chapter 2, "Intentionality and meaning," 44–70.

12. James Michener, *Poland* (New York: Random House, 1983).

13. Ondaatje, *The English patient*, 16.

14. For the English patient, The histories was both literally and figuratively a prosthetic device. Figuratively, it served as a "space" for ideas developed both in his "real world" and in his imagination. This is how most of us use literary texts; they become "cognitive prostheses" for the "extra" we cannot hold in our own minds. For the English patient, however, the book became a prosthetic device in a more literal way since his extensive burns left his body more or less dead; the book became a bodily extension of his very-much alive mind.

15. Geoff Fox, "Dark watchers: Young readers and their fiction," *English in Education* 13, no. 1 (1979). The concept of the "Dark watcher" emerged from an interview which Geoff Fox had with one reader who, in discussing her interaction with a novel, positioned herself as "stand[ing] apart, watching from the shadows" (32). In his analysis of this comment, Fox theorizes that the reader is not merely incidental to the story, but "is the power, not the text: her sensitivities are playing upon the novel and without her the story could not develop" (32).

16. Ondaatje, *The English patient*, 39.

17. Ibid., 222.

18. René Descartes, *Discourse on method and Meditations on first philosophy*, translated by Donald A. Cress (Indianapolis: Hackett Publishing Co, 1980).

19. These are all exceedingly complicated questions which are dealt with, in greater detail in the next chapter where I present some of the literature on cognition and the mind.

20. Jean-Paul Sartre, *Being and nothingness*, translated by Hazel E. Barnes (New York: Pocket Books, 1956).

21. Ondaatje, *The English patient*, 94.

22. Sartre, *Being and nothingness*, 344.

23. These ideas have been summarized from my own reading of chapters one and two of Part III of *Being and nothingness*, with considerable interpretive assistance from the translator Hazel Barnes' introduction to the book, and Michael Hammond, Jane Howarth and Russell Keat's book *Understanding phenomenology*, in which the importance of the work of Sartre, Husserl, and Merleau-Ponty to phenomenological inquiry is explained.

24. This is commonly referred to as "assuming another role" when in a different context. The problem with this "role switching" formulation is that it does not really account for the importance of the relation with "the Other" in these changed behaviors in concert with the change of "location." Changing location changes our relations with the Other, not just because there are differing "social" conditions, but also because there are "spatial" differences. This is why moving to a new city can put a strain on personal relations, particularly if the move is to a very different geographical and temporal location: changes in environment require changes in behavior, which necessarily require changes in the architecture of personal relationships. The way in which "place" becomes fused with "self" also helps us to understand why personal relations are difficult to maintain when partners live in different cities. There is a sense, over time, that there is a "movement away" from the other, which is often accounted for by pointing to "absence." Although absence from the Other is likely a factor in relational disintegration, it is also likely true that the two partners become distanced not by absence, but by the way in which the "place" the "location" of each Self has become woven in and through them.

25. In her introduction to Sartre's *Being and nothingness*, translator Hazel Barnes explains the important distinction Sartre makes between a "sense" of conscious Self as derived from the Ego and the situations that make this sense possible: "According to Sartre, the Ego is not in consciousness, which is utterly translucent, but in the world; and like the world it is the object of consciousness. This is not, of course, to say that the Ego is material but only that it is not a subject which in some sense manipulates or directs consciousness. Strictly speaking, we should never say 'my consciousness' but rather 'consciousness of me'" (xii). For Sartre, consciousness always overflows the "I" which tries to contain it, for consciousness is always related to other consciousness in the world, to which we cannot have direct access. Therefore, although we "experience" our own consciousness, we can never really own it.

26. Merleau-Ponty, *Phenomenology of perception*.

27. Ibid., 347–348.

28. Heidegger, *Being and time*.

29. Merleau-Ponty, *Phenomenology of perception*, 354.
30. Ondaatje, *The English patient*, 261.
31. Merleau-Ponty, *Phenomenology of perception*, 361.
32. Ondaatje, *The English patient*, 194.
33. The distinctions between the use of jouissance by Lacan and Kristeva is explained by Leon S. Roudiez, translator of Julia Kristeva's *Desire in language* (New York: Columbia University Press, 1980), viii. In a forward to Barthes' *The pleasure of the text* (New York: Hill and Wang, 1975), Richard Howard explicates the process of translation used by Richard Miller, making the same distinctions between English and French understandings of jouissance as made by Roudiez. Therefore, although there are important differences between all three writers' (Barthes, Lacan, Kristeva) usage of jouissance, it seems appropriate to suggest that they all meant the term to include physical, emotional, sexual, and cognitive allusions.
34. As coined by Jacques Derrida, différance suggests an alternative to thinking in terms of simple presence. According to Derrida, différance is neither a word nor a concept, but points to a possibility of meaning. This complicated Derridean formulation is clearly explained in Brenda K. Marshall's *Teaching the postmodern* (New York: Routledge, 1992). She writes: "Différance is that which marks and makes possible the passage from one term of opposition to another, and which indicates that each term resides within the other" (75), and goes on to quote Derrida: "One could reconsider all the pairs of opposites on which philosophy is constructed and on which our discourse lives, not in order to see opposition erase itself but to see what indicates that each of the terms must appear as the différance of the other, as the other different and deferred in the economy of the same (the intelligible as differing-deferring the sensible, as the sensible different and deferred; ... culture as nature different and deferred, differing-deferring)" (cited on page 75). Derrida's complete essay, "Différance," is in his *Margins of philosophy*, translated by Alan Bass (Chicago: University of Chicago Press, 1982), 1–27.
35. Ludwig Wittgenstein, in *Philosophical investigations*, translated by G. E. M. Anscombe (New York: Macmillan, 1953), uses the term "language games" to explain why various utterances may be explained/ defined in terms of rules specifying their properties and the uses to which they can be put. Three observations he makes about these games are (1) their rules do not carry within themselves their own legitimation, but are the object of a contract, explicit of not, between players; (2) if there are no rules there is no game; (3) every utterance should be thought of as a move in a game.

36. Jean-François Lyotard, in *The postmodern condition: A report on knowledge* (Minneapolis: Minnesota Press, 1984), argues that the ordinary use of discourse in personal conversation and that which is validated in institutions are played according to radically different sets of rules. Within the former "the interlocutors use any available communication, changing games from one utterance to the next" while in the latter "supplementary constraints for statements to be declared admissible" are always required" (17). It is the additional "game-rules" that delimit and constrain personal conversation and alternate "ways of knowing" that support the imperialism of the grand discourse of scientific rationalism, marginalizing the playful quality of conversational discourse.

37. Foucault's theories about the "limit experience," and the way his views about this changed over his lifetime are discussed in James Miller's biography of Foucault, *The passion of Michel Foucault* (New York: Simon and Schuster, 1993).

38. Gadamer, *Truth and method*, esp. 269–277.

39. Ondaatje, *The English patient*, 217.

40. Ibid., 218.

41. Gadamer, *Truth and method*, 102.

42. Ibid., 103.

43. Ibid., 108.

44. Iser, *Prospecting*, 34.

45. Ondaatje, *The English patient*, 136–137.

46. Ibid., 139.

47. Jane Flax, in *Thinking fragments: Psychoanalysis, feminism and postmodernism in the contemporary west* (Berkeley: University of California Press, 1990), discusses her psychotherapeutic work with patients suffering from "borderline syndrome." "Borderline patients," she suggests, "lack a core self without which the registering of and pleasure in a variety of experiencing of ourselves, others, and the outer world are simply not possible" (218). She criticizes postmodern theorists' call for a "decentered self" as "self deceptively naive and unaware of the basic cohesion within themselves that makes the fragmentation of experiences something other than a terrifying slide into psychosis.... Borderline patients' experiences vividly demonstrate the need for a core self and the damage done by its absence. Only when a core self begins to cohere can one enter into or use the transitional space in which the differences and boundaries between self and other, inner and outer, reality and illusion are bracketed or elided" (218–219).

48. Post-structuralist theorists (particularly Derrida) would reject this

formulation, insisting that there are not borders in language, and therefore any borders in lived experience are illusory. The "desert" metaphor, as it is played out in the balance of this chapter, however, demonstrates more clearly my position between structuralism and post-structuralism.

49.   Michael Ondaatje, *The English patient*, 231.

50.   Ibid., 145.

51.   Such as the work of Jacques Derrida, particularly *Of grammatology*, translated by G. Spivak (Baltimore: The Johns Hopkins University Press, 1976), and *Writing and différance*, translated by A. Bass (London: Routledge and Kegan Paul, 1978); Umberto Eco's *Travels in hyper reality*, translated by William Weaver (San Diego: Harcourt, Brace, Jovanovich, 1983); and Jean-François Lyotard's *The postmodern condition*.

52.   As cited by Pauline Rosenau in *Postmodernism and the social sciences* (Princeton: Princeton University Press, 1992), 97.

53.   This is likely one of the reasons why persons who lose their personal belongings through fire, earthquake, tornado, divorce, feel separated from themselves. It can also account for our desire to carry with us "artifacts" such as photographs, books (I find it impossible to part with books that I have read and loved), for there is a sense the book, the photograph, the Christmas ornament from our youth, contains part of the Self. We remember and know ourselves in and through these artifacts.

54.   See *The Kristeva reader*, edited by Toril Moi (New York: Columbia University Press, 1986).

55.   Ibid., 14.

56.   Ibid.

57.   Julia Kristeva, *Revolution in poetic language*, translated by Margaret Waller (New York: Columbia University Press, 1984).

58.   Cited in Toril Moi (editor), *The Kristeva reader*, 93–94.

59.   Ibid.

60.   Ibid., 110. For Kristeva the "thetic" refers to the primordial moment of language when the signified and the signifier collect into some form which has meaning. The uttering of a word or a sentence is a thetic moment.

61.   Ondaatje, *The English patient*, 136.

62.   Grumet, from the essay "Bodyreading," in *Bitter milk*, 136.

63.   Toril Moi (ed.), *The Kristeva reader*, 112.

64.   Sartre, *Being and nothingness*, 400.

IV. Reading as Embodied Action

1. Ondaatje, *The English patient*, 233.
2. Ibid., 229.
3. Ibid., 36–37.
4. Actually, Margaret Atwood's *Cat's eye* (Toronto: McClelland and Stewart, 1988) was our second choice, and had it not been for the fact that The English patient had just won the Booker prize, we likely would have read it instead.
5. Richard Rorty, in *Contingency, irony, and solidarity* (New York: Cambridge University Press, 1989), makes use of the philosophy of language developed by Donald Davidson to explain that what we consider "literal" language is primarily a set of "dead metaphors" that have been literalized through common usage and that it is only by inventing new metaphors that we will be able to understand our literalized world differently. (See especially pages 13–20.)
6. Ondaatje, *The English patient*, 48.
7. Ibid., 4.
8. Humberto Maturana and Francisco Varela, *The tree of knowledge: The biological roots of human understanding* (Boston: Shambhala, 1987).
9. Francisco Varela, Evan Thompson, and Eleanor Rosch, *The embodied mind: Cognitive science and human experience* (Cambridge, MA: The MIT Press, 1991).
10. These influential texts were introduced to me by Thomas Kieren, professor of mathematics education at the University of Alberta, Canada. It was during a doctoral seminar led by Tom that I came to more deeply understand some of these ideas and, with his support and assistance, develop some of the theory presented in this chapter.
11. My understanding of Gadamer's work was greatly enhanced and influenced by discussions of *Truth and method* that I had with my colleagues Brent Davis, Rose Montgomery-Whicher, Brenda Cameron, Hans Smits, Terry Carson, and Vimbi Nhundu.
12. Maturana and Varela, *The tree of knowledge*.
13. Varela et al., *The embodied mind*, 198.
14. Ibid., 196.
15. Ibid.
16. This of course is represented by the popular "conduit" model of communication offered in many language arts textbooks.
17. For a concise explication of the history of hermeneutics see Richard E. Palmer, *Hermeneutics* (Evanston, IL: Northwestern University Press,

1969).

18.   Marvin Minsky, *The society of mind* (New York: Simon and Schuster, 1986).

19.   Varela et al., *The embodied mind*, 172–173.

20.   Maurice Merleau-Ponty, *The primacy of perception* (Evanston, IL: Northwestern University Press, 1964).

21.   In his essay "The child's relations with others" (in *The primacy of perception*, 96-155), Merleau-Ponty highlights the essence of the bodily relationship that we have to the world and to each other: "The enigma is that my body simultaneously sees and is seen. That which looks at all things can also look at itself and recognize, in what it sees, the 'other side' of its power of looking. It sees itself seeing; it touches itself touching; it is visible and sensitive for itself" (152). In this essay, Merleau-Ponty becomes very Sartrian (see chapter three), reinforcing Sartre's idea that we can only know our Selves through the relations that we have with others, and the others can only know themselves through their relations with us. It is indeed a continual circle of understanding.

22.   Merleau-Ponty, *Phenomenology of perception*, 430, as cited by Varela et al. in *The embodied mind*, 4.

23.   For Heidegger, "Being" forms the ontological ground for all human understanding. In *Basic writings* (San Francisco: HarperCollins, 1977), he defines it as "Being is always the Being of an entity" (29). By this he means that Being is different from being in that Being is the opening created in being through which all objects may become present. In other words, what distinguishes human beings from other living entities is that human beings are able to reflect on their own existence. Human beings have the capacity to think about what it is to "be."

24.   Martin Heidegger, *Being and time*.

25.   In his essay, "The question concerning technology" (in *Basic writings*, 283—318), Heidegger suggests that each thinker goes a way that is uniquely her or his own, and that this way is built through questioning. He suggests that "Questioning builds a way. We would be advised, therefore, above all to pay heed to the way, and not to fix our attention on isolated sentences and topics. The way is a way of thinking" (283). By this, he means that it is the way and not the individual person that assembles what is thought that provides the structure of a person's thinking and allows her or him to see everything in a particular relation to everything else.

26.   As described in *Truth and method*, 306–307.

27.   Varela et al., *The embodied mind*, 150.

28. Oliver Sacks, "A neurologist's notebook: To see and not see," *The New Yorker*, 10 May 1993, 59–73.

29. Varela et al., *The embodied mind*, 183.

30. Ibid., 195.

31. Ibid.

32. Madeleine Grumet, "Lost places, potential spaces and possible worlds."

33. Ong, *Orality and literacy*.

34. For a useful summary see chapter five of Stephen Bonnycastle's *In search of authority: An introductory guide to literary theory* (Peterborough, ON: Broadview Press, 1991).

35. Most prominent of the New Critics were F. R. Leavis, *New bearings in English poetry* (London: Chatto and Windus, 1950 [1932]) and I. A. Richards, *Practical criticism*.

36. First described by W. Wimsatt and M. Beardsley, "The intentional fallacy, the affective fallacy," in *Critical theory since Plato*, edited by Hazard Adams (New York: Harcourt, Brace, Jovanovich, 1958).

37. Ferdinand de Saussure, *Course in general linguistics*, translated by Wade Baskin (London: Fontana, 1974 [1916]).

38. Northrop Frye, *Anatomy of criticism: Four essays* (Princeton: Princeton University Press, 1957).

39. Particularly Jacques Derrida with his influential *Of grammatology*.

40. For an excellent summary of deconstruction see Sharon Crowley's *A teacher's guide to deconstruction* (Urbana, IL: National Council of Teachers of English, 1989).

41. As Norman Holland first described in his book *The dynamics of literary response* (New York: Oxford University Press, 1968), and later in *Five readers reading* (New Haven: Yale University Press, 1975).

42. David Bleich, *Subjective criticism* (Baltimore: The Johns Hopkins University Press, 1978).

43. First appearing in Rosenblatt, *The reader, the text, the poem*.

44. Iser, *The act of reading*, 128–129.

45. Iser, Prospecting (1989); *The fictive and the imaginary* (1993).

46. Ondaatje, *The English patient*, 12.

V. Bringing Forth a World of Understanding

1. Smith, "Hermeneutic inquiry," 201.

2. Ibid.

3. Ibid., 189.

4. Gregory Bateson, *Steps to an ecology of mind* (New York: Ballantine Books, 1972), 315.

5. Gadamer, *Truth and method*, esp. 269–277.

6. Gary Madison, *The hermeneutics of postmodernity: Figures and themes* (Bloomington, Indiana University Press, 1988), 189.

7. Paulo Freire, *Pedagogy of the oppressed* (New York: Herder and Herder, 1970).

8. David Jardine, "Reflections on education, hermeneutics, and ambiguity: Hermeneutics as a restoring of life to its original difficulty," in *Understanding curriculum as phenomenological and deconstructed text*, edited by William Pinar and William Reynolds (New York: Teachers College Press, 1992), 116.

9. Gadamer, *Truth and method*. In his introduction, Gadamer explains the fundamental circularity between the ideas of truth and method, insisting that neither truth nor method can pre-exist one another, but rather, must always co-arise together through the process of living through a world.

10. Martin Heidegger, *Basic writings*, 113–142.

11. Gadamer, *Truth and method*, 432.

12. Rorty, *Contingency, irony, and solidarity*, 5.

13. Ibid., 6–7.

14. Smith, "Hermeneutic inquiry."

15. Jardine, "Reflections on education, hermeneutics and difficulty."

16. Maturana and Varela, *The tree of knowledge*; Varela et al., *The embodied mind*.

17. Madeleine Grumet, "Curriculum and the art of daily life," in *Reflections from the heart of educational inquiry: Understanding curriculum and teaching through the arts*, edited by George Willis and William Schubert (Albany, NY: State University of New York Press, 1991), 74.

18. Ibid.

19. Jacques Derrida, *Of grammatology*. See chapter three for a more detailed description of the Derrida's use of the word différance.

20. Charles Taylor, *The malaise of modernity* (Concord, ON: Anansi, 1991).

21. Albert Borgmann, *Crossing the postmodern divide*.

22. Ibid., 7.

23. Ibid., 12.

24. Sartre, *Being and nothingness*.

25. Merleau-Ponty, *Phenomenology of perception*.

26. Anthony Kerby, *Narrative and the self* (Bloomington: Indiana University Press, 1991).

27.   Jean Clandinin and Michael Connelly have attempted to render visible the
       largely de-legitimized and often invisible work of teachers by developing
       methods of narrative inquiry. For a good overview see Michael F.
       Connelly and D. Jean Clandinin, *Teachers as curriculum planners:
       Narratives of experience* (New York: Teachers College Press, 1988) and
       D. Jean Clandinin and Michael F. Connelly, "Teacher as curriculum
       maker," in *Handbook of research on curriculum*, edited by Philip W.
       Jackson (New York: Macmillan, 1992).
28.   Kerby, *Narrative and the self.*
29.   Smith, "Hermeneutic inquiry."
30.   Ibid.
31.   Ibid., 196.
32.   Ibid., 188.
33.   Ibid., 201.
34.   Although they do not specifically describe bricolage as hermeneutic
       Denzin and Lincoln, in the introduction to their edited collection
       Handbook of qualitative research, explain the importance of this approach
       to qualitative research in a postmodern era.
35.   Gadamer, *Truth and method*, 383.
36.   Ted Aoki, *Inspiriting curriculum and pedagogy: Talks to teachers*
       (Edmonton, AB: University of Alberta Press, 1991), 7–10.
37.   Gadamer, *Philosophical hermeneutics*, 12.
38.   Roland Barthes, *S/Z.*
39.   Brent Davis, in *Teaching mathematics: Toward a sound alternative* (New
       York: Garland Publishing, 1996), discusses the need for teaching and
       research into teaching to move away from metaphors of "telling" to those
       of "listening."
40.   Ondaatje, *The English patient*, 139.
41.   I later learned that this was one of the reasons two members dropped out.
42.   Ibid., 117.
43.   Jerome Bruner, *Acts of meaning* (Cambridge, MA: Harvard University
       Press, 1990).
44.   Borgmann, *Crossing the postmodern divide.*
45.   Francis Bacon, *The great instaurition and New Atlantis*, edited by J.
       Weinberger (Arlington Heights, IL: Harlan Davidson, 1980).
46.   Descartes, *Discourse on Method.*
47.   John Locke, *Treatise of civil government and a letter concerning
       toleration*, edited by Charles L. Sherman (New York: Appleton-Century-
       Crofts, 1965).
48.   Borgmann, *Crossing the postmodern divide*, 25.

49.   Ibid., 41.

50.   Ibid., 45.

51.   As promoted by literary theorists Bleich in Subjective criticism, Stanley Fish in Is there a text in this class? (Cambridge, MA: Harvard University Press, 1980), and Holland in *The dynamics of literary response.*

52.   Bleich, *Subjective criticism.*

53.   Fish, *Is there a text in this class?*

54.   Ondaatje, *The English patient,* 195.

55.   As discussed by Nancie Atwell in *In the middle: Writing, reading and learning with adolescents* (Upper Montclair, NJ: Boynton Cook, 1987); T. Cairney and S. Langbien in "Building communities of readers and writers," *The Reading Teacher* 42 (1989): 560–567; Donald Graves in *Writing: Children and teachers at work* (Portsmouth, NH: Heinemann, 1983); and Constance Weaver in *Understanding whole language* (Toronto: Irwin, 1990).

56.   As depicted in Carr and Kemmis, *Becoming critical,* and in Elliott, *Action research for educational change.*

57.   1991 edition.

58.   Bruner, *Acts of meaning.*

59.   Ibid., 131.

60.   Ondaatje, *The English patient,* 94.

61.   Hunsberger, "The time of texts," 64.

62.   Deborah Britzman, *Practice makes practice: A critical study of learning to teach* (New York: State University of New York Press, 1991).

63.   This stylized list represents "bits" from a number of comments made by all of the readers in our group.

64.   For example, Bill Corcoran, "Reading, re-reading, resistance: Versions of reader response," in *Reading and response,* edited by M. Hayhoe and S. Parker (Milton Keynes: Open University Press, 1990); Suzanne de Castell, Allan Luke and Carmen Luke, editors, *Language, authority , and criticism: Readings on the school textbook* (New York: Falmer, 1989); E. A. Flynn and P. P. Schweickart, editors, *Gender and reading: Essays on readers, texts and contexts* (Baltimore: The Johns Hopkins University Press, 1986); Elaine Showalter, editor, *The new feminist criticism: Essays on women, literature, and theory* (New York: Pantheon, 1985).

65.   Margaret Mackey provides an insightful discussion of this phenomenon in her article "The Many Faces of Resistance," *English Journal* 82 (1993): 69–74.

66.   Varela et al., *The embodied mind.*

67.   Ondaatje, *The English patient,* 157.

68. It is important to understand that, although I have listed "living and perceiving" one after the other, I do not mean that the former causes the latter. Rather, they co-emerge together (mutually specify one another).

69. I develop this idea more fully in my article "Of seagulls and glass roses: Teachers' relationships with literary texts as transformational space," *JCT: Journal of Curriculum Theory and Classroom Practice* 10, no. 3 (1994): 153–182.

70. Grumet, *Bitter milk*, 144.

71. Ibid., 96.

72. Heidegger, "Building Dwelling Thinking" (in *Basic writings*, 319–340).

73. Ibid., 326.

74. Ibid., 332.

75. Ibid., 330 (original emphasis).

76. Ondaatje, *The English patient*, 117.

77. Ibid., 8.

VI. Laying Down a Path While Walking

1. William Pinar and Madeleine Grumet, *Toward a poor curriculum* (Dubuque, IA: Kendall Hunt, 1976).

2. Philip Jackson, "Conceptions of curriculum and curriculum specialists," in *Handbook of research on curriculum*, edited by Philip Jackson (New York: Macmillan, 1992), 3.

3. For example, James Macdonald, "Curriculum theory," in *Curriculum theorizing*, edited by William Pinar (Berkeley, CA: McCutchan, 1975) and Hilda Taba, *Curriculum development: Theory and practice* (New York: Harcourt, Brace and World, 1962).

4. Kieran Egan, "What is curriculum?" *Curriculum Inquiry* 8, no. 1 (1978): 65–72; and Elliot Eisner and Elizabeth Vallance, editors, *Conflicting conceptions of curriculum* (Berkeley, CA: McCutchan, 1974).

5. John Goodlad, "Curriculum as a field of study," in *International encyclopedia of education*, volume 2, edited by Torsten Husen and T. Neville Postlethwaite (Oxford: Pergamon, 1985).

6. Joseph Schwab, "The practical: Arts of eclectic," *School Review* 79, no. 4 (1969): 493–542.

7. William Pinar, William Reynolds, Patrick Slattery, and Peter Taubman, *Understanding curriculum* (New York: Peter Lang, 1995), 848.

8. John Dewey, *The child and the curriculum* (Chicago: University of Chicago Press, 1956 [1902]), 5.

9. William H. Schubert, *Curriculum: Perspective, paradigm, possibility* (New York: Macmillan, 1986), 72.

10. John Dewey, *Democracy and education* (New York: Macmillan, 1966 [1916]).

11. Franklin Bobbitt, *The curriculum* (Boston: Houghton Mifflin, 1918).

12. Franklin Bobbitt, *How to make a curriculum* (Boston: Houghton Mifflin, 1924).

13. Bobbitt, *The curriculum*, v.

14. Ibid., 41.

15. Ralph Tyler, *Basic principles of curriculum and instruction* (Chicago: University of Chicago Press, 1949).

16. Pinar et al., *Understanding curriculum*.

17. Herbert Kliebard, *The struggle for the American curriculum, 1893–1958* (New York: Routledge, 1986).

18. Schubert, *Curriculum*.

19. Tyler, *Basic principles of curriculum and instruction*, 128.

20. Schubert, *Curriculum*.

21. W. W. Charters, *Curriculum construction* (New York: Macmillan, 1923).

22. Henry Harap, *The changing curriculum* (New York: Appleton-Century, 1937).

23. Harold Rugg, *Curriculum making: Past and present* , *Twenty-sixth yearbook of the National Society for the Study of Education, part 1* (Bloomington, IL: Public School Publishing, 1926); and *The foundations of curriculum-making, Twenty-sixth yearbook of the National Society for the Study of Education, part 2* (Bloomington, IL: Public School Publishing, 1926).

24. In Jackson, "Conceptions of curriculum and curriculum specialists"; Kliebard, *The struggle for the American curriculum*; and Schubert, *Curriculum*.

25. Schwab published four influential essays on curriculum over a fourteen year period: "The practical: A language for curriculum," *School Review* 78 (1969): 1–23; "The practical: Arts of eclectic" (1971); "The practical 3: Translation into curriculum," *School Review* 81, no. 4 (1973): 501–522; "The practical 4: Something for curriculum professors to do," *Curriculum Inquiry* 13 (1983): 239–265.

26. William Pinar, editor, *Curriculum theorizing: The reconceptualists* (Berkeley, CA: McCutchan, 1975).

27. Pinar announces this in the introduction to *Curriculum theorizing*.

28. Pinar, in the essay "Currere: Toward reconceptualization" (in *Curriculum theorizing*, 396–414).

29.   Pinar and Grumet, *Toward a poor curriculum.*
30.   Ibid., 45.
31.   Ibid.
32.   For a full description of this, see William Pinar's essay, "The method of currere" in *Autobiography, politics and sexuality* (New York: Peter Lang, 1994).
33.   William Pinar, in Pinar and Grumet, *Toward a poor curriculum*, ix.
34.   For a summary of the contribution of Pinar's reconceptualist work, as well as an excellent review of the use of autobiography in educational inquiry, see Robert Graham's *Reading and writing the self: Autobiography in education and the curriculum* (New York: Teachers College Press, 1991).
35.   This is discussed in Varela et al., *The embodied mind*, particularly in chapters 10 and 11.
36.   Anne Berthoff, *The sense of learning* (Portsmouth, NH: Heinemann, 1990), 86.
37.   See James Gleick, *Chaos: Making a new science* (New York: Penguin, 1987), for an accessible description of chaos theory.
38.   See David Smith's collection of essays, *Pedagon: Meditations on pedagogy and culture* (Bragg Creek, AB: Makyo press, 1994), as well as his most recent essay, "Interpreting educational reality," in *Hermeneutics in educational discourse*, edited by H. Danner (Durban, SA: Butterworths Press, 1995).
39.   Joel Weinsheimer, *Gadamer's hermeneutics*, 8.
40.   Gadamer, *Truth and method*, xxi.
41.   The idea of currere as embodied action was used as the theoretical centerpiece for a chapter I wrote entitled "A path laid down while walking: Curriculum development in high school English programs," in *Curriculum planning in the language arts K–12: An holistic perspective*, edited by Trevor J. Gambell and Mary Clare Courtland (North York, ON: Captus Press, 1994). It was in during the writing of this piece that I began to understand the contribution that enactivist theory might make to curriculum theorizing.
42.   Arthur Applebee, "The background for reform," in *Literature instruction: A focus on student response*, edited by Judith A. Langer (Urbana, IL: National Council of Teachers of English, 1992).
43.   James Britton and Merron Chorny, "Current issues and future directions," in *Handbook of research on teaching the English language arts*, editors, James Flood, Julie M. Jensen, Diane Lapp and James R. Squire (New York: Macmillan, 1991).

44. For a good overview of various theories of reader response see Richard Beach, *A teacher's introduction to reader-response theories* (Urbana, IL: National Council of Teachers of English, 1993).

45. Merleau-Ponty, in his essay "The child's relations with others" (in *The Primacy of perception*), suggests that the psyche is not a series of "states of consciousness" that are closed and inaccessible to others, but rather that a person's consciousness is "turned primarily toward the world, turned toward things; it is above all a relation to the world" (117). It is through the noticing of the ways in which others engage in a relation with the world (their "conducts") that I am able to know them.

46. Grumet, *Bitter milk*, 81.

47. Susan Sontag, *Against interpretation* (New York: Anchor Books, 1990), 8. With this phrase Sontag points to the way in which the artwork can speak ontologically. I use it here to signify the inherent ontological value that many of us who read and teach literature see in the literary work of art and its potential to help us to understand ourselves differently (perhaps nervously).

48. See John D. Caputo's introduction, "Restoring life to its original difficulty," in *Radical hermeneutics* (Bloomington: Indiana University Press, 1987), for an insightful commentary on the avoidance of difficulty and ambiguity in Western cultures.

49. Yes, Harper Lee's *To kill a mockingbird* (New York: F. Watts, 1960) had a very active life in this school.

50. This has been well documented by a number of writers in the field. See, for example, Beach, *A teacher's introduction to reader-response theories*; Patrick Dias and Michael Hayhoe, *Developing response to poetry* (Milton Keynes, UK: Open University Press, 1988); and Robert Probst, "Response to literature," in *Handbook of research on teaching the English language arts*, edited by James Flood, Julie M. Jensen, Diane Lapp and James R. Squire (New York: Macmillan, 1991).

51. John Wyndham, *The chrysalids* (Markham, ON: Penguin Books, 1955).

52. Bell, *Forbidden city*.

53. For example, Appleyard, *Becoming a reader*; Victor Nell, *Lost in a book: The psychology of reading for pleasure* (New Haven: Yale University Press, 1988); and Rabinowitz, *Before reading*.

54. For an insightful essay on the experience of re-reading see Margaret Hunsberger, "The experience of re-reading."

55. Dixon, in *Growth through English*, summarizes the proceedings of the three week Anglo-American seminar on the teaching of English held in Dartmouth, New Hampshire in 1966. In it, he outlines three models of

instruction that were in evidence in English language arts classrooms in both the United States and Great Britain: a "growth" model, a "skills" model, and a "cultural transmission" model.

56. Emerging primarily from the work of Rosenblatt, *Literature as exploration* and *The reader, the text, the poem*; Bleich, *Subjective criticism*; Holland, *The dynamics of literary response*; and Iser, *The act of reading*.

57. For example, de Castell et al., editors, *Language, authority and criticism*; Mackey, "The many faces of resistance"; Flynn and Schweickart, editors, *Gender and reading*; Showalter, editor, *The new feminist criticism*; Corcoran, "Reading, re-reading, resistance."

58. Dias and Hayhoe give a thoughtful and insightful overview of some of the difficulties arising from these competing literary theories in *Developing response to poetry*.

59. Judith Langer discusses these questions in *Literature instruction: A focus on student response* (Urbana, IL: National Council of Teachers of English, 1992), 42.

60. Ondaatje, *The English patient*, 283.

61. In addition to taking up *Forbidden city* and *The chrysalids* in our reading group, I interviewed Anna and Ingrid several times. The interviews focused on their personal response to the novels, their plans for teaching it, and their experience of teaching it.

62. Maturana and Varela, *The tree of knowledge*, 242.

63. Grumet, *Bitter milk*, 141.

64. Borgmann, *Crossing the postmodern divide*, 141–143.

65. Iser, *Prospecting*, 208.

66. Madeleine Grumet, "Lost places, potential spaces and possible worlds," 40.

67. Ibid.

68. Martin Heidegger, "Building Dwelling Thinking" (in *Basic writings*), 340.

69. Gadamer, *Philosophical hermeneutics*, 9.

70. Barthes, *S/Z*. For Barthes, the writerly text is a plural text, so open as to yield an infinite number of interpretations. It is called "writerly" because it is more able to be re-written with every reading. This is the opposite of the "readerly" text which is much more closed, much tighter, much more didactic than its counterpart, the writerly text.

71. Humberto Maturana, "Everything is said by an observer," in *Gaia, a way of knowing: Political implications of the new biology*, edited by William I. Thompson (Hudson, NY: Lindisfarne Press, 1987), 73–74.

72. Twelve out of twenty-five students agreed to be interviewed about their experience of reading the novel and the other activities which made up the

unit. Each interview was between 25–40 minutes in length.

73. It was Tom Kieren who introduced me to the work of Maturana and Varela (*The tree of knowledge*) and Varela, Thompson, and Rosch (*The embodied mind*). Obviously, it has been influential in this work. In addition, many conversations between Tom and myself (usually in the hallway by the elevators!) helped me to develop my understanding of an "enactivist" approach to cognition and curriculum theorizing.

74. Francisco Varela, "Laying down a path in walking," in *Gaia, a way of knowing: Political implications of the new biology*, edited by William I. Thompson (Hudson, NY: Lindisfarne Press, 1987), 50.

75. Langer, *Problems of art*, 48 (original emphasis).

76. Grumet, *Bitter milk*, 172.

77. Goldberg, *Long quiet highway*, 17.

78. Ondaatje, *The English patient*, 117.

79. Appleyard, *Becoming a reader*.

80. Elliott, *Action research for educational change*, 14.

81. For an excellent overview of the history of English teaching see Arthur Applebee and Alan Purves, "Literature and the language arts," in *Handbook of research in curriculum*, edited by Philip W. Jackson (New York: Macmillan, 1992).

82. Richard's *Practical criticism* (published in 1929) was one of the first texts of literary theory to address the importance of the reader's response to a literary work.

83. Michel Foucault, *Discipline and punish: The birth of the prison*, translated by Alan Sheridan (New York: Vintage Books, 1979).

84. Ibid., 200.

85. Ibid., 205.

86. Ondaatje, *The English patient*, 253.

87. Iser, *The fictive and the imaginary*, 3.

88. Ondaatje, *The English patient*, 111.

89. Kerby, *Narrative and the self*, 46.

90. Britzman, *Practice makes practice*, 4.

91. Max van Manen, *The tact of teaching* (London, ON: The Althouse Press, 1991).

92. Although a thorough discussion of pedagogy is provided in *The tact of teaching*, van Manen has recently elaborated on some of his ideas, particularly in relation to different conceptions of pedagogy in North America and The Netherlands in a recent article entitled "Pedagogy, virtue, and narrative identity in teaching," *Curriculum Inquiry* 24, no. 2 (Summer 1994): 135–170.

93.   Ondaatje, *The English patient*, 178.
94.   Britzman, *Practice makes practice*, 7.
95.   In "(Un)becoming a teacher: Negotiating identities while learning to teach" (in press in *Canadian Journal of Education*), Rebecca Luce-Kapler and I discuss the way in which multiple identities are negotiated by beginning teachers and, particularly, describe the influence of the "fictive" identity during the process of learning to teach.
96.   For more information on this subject see M. D. Khayatt's *Lesbian teachers: An invisible presence* (Albany, NY: State University of New York Press, 1992) and James Sears' "Educators, homosexuality, and homosexual students: Are personal feelings related to professional beliefs?" in *Coming out of the classroom closet: Gay and lesbian students, teachers and curricula*, edited by Karen Harbeck (Binghamton, NY: Harrington Park Press, 1992).
97.   Grumet, *Bitter milk*, 92–93.
98.   Smith , "Hermeneutic inquiry," 187.
99.   Ondaatje, *The English patient*, 12.

VII.   Unskinning Curriculum

1.   Pinar, "The lost language of cranes: Windows and mirrors in the regressive phase of currere," in *Autobiography, politics and sexuality*, 266.
2.   Ibid.
3.   David Leavitt, *The lost language of cranes* (New York: Knopf, 1986).
4.   Pinar, *Autobiography, politics and sexuality*, 265.
5.   Suzanne de Castell, "6 December 1989/1993, Je me souviens," *Canadian Journal of Education/Revue canadienne de l'éducation* 18, no. 3 (1993): 185–188, 186. This essay is the introduction to this issue of *CJE/RCE* that de Castell has edited entitled "Against the grain: Narratives of resistance."
6.   Patti Lather, *Getting smart: Feminist research and pedagogy with/in the postmodern* (New York: Routledge, 1991).
7.   Sontag, *Against interpretation*, 8.
8.   Goldberg, *Long quiet highway*, 46.
9.   See, in particular, David Smith's book *Pedagon* and his essay "Interpreting educational reality."
10.   Personal communication.
11.   Smith, "Hermeneutic inquiry," 198.
12.   Brent Davis, *Teaching mathematics*.
13.   Mary Catherine Bateson, *Peripheral visions: Learning along the way*

(New York: HarperCollins, 1994). Bateson discusses the importance of allowing children to follow their interest rather than touring through the typical school curriculum in her chapter entitled "Learning as coming home" (195–213).

14. Pinar, *Autobiography, politics and sexuality*, 265.
15. Michael Ondaatje, *The cinnamon peeler* (Toronto: McClelland and Stewart, 1989).
16. Ondaatje, "Light," in *The cinnamon peeler*, 3.
17. Freire, *Pedagogy of the oppressed*.
18. Alan Block, *Occupied reading: Critical foundations for an ecological theory* (New York: Garland Publishing, 1995).
19. Ibid., 222.
20. Iser, *The fictive and the imaginary*.
21. Block, *Occupied reading*.
22. W. O. Mitchell, *Roses are difficult here* (Toronto: McClelland and Stewart, 1990), 10.

Bibliography

Aoki, Ted. *Inspiriting the curriculum: Talks to teachers.* Edmonton, AB: University of Alberta Press, 1991.

Applebee, Arthur. "The background for reform." In *Literature instruction: A focus on student response.* Edited by Judith A. Langer. Urbana, IL: National Council of Teachers of English, 1992.

Applebee, Arthur and Alan Purves. "Literature and the language arts." In *Handbook on research in curriculum.* Edited by Philip W. Jackson. New York: Macmillan, 1992.

Appleyard, J. A. *Becoming a reader: The experience of fiction from childhood to adulthood.* New York: Cambridge University Press, 1990.

Aristotle. *On poetry and music.* Translated by S. H. Butcher. New York: Bobs-Merrill, 1948.

Ashton-Warner, Sylvia. *Teacher.* New York: Simon and Schuster, 1963.

Atwell, Nancie. *In the middle: Writing, reading and learning with adolescents.* Upper Montclair, NJ: Boynton Cook, 1987.

Atwood, Margaret. *The journals of Susanna Moodie.* Toronto: Oxford University Press, 1970.

Atwood, Margaret. *Cat's eye.* Toronto: McClelland and Stewart, 1988.

Bach, Richard. *Jonathan Livingston Seagull.* New York: Macmillan, 1970.

Bacon, Francis. *The great instaurition and New Atlantis.* Edited by J. Weinberger. Arlington Heights, IL: Harlan Davidson, 1980.

Barthes, Roland. *S/Z.* New York: Hill and Wang, 1974.

Barthes, Roland. *The pleasure of the text.* New York: Hill and Wang, 1975.

Bateson, Gregory. *Steps to an ecology of mind.* New York: Ballantine Books, 1972.

Bateson, Mary Catherine. *Peripheral visions: Learning along the way.* New York: HarperCollins, 1994.

Beach, Richard. *A teacher's guide to reader-response theories.* Urbana, IL: National Council of Teachers of English, 1993.

Bell, William. *Forbidden city.* Toronto: Doubleday, 1990.

Berry, Wendell. "The futility of global thinking." *Harpers* (June, 1990): 16–22.

Berthoff, Anne. *The sense of learning.* Portsmouth, NH: Heinemann, 1990.

Bleich, David. *Subjective criticism.* Baltimore: The Johns Hopkins University Press, 1978.

Block, Alan. *Occupied reading: Critical foundations for an ecological theory.* New York: Garland Publishing, 1995.

278 *Private Readings in Public*

Bobbitt, Franklin. *The curriculum.* Boston: Houghton Mifflin, 1918.

Bobbitt, Franklin. *How to make a curriculum.* Boston: Houghton Mifflin, 1924.

Bonnycastle, Stephen. *In search of authority: An introductory guide to literary theory.* Peterborough, ON: Broadview Press, 1991.

Borgmann, Albert. *Crossing the postmodern divide.* Chicago: The University of Chicago Press, 1992.

Britton, James and Merron Chorny. "Current issues and future directions." In *Handbook of research on teaching the English language arts.* Edited by James Flood, Julie M. Jensen, Diane Lapp and James R. Squire. New York: Macmillan, 1991.

Britzman, Deborah. *Practice makes practice: A critical study of learning to teach.* New York: State University of New York Press, 1991.

Britzman, Deborah. "The question of belief: Writing post-structural ethnography." *Educational Theory* 8, no. 3 (1995): 229–238.

Bruner, Jerome. *Actual minds, possible worlds.* Cambridge, MA: Harvard University Press, 1986.

Bruner, Jerome. *Acts of meaning.* Cambridge, MA: Harvard University Press, 1990.

Cairney, Trevor and S. Langbien. "Building communities of readers and writers." *The Reading Teacher* 42 (1989): 560–567.

Caputo, John. *Radical hermeneutics.* Bloomington: Indiana University Press, 1987.

Carr, William and Stephen Kemmis. *Becoming critical: Education,knowledge and action research.* Philadelphia: The Falmer Press, 1986.

Carson, Terrance and Jean-Claude Couture, editors. *Collaborative action research: Experience and reflections* (Improvement of Instruction Series, Monograph no. 18). Edmonton, AB: Alberta Teachers' Association, 1988.

Chambers, Cynthia. "Student journals: Private lessons in public." In *WestCAST Proceedings.* Edited by Louisa M. Kozey and Caroline D. Krentz. Regina, SK: Saskatchewan Instructional and Development Research Unit, 1992.

Chambers, Cynthia. "Private lessons in public." *Analytic Teaching 42,* no. 4 (1993): 37–42.

Charters, William W. *Curriculum construction.* New York: Macmillan, 1923.

Clandinin, D. Jean and Michael F. Connelly. "Teacher as curriculum maker." In *Handbook of research on curriculum.* Edited by Philip W. Jackson. New York: Macmillan, 1992.

Clifford, James and George E. Marcus, editors. *Writing culture: The poetics and politics of ethnography.* Los Angeles: University of California Press, 1986.

Connelly, Michael F. and D. Jean Clandinin. *Teachers as curriculum planners: Narratives of experience.* New York: Teachers College Press, 1988.

Corcoran, Bill. "Reading, re-reading, resistance: Versions of reader response." In *Reading and response.* Edited by Michael Hayhoe and S. Parker. Milton Keynes, UK: Open University Press, 1990.

Crowley, Sharon. *A teacher's guide to deconstruction.* Urbana, IL: National Council of Teachers of English, 1990.

Davis, Brent. *Teaching mathematics: Toward a sound alternative.* New York: Garland Publishing, 1996.

Davis, Brent, Dennis Sumara, and Thomas Kieren. "Cognition, co-emergence, curriculum." *Journal of Curriculum Studies,* in press.

de Castell, Suzanne. "6 December 1989/1993, Je me souviens," *Canadian Journal of Education/Revue canadienne de l'éducation* 18, no. 3 (1993): 185–188.

de Castell, Suzanne, Allan Luke and Carmen Luke, editors. *Language, authority, and criticism: Readings on the school textbook.* New York: The Falmer Press, 1989.

de Saint-Exupery, Antoine. *Le petit prince.* Bourges, France: Editions Gallimard, 1946.

de Saussure, Ferdinand. *Course in general linguistics.* London: Fontana, 1975 [1916].

Derrida, Jacques. *Of grammatology.* Baltimore: The Johns Hopkins University Press, 1976.

Derrida, Jacques. *Writing and différance.* London: Routledge, 1978.

Derrida, Jacques. *Positions.* London: Athlone, 1981.

Derrida, Jacques. *Margins of philosophy.* Translated by Alan Bass. Chicago: University of Chicago Press, 1982.

Derrida, Jacques. *Acts of literature.* New York: Routledge, 1992.

Denzin, Norman K and Yvonna S. Lincoln, editors. *Handbook of qualitative research.* Thousand Oaks, CA: Sage, 1994.

Descartes, René. *Discourse on method* and *Meditations on first philosophy.* Indianapolis: Hackett Publishing Company, 1980.

Dewey, John. *The child and the curriculum.* Chicago: The University of Chicago Press, 1956 [1902].

Dewey, John. *Democracy and education.* New York: The Free Press, 1966 [1916].

Dias, Patrick and Michael Hayhoe. *Developing response to poetry.* Milton Keynes, UK: Open University Press, 1988.

Dixon, John. *Growth through English.* Oxford: Oxford University Press, 1967.

Eagleton, Terry. *Literary theory.* Minneapolis: University of Minnesota Press, 1983.

Eco, Umberto. *Travels in hyper reality.* San Diego: Harcourt, Brace, Jovanovich, 1983.

Egan, Kieren. "What is curriculum?" *Curriculum Inquiry* 8, no. 1 (1978): 65–72.

Eisner, Elliot and Elizabeth Vallance, editors. *Conflicting conceptions of curriculum.* Berkeley: McCutchan, 1974.

Elliott, John. *Action research for educational change.* Milton Keynes, UK: The Open University Press, 1991.

Fish, Stanley. *Is there a text in this class?* Cambridge, MA: Harvard University Press, 1980.

Flax, Jane. *Thinking fragments: Psychoanalysis, feminism and postmodernism in the contemporary west.* Berkeley: University of California Press, 1990.

Flynn, Elizabeth A. and Patricia. P. Schweickart, editors. *Gender and reading: Essays on readers, texts and contexts.* Baltimore: The John Hopkins University Press, 1986.

Foucault, Michel. *Discipline and punish: The birth of the prison.* New York: Vintage Books, 1979.

Fox, Geoff. "Dark watchers: Young readers and their fiction." *English in Education* 13 (1979): 32–36.

Frank, Anne. *Anne Frank: Diary of a young girl.* New York: Pocket Books, 1958.

Franklin, Ursula. *The real world of technology.* Concord, ON: Anansi, 1990.

Freire, Paulo. *Pedagogy of the oppressed.* New York: Herder and Herder, 1970.

Frye, Northrop. *Anatomy of criticism: Four essays.* Princeton: Princeton University Press, 1957.

Gadamer, Hans-Georg. *Philosophical hermeneutics.* Los Angeles:University of California Press, 1976.

Gadamer, Hans-Georg. *Truth and method* (2nd revised edition). Translated by Joel Weinsheimer and Donald Marshall. New York: Crossroad, 1990.

Gallagher, Shaun. *Hermeneutics and education.* Albany: State Univeristy of New York Press, 1992.

Geertz, Clifford. *Works and lives: The anthropologist as author.* Stanford, CA: Stanford University Press, 1988.

Gleick, James. *Chaos: Making a new science.* New York: Penguin Books, 1987.

Goldberg, Natalie. *Long quiet highway: Waking up in America.* New York: Bantam Books, 1993.

Goodlad, John. "Curriculum as a field of study." In *International encyclopedia of education,* volume 2. Edited by Torsten Husen and T. Neville Postlewhaite. Oxford: Pergamon, 1985.

Gould, John. *Herodotus.* London: Weidenfeld and Nicolson, 1989.

Graham, Robert. *Reading and writing the self: Autobiography in education and the curriculum.* New York: Teachers College Press, 1991.

Graves, Donald. *Writing: Children and teachers at work.* Portsmouth, NH: Heinemann, 1983.

Grumet, Madeleine. *Bitter milk: Women and teaching.* Amherst: University of Massachusetts Press, 1988.

Grumet, Madeleine. "Curriculum and the art of daily life." In *Reflections from the heart of educational inquiry: Understanding curriculum and teaching through the arts.* Edited by George Willis and William Schubert. Albany, NY: State University of New York Press, 1991.

Grumet, Madeleine. "Lost places, potential spaces and possible worlds: Why we read books with other people." *Margins* 1, no. 1 (Spring, 1991): 35–53.

Hammond, Michael, Jane Howarth and Russell Keat. *Understanding phenomenology.* Oxford: Blackwell, 1991.

Harap, Henry. *The changing curriculum.* New York: Appleton-Century, 1937.

Heidegger, Martin. *Being and time.* New York: Harper and Row, 1966.

Heidegger, Martin. *Basic writings.* San Francisco: HarperCollins, 1977.

Herodotus. *Histories.* Middlesex, UK: Penguin Books, 1954.

Hirsch, Eric Donald. *The aims of interpretation.* Chicago: The University of Chicago Press, 1976.

Holland, Norman. *The dynamics of literary response.* New York: Oxford University Press, 1968.

Holland, Norman. *Five teachers teaching.* New Haven: Yale University Press, 1975.

Hunsberger, Margaret. "The experience of re-reading." *Phenomenology + Pedagogy* 3 (1985): 161–166.

Hunsberger, Margaret. "The time of texts." In *Understanding curriculum as phenomenological and deconstructed text.* Edited by William F. Pinar and William M. Reynolds. New York: Teachers College Press, 1992.

Iser, Wolfgang. *The implied reader.* Baltimore: The Johns Hopkins University Press, 1975.

Iser, Wolfgang. *The act of reading.* Baltimore: The Johns Hopkins University Press, 1978.

Iser, Wolfgang. *Prospecting: From reader response to literary anthropology.* Baltimore: The Johns Hopkins University Press, 1989.

Iser, Wolfgang. *The fictive and the imaginary: Charting literary anthropology.* Baltimore: The Johns Hopkins University Press, 1993.

Jackson, Philip. "Conceptions of curriculum and curriculum specialists." In *Handbook of research on curriculum.* Edited by Philip Jackson. New York: Macmillan, 1992.

Jardine, David. "Reflections on education, hermeneutics, and ambiguity: Hermeneutics as a restoring of life to its original difficulty." In *Understanding curriculum as phenomenological and deconstructed text.* Edited by William F. Pinar and William M. Reynolds. New York: Teachers College Press, 1992.

Jardine, David. *Speaking with a boneless tongue*. Bragg Creek, AB: Makyo Press, 1993.

Kemmis, Stephen and Robin McTaggart, editors. *The action research planner*. Victoria, Australia: Deakin University Press, 1988.

Kerby, Anthony. *Narrative and the self*. Bloomington: Indiana University Press, 1991.

Khayatt, M. D. *Lesbian teachers: An invisible presence*. Albany: State University of New York Press, 1992.

Kliebard, Herbert. *The struggle for the American curriculum, 1893–1958*. New York: Routledge, 1986.

Kristeva, Julia. *Desire in language*. New York: Columbia University Press, 1980.

Kristeva, Julia. *Revolution in poetic language*. New York: Columbia University Press, 1984.

Langer, Judith, editor. *Literature instruction: A focus on student response*. Urbana, IL: National Council of Teachers of English, 1992.

Langer, Susanne. *Problems of art*. New York: Charles Scribner's Sons, 1957.

Lather, Patti. *Getting smart: Feminist research and pedagogy with/in the postmodern*. New York: Routledge, 1991.

Leavis, Frank R. *New bearings in English poetry*. London: Chatto and Windus, 1950 [1932].

Leavitt, David. *The lost language of cranes*. New York: Knopf, 1986.

Lee, Harper. *To kill a mockingbird*. New York: F. Watts, 1960.

Lightman, Alan. *Einstein's dreams*. Toronto: Alfred A. Knopf Canada, 1993.

Locke, John. *Treatise of civil government and a letter concerning toleration*. Edited by Charles L. Sherman. New York: Appleton-Century-Crofts, 1965.

Lyotard, Jean-François. *The postmodern condition: A report on knowledge*. Minneapolis: Minnesota Press, 1984.

Macdonald, James. "Curriculum theory." In *Curriculum theorizing: The reconceptualists*. Edited by William F. Pinar. Berkeley, CA: McCutchan, 1975.

Mackey, Margaret. "The many faces of resistant reading." *English Journal* 82 (1993): 69–74.

Madison, Gary. *The hermeneutics of postmodernity: Figures and themes*. Bloomington: Indiana University Press, 1988.

Marshall, Brenda. *Teaching the postmodern*. New York: Routledge, 1992.

Maturana, Humberto. "Everything is said by an observer." In *Gaia, a way of knowing: Political implications of the new biology*. Edited by William I. Thompson. Hudson, NY: Lindisfarne Press, 1987.

Maturana, Humberto and Francisco Varela. *The tree of knowledge: The biological roots of human understanding*. Boston: Shambhala, 1987.

Merleau-Ponty, Maurice. *Phenomenology of perception*. London: Routledge, 1962.

Merleau-Ponty, Maurice. *The primacy of perception.* Evanston, IL: Northwestern University Press, 1964.

Michener, James. *Poland.* New York: Random House, 1983.

Miller, James. *The passion of Michel Foucault.* New York: Simon and Schuster, 1993.

Mills, Gordon. *Hamlet's castle: The study of literature as a social experience.* Austin: University of Texas Press, 1976.

Minsky, Marvin. *The society of mind.* New York: Simon and Schuster, 1986.

Mitchell, W. O. *Roses are difficult here.* Toronto: McClelland and Stewart, 1990.

Moi, Toril, editor. *The Kristeva reader.* New York: Columbia University Press, 1986.

Moodie, Susanna. *Roughing it in the bush.* Toronto: McClelland and Stewart, 1962.

Nell, Victor. *Lost in a book: The psychology of reading for pleasure.* New Haven, CT: Yale University Press, 1988.

Ondaatje, Michael. *The cinnamon peeler.* Toronto: McClelland and Stewart, 1989.

Ondaatje, Michael. *The English patient.* Toronto: McClelland and Stewart, 1992.

Ong, Walter. *Orality and literacy: The technologizing of the word.* New York: Methuen, 1982.

Palmer, Richard. *Hermeneutics.* Evanston, IL: Northwestern University Press, 1969.

Paterson, Katherine. *Bridge to Teribithia.* New York: Harper and Row, 1977.

Pinar, William, F. editor. *Curriculum theorizing: The reconceptualists.* Berkeley, McCutchan, 1975.

Pinar, William F. *Autobiography, politics and sexuality: Essays in curriculum theory, 1972–1992.* New York: Peter Lang, 1994.

Pinar, William F. and Madeleine R. Grumet. *Toward a poor curriculum.* Dubuque, IA: Kendall/Hunt Publishing Company, 1976.

Pinar, William F. and William M. Reynolds, editors. *Understanding curriculum as phenomenological and deconstructed text.* New York: Teachers College Press, 1992.

Pinar, William F., William M. Reynolds, Patrick Slattery and Peter Taubman, editors. *Understanding curriculum.* New York: Peter Lang, 1995.

Plato. *The republic.* Translated and introduced by Francis MacDonald Cornford. Oxford: Clarendon Press, 1945.

Probst, Robert. "Response to literature." In *Handbook of research on teaching the English language arts.* Edited by James Flood, Julie M. Jensen, Diane Lapp and James R. Squire. New York: Macmillan, 1991.

Rabinowitz, Peter. *Before reading: Narrative conventions and the politics of interpretation.* Ithaca, NY: Cornell University Press, 1987.

Richards, Ivor A. *Practical criticism.* New York: Harcourt Brace, 1929.

Rorty, Richard. *Contingency, irony, and solidarity.* New York: Cambridge University Press, 1989.

Rosenau, Pauline. *Postmodernism and the social sciences.* Princeton: Princeton University Press, 1992.

Rosenblatt, Louise. *Literature as exploration.* New York: Appleton-Century, 1938.

Rosenblatt, Louise. *The reader, the text, the poem.* Carbondale, IL: Southern Illinois University Press, 1978.

Rugg, Harold. *Curriculum making: Past and present. Twenty-sixth yearbook of the National Society for the Study of Education, part 1.* Bloomington, IL: Public School Publishing, 1926.

Rugg, Harold. *The foundations of curriculum making. Twenty-sixth yearbook of the National Society for the Study of Education, part 2.* Bloomington, IL: Public School Publishing, 1926.

Sacks, Oliver. "A neurologist's notebook: To see and not see." *The New Yorker* 10 (May 1993): 59–73.

Salvio, Paula M. "Transgressive daughters: Student autobiography and the project of self-creation." *Cambridge Journal of Education* 20, no. 3 (1990): 283–290.

Salvio, Paula M. "On the forbidden pleasures and hidden dangers of covert reading."*English Quarterly* 27, no. 3 (Spring 1995): 8–15

Sartre, Jean-Paul. *Being and nothingness.* New York: Pocket Books, 1956.

Schubert, William H. *Curriculum: Perspective, paradigm, and possibility.* New York: Macmillan Publishing Company, 1986.

Schwab, Joseph. "The practical: A language for curriculum." *School Review* 78 (1969): 1–23.

Schwab, Joseph. "The practical: Arts of the eclectic." *School Review* 79, no. 4 (1971): 493–542.

Schwab, Joseph. "The practical 3: Translation into curriculum." *School Review* 81, no. 4 (1973): 501–522.

Schwab, Joseph. "The practical 4: Something for curriculum professors to do." *Curriculum Inquiry* 13 (1983): 239–265.

Sears, James. "Educators, homosexuality, and homosexual students: Are personal feelings related to professional beliefs?" In *Coming out of the classroom closet: Gay and lesbian students, teachers and curricula.* Edited by Karen Harbeck. Binghamton, NY: Harrington Park Press, 1992.

Showalter, Elaine, editor. *The new feminist criticism: Essays on women, literature, and theory.* New York: Pantheon, 1985.

Smith, David. "Hermeneutic inquiry: The hermeneutic imagination and the pedagogic text." *Forms of curriculum inquiry.* Edited by Edmund Short. New York: State University of New York Press, 1991.

Smith, David. *Pedagon: Meditations on pedagogy and culture.* Bragg Creek, AB: Makyo Press, 1994.

Smith, David. "Interpreting educational reality." In *Hermeneutics in educational discourse.* Edited by H. Danner. Durban, SA: Butterworths Press, 1995.

Sontag, Susan. *Against interpretation.* New York: Anchor Books, 1990.

Sumara, Dennis. "Of seagulls and glass roses: Teachers' relationships with literary texts as transformational space." *JCT: An Interdisciplinary Journal of Curriculum Studies* 10, no. 3 (1994): 153–182.

Sumara, Dennis. "A path laid down while walking: Curriculum development in high school English programs." In *Curriculum planning in the language arts K–12.* Edited by Trevor J. Gambell and Mary Clare Courtland. North York, ON: Captus Press, 1994.

Sumara, Dennis. "Resisting the tourist gaze: Literature reading as dwelling. *English Journal* 83, no. 8 (1994): 41–46.

Sumara, Dennis. "Schooling the literary imagination." *English Quarterly* 26, no. 4 (1994): 13–21.

Sumara, Dennis. "Counterfeiting." *Taboo: The Journal of Cultural Studies and Education,* 1, no. 1 (1995): 94–122.

Sumara, Dennis and Rebecca Luce-Kapler. "Action research as a writerly text: Locating co-labouring in collaboration." *Educational Action Research* 1. no. 3 (1993): 387–396.

Sumara, Dennis and Rebecca Luce-Kapler. "(Un)becoming a teacher: Negotiating identities while learning to teach." *Canadian Journal of Education*, in press.

Taba, Hilda. *Curriculum development: Theory and practice.* New York: Harcourt, Brace and World, 1962.

Taylor, Charles. *The malaise of modernity.* Concord, ON: Anansi, 1991.

Thompson, William Irwin, editor. *Gaia, a way of knowing: Political implications of the new biology.* Hudson, NY: Lindisfarne Press, 1987.

Todorov, Tzvetan. *The poetics of prose.* Ithaca: Cornell University Press, 1977.

Tyler, Ralph. *Basic principles of curriculum and instruction.* Chicago: University of Chicago Press, 1949.

van Manen, Max. "Phenomenology of the novel, or how do novels teach?" *Phenomenology + Pedagogy 3*, no. 3 (1985): 167–181.

van Manen, Max. *Researching lived experience.* New York: State University of New York Press, 1990.

van Manen, Max. *The tact of teaching.* London, ON: The Althouse Press, 1991.

van Manen, Max. "Pedagogy, virtue, and narrative identity in teaching." Curriculum Inquiry 24, no. 2 (Summer 1994): 135–170.

Varela, Francisco. "Laying down a path in walking." In *Gaia, a way of knowing: Political implications of the new biology.* Edited by William I. Thompson. Hudson, NY: Lindisfarne Press, 1987.

Varela, Francisco, Evan Thompson and Eleanor Rosch. *The embodied mind: Cognitive science and human experience.* Cambridge: The MIT Press, 1991.

Weaver, Constance. *Understanding whole language.* Toronto: Irwin, 1990.

Weinsheimer, Joel. *Gadamer's hermeneutics: A reading of "Truth and method."* New Haven, CT: Yale University Press, 1985.

Willinsky, John. *The new literacy.* New York: Routledge, 1990.

Wimsatt, William and Monroe Beardsley. "The intentional fallacy, the affective fallacy." In *Critical theory since Plato.* Edited by Hazard Adams. New York: Harcourt, Brace, Jovanovich, 1958.

Wittgenstein, Ludwig. *Philosophical investigations.* New York: Macmillan, 1953.

Wyndham, John. *The chrysalids.* London: Penguin Books, 1955.

Index

action, perceptually guided, 105, 180
action research, 11–13, 142
adolescent, experience of reading,
    206–207
adult, experience of reading, 206
aesthetic experience, 27, 255;
    and school, 199;
    of reading, 26–28, 199;
    response, 35
AIDS, 247
Alberta, southwestern:
    agricultural practices, 244;
    geography of, 244
aletheia, 119
allatonce, 174, 175, 204
ambiguity:
    of private & public, 137;
    of research processes, 129;
    while reading, 68, 70, 147
analysis:
    deconstructive, 124;
    feminist, 124;
    psychoanalytic, 124
Anglo-American Conference, 27
anomalies, physical, 207
anxiety:
    felt by teachers, 223, 225;
    while reading, 54
Aoki, Ted, 126, 250
Applebee, Arthur, 179, 274
Appleyard, J.A., 28, 206, 253
Aristotle, 45
art:
    as extension of artist, 215;
    effects of, 235;
    function of, 180–181, 256–257;
    historical interpretation, 29;
    interpretation, 30;
    literary work of, 22, 29–30;

perception of, 29
artist, task of, 148
Ashton-Warner, Sylvia, 1, 14
attitudes:
    homophobic, 195;
    racist, 195;
    sexist, 195
Attridge, Derek, 32
Atwell, Nancie, 268
Atwood, Margaret, 26, 87, 251–252
Auschwitz, 240
autobiographical inquiry, 173

Bacon, Francis, 135
Barnes, Hazel, 259
Barthes, Roland, 14, 26, 62, 127, 196,
    254, 273
Bateson, Gregory, 118
Bateson, Mary Catherine, 237, 275–
    276
Beijing, 19, 252
Being, Heideggerian philosophy of,
    264
being-in-the-world, ecologies of, 59
behaviorism, 97
Bell, William, 17
Bentham, Jeremy, 209
Berthoff, Ann, 174
Berry Wendell, 8
Bleich, David, 110, 138
Block, 241, 243
Bobbitt, Franklin, 169
bodies of knowledge, 115
body:
    as biological structure, 92;
    as chamber for text, 190, 194;
    as collecting place for knowledge,
        85;
    as environment, 90;

as embodied action, 100–106,
123;
as emergent system, 98–100;
as information processing, 96–97;
as representation, 96–98;
commonsense views of, 96, 99
cognitive science, 102
cognitive system, 92, 95
co-laboring, 144–146;
with text, 163
collaboration:
as difficulty, 142;
character of, 142–143
collective experience, 113
commitment:
communal, 141–146;
to literary fictions, 43, 68, 152,
162, 179, 181, 218;
to other persons, 92;
to reading, 68, 193–194
Commonplace Book, 48, 72–73;
in *The English Patient*, 49, 53,
107, 133, 161, 163, 164, 181,
235
commonplace location, 49, 126, 131–
133, 145, 159, 160, 162, 166, 185,
194, 218, 222, 242;
borders of, 163
commonplaces:
for sense of self, 49–50;
of inquiry, 126;
for interpretation, 179;
of reading, 50, 85
communal:
commitment in families, 143;
experiences of, 139–140;
reading practices, 140, 156;
relationship to public, 143
community:
characteristics of, 141–142;
of gays & lesbians, 201;
of readers, 141, 158
complexity of curriculum, 8
complicity within lived experiences,

122
conditioning:
biological, 103;
cultural, 103
conducts, 180
Connelly, Michael, 267
consciousness, 257–258, 259;
aesthetic, 39;
development of, 57;
historically-effected, 57;
tradition of, 123–124;
world, 59
constraints, liberating, 23
constructivism, 98
consumerism in modern culture, 136
continental philosophy, 102
contingencies, in curriculum, 178
contract, character of, 154
control, desire for, 151
convergence, during lived cognition,
106
conversation, 53;
as metaphor for inquiry, 126;
qualities of, 125;
reflecting on, 59
core self, 76, 261–262
correspondence of world & perception,
38, 105
co-specification, 87;
and curriculum, 174
counterfeiting:
consequences of, 228;
response to literary fiction,
212–224
countersigning, 33
course, running of, 177
critical:
practices, 182;
traditions, 123–124
criticism, literary, 109
cultural artifacts, 20, 132, 214, 242;
as mediator, 132;
as tools, 58;
importance of, 262

About the Cover Drawing

This drawing traces in graphite the course of an autumn afternoon when, between spaces filled with tea and conversation (her dream of the night before, the retelling of a story told by an elderly neighbour), a young reader curled, one limb at a time, into a wicker chair with a book. As she was gradually drawn in to the text, I was drawn to render her quiet absorption— drawn to wonder at how, while reading a work of literary fiction, she was simultaneously here, yet not here. As my graphite edged softly around skin, hair, book cover, aspects of her that I had not yet seen in the nineteen years I have known her, were suddenly exposed—in the tilt of her head, the flicker of expression across her face—and then, just as suddenly, hidden and covered. Perhaps drawing, like reading, is also a matter of unskinning. For drawing peels off the covers behind which both artist and subject usually hide. To draw another reading is to draw one who is already, partially unmasked. It is not surprising then, that as she and I got up from our chairs, gathering teacups and books, we were unusually quiet, and exchanged shy smiles. Thank you, Anne.

Rose Montgomery-Whicher